J. William Pfeiffer
Richard Heslin

INSTRUMENTATION IN HUMAN RELATIONS TRAINING

A Guide to 75 Instruments with
Wide Application to the
Behavioral Sciences

311

$8.50

SERIES IN HUMAN RELATIONS TRAINING

INSTRUMENTATION IN HUMAN RELATIONS TRAINING

A Guide to 75 Instruments with
Wide Application to the
Behavioral Sciences

J. William Pfeiffer
Human Relations Consultant

and

Richard Heslin
Associate Professor
Department of Psychology
Purdue University

UNIVERSITY ASSOCIATES

Publishers and Consultants
P.O. Box 615, Iowa City, Iowa 52240

UNIVERSITY ASSOCIATES is an educational organization engaged in human relations training, research, consulting, publication, and both pre-service and in-service education. The organization consists of university-affiliated educational consultants and experienced facilitators in human relations and leadership training.

In addition to offering general laboratory experiences, University Associates designs and carries out programs on a contractual basis for various organizations. These programs fall under the following areas of specialization: Human Relations Training, Leadership Development, Organization Development, Community Development, and Educational Research.

Library of Congress catalog number 73-79392

ISBN 0-88390-023-8

Acknowledgements

Instrumentation in Human Relations Training is the result of the cumulative efforts of many people. We wish to acknowledge the contribution of group participants and students whose involvement with the research was of great importance to our effort.

We wish to express our appreciation to Sandra L. Pfeiffer, Ed.S., whose continuous editorial supervision through all phases of this project was invaluable.

We are especially grateful for the support and advice of our consulting editor, John E. Jones, Ph.D., whose efforts toward completion of the final draft are responsible for a uniformly strong volume.

PREFACE

When human relations training began a quarter of a century ago, most of the practitioners were clinicians or academicians with relatively solid backgrounds in research design and measurement. The earliest uses of instruments were to generate research-oriented data to assess behavioral changes in training groups. Over the years this practice evolved into a more common use of instruments to generate data for "group consumption." Instrumentation has become an invaluable aid in the laboratory training setting, not only for its original purpose of research, but also for increasing participants' self-understanding and helping to identify behaviors or patterns of behavior which might be perceived as dysfunctional to interpersonal relations or to the accomplishment of group tasks.

In recent years, human relations training has reached out beyond the realm of the social sciences into nearly every phase of contemporary life. It has been shown to be valuable in industry, education, community development, the church, business, the military, and, in fact, any setting where the effects of human behavior are acknowledged. Group facilitators currently represent a rich diversity of educational and training backgrounds. The influx of individuals from orientations other than the social sciences has greatly enlarged the scope and usefulness of training and predisposes the field to continuous growth.

One result of the appearance within the human relations training field of facilitators with a variety of backgrounds is that many individuals with little or no knowledge of research design and measurement are in positions of responsibility for human relations training activities. Their lack of expertise in measurement theory and application may prevent them from using instruments in laboratory designs or may promote inappropriate uses. While it is perfectly legitimate for a facilitator—regardless of his background—to use instrumentation, it is of no use to him or to the participants in his groups if he fails to provide the opportunity for a learning experience. This book is designed to introduce group facilitators from a variety of orientations to the use of instruments in human relations training. The intent is to provide some groundwork in methodology and theory so that facilitators will feel comfortable and, hopefully, confident in applying this valuable tool in their work with groups.

It was the decision to design this book for practitioners rather than for researchers which led us to a practical approach. We wanted to provide essential learnings pertinent to the specific instruments discussed without becoming involved in excessive theory. A major, continuing concern of University Associates is to provide tools for the practitioner in human relations training. The response to our initial publications, *A Handbook of Structured Experiences for Human Relations Training* and *The Annual Handbook for Group Facilitators* has supported the contention that facilitators value and use materials which are presented rather simplistically. The assumption is that facilitators are designing laboratory experiences which are compatible with current theories of human behavior and that numerous sources for full discussions of such theories are available to the facilitator. *Instrumentation in Human Relations Training* is principally concerned with exploring a number of instruments which we have found to be highly useful in actual training settings and suggesting ways in which instrumented feedback may be applied in an effective manner. Nevertheless, we have some mixed feelings about how non-sophisticated we should be in the introductory chapters. There is a potential danger of insulting part of our target audience by the relatively simplistic approach we have taken on some technical considerations; on the other hand, we view it as very important that those facilitators who lack knowledge of research design and techniques have a "basic course" or "review" before they begin to use more instrumentation in their training designs. This increases the chances that instrumentation will be used appropriately to promote learning experiences for participants. It may also help to defuse some of the anxiety and suspicion which often accompanies the introduction of instrumentation in human relations groups by allowing the facilitator to assume a comfortably knowledgeable posture in administering and interpreting instruments.

Our interest in writing this book came out of an awareness of the plethora of information about the uses of instrumentation in human relations training. Since the inception of University Associates, the senior author has been integrally involved in development of structured approaches to training, including instrumentation. Our enthusiasm in discovering and finding reinforcement for instrumentation in the data-gathering and feedback process in our own training experiences has led us to a personal involvement in experimenting with instrument design and modification as well as in the use of commercial instruments. In addition, the outgrowth of instrumentation has been simultaneous with the development of structured experiences, and our laboratory designs reflect this interrelationship. In a very real sense, *Instrumentation in Human Relations Training* extends the work and intent of the *Handbook* and the *Annual* since the impetus toward including instrumentation as part of the learning structure comes from our involvement with structured experiences. As University Associates became more involved with and committed to instrumentation as a growthful part of laboratory learning, we became increasingly aware that while instruments were being used because it seemed to be "a great idea," little had been done about discovering their most effective uses. Many well-intentioned group facilitators have been and are currently in the practice of administering an instrument such as the *FIRO-B* to a group and then handling (or more precisely not handling) interpretations by saying to the participants, "You may want to discuss some of the scores which seem significant to you." We contend that such an approach very significantly decreases the potential learning for the person to whom the instrument is given.

A couple of years ago, we began to explore how we might respond to what we perceived as this unmet need in facilitator development. The result was that in February, 1971, we conducted our first "Uses of Instrumentation in Human Relations Training" workshop at Yokefellow Institute, Earlham College, Richmond, Indiana. About twenty people participated in that training event and were systematically overloaded with instrumented feedback. The Personal Orientation Inventory, Adjective Check List, and Jackson's Personality Research Form were given in the first nine hours of training. In subsequent versions of the workshop we have exchanged some instruments for others, gathered first-hand reactions to the instruments, and shared many ideas about uses and limitations of large numbers of instruments with scores of participants who have had widely varied backgrounds. The research has not been limited to the instrumentation workshop; we are continually incorporating new instruments into a variety of training designs. We have also taken opportunities in our consulting activities to develop uses of instrumentation and have brought instrumentation into the classroom when it was appropriate. We believe that we have researched uses of instrumentation in nearly every conceivable human relations setting and group. It is our aspiration that this book will aid facilitators in developing their sophistication with instrumentation uses. It should enlarge their instrument repertoire and allow them to experiment with instrument development.

This book is one that can never really be completed; we keep discovering "new" instruments and new uses for "old" instruments. It does, however, represent the results of years of practical work filled with a lot of pragmatic questions. We believe that it will begin to fill a void in the rapidly evolving profession of group facilitation. One of our hopes is that we may stimulate interest on the part of group facilitators that may result in a second volume of the book. Our primary goal in presenting the material is to encourage the expansion of instrumentation usage in human relations training. We believe it to have a potentially enormous impact on the understanding of individual, interpersonal, and organization behavior. The concept of widely disseminating the learnings derived from human relations training settings has always been uppermost in our minds. The materials in the previous publications in this series have carried with them the permission and encouragement to reproduce them for workshop and educational uses. It is our belief that through such non-possessive sharing of learning, the widespread incorporation of instrumentation in the field of human relations can happen. To that end, we ask you to share with us your instruments, ideas, and experiences about the use of instrumentation in laboratory designs so that the field can be enriched synergistically.

Indianapolis, Indiana
February, 1973

J. William Pfeiffer
Richard Heslin

TABLE
OF
CONTENTS

Preface vii

Introduction 1

PART I INSTRUMENTATION

Chapter One   A Perspective on Instrumentation 7

Chapter Two   Instrumentation 19

Chapter Three   Technical Considerations 27

Chapter Four   Instrument Development 33

Chapter Five   Research Uses of Instrumentation in Human
Relations Training 41

PART II INSTRUMENTS

Introduction to Part II 53

SECTION A   INSTRUMENTS WITH A PERSONAL FOCUS

Short and Uni-Scaled Instruments

Survey of Personal Values 59

Study of Values 62

Gordon Personal Inventory 64

Gordon Personal Profile 67

Personal Value Scales 69

The Personality Inventory 72

Personal Growth Inventory 74

Eysenck Personality Inventory 76

How Well Do You Know Yourself 78

Self Actualization Test 80

The Involvement Inventory 82

Coping Operations Preference Enquiry 85

Inventory of Affective Tolerance 89

Multiple Affect Adjective Check List 90

California F Scale 92

Dogmatism Scale 94

Social Desirability Scale 95

Repression-Sensitization Scale 96

Long, Multiple-Scaled Instruments

Personal Orientation Inventory 99

Myers-Briggs Type Indicator 101

Self-Disclosure Questionnaire 104

Taylor-Johnson Temperament Analysis 106

The Sixteen Personality Factor Test 108

The Adjustment Inventory 110

Thurstone Temperament Schedule 112

The Adjective Check List 114

Profile of Mood States 118

Dimensions of Temperament 120

Edwards Personal Preference Schedule 122

California Test of Personality 124

California Psychological Inventory 126

Omnibus Personality Inventory 129

Personality Research Form 131

Minnesota Multiphasic Personality Inventory 134

SECTION B   INSTRUMENTS WITH AN INTERPERSONAL FOCUS

General

Fundamental Interpersonal Relations—Behavior 139

Fundamental Interpersonal Relations—Feeling 152

Survey of Interpersonal Values 158

Interpersonal Check List 161

Interpersonal Rating Form 164

Psychological Audit for Interpersonal Relations 171

The A-S Reaction Study in Personality 175

Pre-Marriage, Marriage, and Family

Marital Attitudes Evaluation 179

Scale of Feelings and Behavior of Love 190

The Marriage Prediction Schedule 192

The Marriage Adjustment Schedule 195

Life Interpersonal History Enquiry 197

The Family Scale 202

Elias Family Opinion Survey 203

Group Dynamics

Hill Interaction Matrix—B 207
Hill Interaction Matrix—Group 217
Reactions to Group Situations 221
Group Leadership Questionnaire 223
Helping Relationship Inventory 228
Group Encounter Survey 230
Team Effectiveness Survey 232
Group Dimensions Descriptions Questionnaire 233

SECTION C   INSTRUMENTS WITH AN ORGANIZATIONAL FOCUS

Organizational Climate

Organization Health Survey 239
Organizational Climate 241
Educational Values 243
Organizational Climate Index 250
Organizational Climate Questionnaire 253

Management/Leadership Style

The Orientation Inventory 257
A Survey of Life Orientations 260
Management Style Diagnosis Test 263
X-Y-Z Test 265
Leadership Appraisal Survey 267
Management Appraisal Survey 269
Leadership Opinion Questionnaire 271
The Leadership Ability Evaluation 272

Supervisor-Subordinate Relations

Leadership: Employee-Orientation and Differentiation Questionnaire ... 277
Rate Your Boss As A Leader 279
Personnel Relations Survey 280
Management of Motives Index 282
Work Motivation Inventory 283
Supervisory Index 284

PART III APPENDICES

Appendix A   List of Authors 289
Appendix B   List of Instruments 291
Appendix C   List of Scales 293
Appendix D   List of Publishers 301
Appendix E   Resources 305

INTRODUCTION

ORGANIZATION

Our purpose in writing this book is threefold: (1) to provide reference material for a different sort of consumer of instruments than traditional researchers, (2) to spread consciousness of the availability of instruments that traditionally have had narrow applications, *e.g.*, therapeutic diagnosis, and (3) to provide ideas on applications of instruments in a variety of training events.

We are directing this book specifically toward human relations trainers and consultants of all orientations: counselors, clergymen, personnel administrators, teachers, psychiatrists, social workers, psychologists, and others in clinically-oriented professions. It is our contention that the need for a reference on instrumentation which could be easily used by group facilitators has not been met in spite of the fact that the use of instrumentation has become increasingly common in all types of group efforts. What we have done is to bring together in this volume descriptions of instruments that have high applicability to group work and to individuals within the general group context. The format for the entry of each instrument should, we hope, promote the discriminating ability of the group facilitator and assist him in making intelligent decisions as to which instruments are appropriate given the needs and goals of a particular clientele with a particular time limitation. The first chapter of *Instrumentation in Human Relations Training* points toward the basic understanding of how instruments work. We include some very rudimentary statistical information for those who are uneasy in dealing with instruments because they are uncomfortable about how to answer when a participant asks "What's the norm group for this particular instrument?" or "What's the reliability of this instrument?" We wish to give these facilitators some means of dealing with statistical questions in productive ways. The core of this volume, however, is the presentation of a selective description of instruments, and the primary goal is to examine the usage and application of these instruments within particular groups.

One of the first things that you will observe as you use this book is that the instruments are handled with non-uniform attention. Some instruments have a one-page description while others, for example, *FIRO-B*, has a multiple-page description. The decision not to deal with all instruments at a uniform depth was based on the awareness that some instruments are more useful in human relations training than others.

We have chosen to review instruments on three levels. The first level contains instruments which have been shown to have exceptionally high currency in groups. The treatment that we have given those particular instruments is rather full-blown. The second level of instruments has less general utility in groups; however, depending upon the special focus of the group, they may be extremely appropriate. These instruments are less fully described. At the third level are instruments which, for the most part, have value only to groups with very specific training needs. The descriptions of these instruments are, at best, cursory. Within this last category, we have included such "heavies" as the Minnesota Multiphasic Personality Inventory and the California Psychological Inventory, limiting their description on the basis that they are primarily associated with individual therapy, personnel selection, and career counseling. By a similar determination, we have excluded any mention of projective tests such as the Thematic Apperception Test and the Rorschach. We have also restricted the number of instruments that have exclusively pathological scales.

We have taken this opportunity to write a fully-developed description of one particular instrument—*FIRO-B*. Our decision to use *FIRO-B* as a prototype is based on our opinion that it is the most generally useable instrument in training. Our contention is that you can extrapolate similarly useful information from any particular instrument that you wish to fully explore. Our detailed treatment of this instrument is the most extensive guide available on non-therapy uses of *FIRO-B*.

The instruments selected to be included in this book, then, are those that seem to have the most applicability for groups and group-related activities. There has been a consistent attempt to include instruments that can be used productively in personal growth groups, group dynamics groups, counseling groups, therapy groups, training/education groups and all phases of organization development activities as well as those endeavors subsumed under such vague labels as leadership and management development workshops. In order to allow for easy reference for facilitators who are designing group activities which fall into one of the above group types, we have chosen to divide the instruments into three sections: personal focus, interpersonal focus, and organizational focus. These categories have very permeable boundaries, and the decision to organize the instrument content into this format was, in part, a trade-off, *i.e.*, it seems to us to be more advantageous to have some general listing even if the categories are less than exact. A straight alphabetical listing, which was another option, appears in Appendix B.

One of the difficulties in discussing instruments is that a large number of terms can be applied to various types of instruments; they are known as tests, surveys, questionnaires, inventories and opinionnaires. For the purposes of this book, we make a distinction between tests and other types of instruments. A test, to our way of thinking, is an instrument which has *correct* answers (as defined by the test constructor). The other types of instruments—surveys, questionnaires, inventories, and opinionnaires—are those which do not have a specific correct answer for any given item. A further clarification is required for the use of the word instrumentation. *Instrumentation, by our definition, is the use of various types of instruments to generate data and to personalize theory input within a group setting.*

USING THE BOOK

An important concern to us when we were organizing and writing this book was that readers would be able to use this volume in ways that would meet their particular needs. It is our recommendation that you examine the opening chapters first and read them at the level that is appropriate to your personal level of sophistication. For some readers, these chapters may be useful as a reinforcement or review, while for others, much of the material may be new and require more detailed reading. Once the initial acquaintance has been made with the opening chapters and there is a genuine contextual reference point for what instrumentation attempts to accomplish, we recommend that you (1) look through the scale listing and become familiar with the traits that the instruments are measuring, (2) choose some traits of particular interest to you, and (3) explore the description of the specific instruments which measure those traits. At this point, you can evaluate the dimensions included in the first section of each instrument, "Description," making note of those instruments that seem promising in terms of time, cost, and complexity. You might follow this by finding alternative instruments to use in dealing with the traits that you are interested in measuring.

ORDERING INSTRUMENTS

At the point at which you have chosen specific instruments for a particular training activity, we would suggest that you order a specimen set of each one. A specimen set usually contains the instrument itself, a scoring key, an answer sheet if the answering mechanism is not self-contained, and a manual. We very strongly recommend that you complete the instrument yourself under the most simulative kind of conditions that are available. Pay special attention to the elements that you have understood clearly from the directions given and those that were potential misunderstandings for you. If you can alert the participants in your workshops to these elements, you can defuse some of the negative affect that the instruments may generate. Once you have completed and scored an instrument, you will have a much better sense of its ability to measure accurately the traits it is purporting to measure. After you have evaluated the instruments in this manner, order the instruments that you are going to use for a workshop. It usually takes at least two weeks to receive an order. This time lag can be cut by placing your order by telephone and requesting special handling. In our estimation, too many people order instruments and then try to adapt them for the group rather than to select the correct instrument for the particular group.

PART I
Instrumentation

Chapter
One

A PERSPECTIVE
ON INSTRUMENTATION

RATIONALE

The inclusion of feedback data derived from instruments in human relations training designs is a relatively new innovation. For those group facilitators with a heavy personal growth orientation, instrumentation was, and still is, considered a radical departure from "pure" laboratory methodology. It is sometimes felt that the only legitimate data in a laboratory are internally derived and that the interjection of instrumented data interferes with the natural progression of the learning process. It is important for facilitators of every orientation to understand the appropriate uses of instrumentation and for them to take a fresh look at the issues of feedback sources. Externally-derived data can provide the basis for potentially significant growth experiences if the facilitator is aware of the ramifications of using instruments: he must be personally familiar with the specific instrument he is administering, he must choose the instrument solely on the basis of the expressed needs and goals of his particular client group, and he must be competent to interpret the data which emerge in order that the feedback can be used in functional ways.

In discussing the origins of instrumented approaches to laboratory learning, Hall states:

> Blake and Mouton found that by using well-constructed reaction forms, surveys, interpersonal ratings and the like, attention could be directed to the elements of group life which were most important in group development. This was the initial focus of instrumentation—plotting the session-by-session building of climate, power hierarchy, and other facets of the developing group . . . It was only later that Blake, Mouton, and others began to recognize that the use of instruments for sampling feedback data afforded a precision and specificity not possible previously; moreover, it was realized that feedback on the reactions of participants to a number of situations—both natural and contrived —could be obtained via instrumentation. (*Training and Development Journal,* May, 1970, pp. 48-55.)

It is our contention that more growth can occur for a group participant if he is provided with a method for specifically focusing on his own behavior. This is in addition to the feedback he receives from fellow group members which can be growthful on a different and equally important level.

It is not enough that an individual leave a laboratory learning situation feeling exhilarated, more open, changed, and so on. He must have been given the opportunity to understand himself and his behaviors in highly specific ways and be able to make decisions concerning behavior change based upon this learning. Being able to relate to the particular outcomes of instruments he has taken may serve to reinforce new behavior patterns and positive self-concepts when the glow of the group experience has faded with his return to the real world, and the concerns and personal impact of fellow participants becomes diffused with the on-going demands of old relationships.

Instrumented feedback can be more useful than the typical kinds of verbal feedback one receives in groups. Well-constructed scales can provide feedback on behavioral continua; for example, the extremes on the two major dimensions of the *Personal Orientation Inventory*—Inner-Other Directed and Time Competent-Incompetent—can be seen to be equally dysfunctional. This concept underlies the development of *A Survey of Life Orientations* in which one's strengths in excess are viewed as weaknesses. Too often participants (and facilitators) give feedback that is absolute; that is, it does not locate the person in reference to degrees of a trait or to a norm group. It is not uncommon to hear such statements as the following: "You talk too much." "You are too quiet." "Your aggressiveness turns me off."

Perhaps the primary value of instrumentation, then, is as a source of personal feedback for individuals in a laboratory group. This use involves the rather straightforward completion, scoring, and interpretation of scales. This is, however, just the basis for a more extensive number of uses of instrumentation. Instruments can also be used as vehicles for giving and receiving feedback among group members. For example, participants can be asked to predict each other's scores so that individuals become more aware of their facades and of the impact they have on others. It is also possible for participants to complete entire instruments for each other for a more in-depth examination of interpersonal perceptions.

A related use of instruments is to help participants to study here-and-now process within the group and to assist the group in diagnosing its own internal functioning. These instrumented data can focus on what is happening in the life of the group and may specify what changes are desirable. In this way, the group can more quickly arrive at optimal functioning so that more learning can take place. Again, the unique advantage of specificity with instrumented feedback greatly enhances the probability that the group will be able to monitor and manage its own processes effectively.

Many instruments can be used to teach theory, concepts, and terminology that are intrinsic to the description and interpretation of interpersonal functioning. Some brief instruments are intended primarily to introduce concepts rather than to be used as a source of feedback. For example, the T-P Leadership Questionnaire in Volume I of *A Handbook of Structured Experiences for Human Relations Training* is designed to demonstrate the interplay between task and person concerns in leadership.

Participants learn more when they are actively involved in the learning process, and instruments predetermine an active role in the learning. When participants have invested time and energy in an activity such as completing an inventory related to the model being explored, they have also invested in learning the theory, and the entire process becomes more meaningful and easily relatable in terms of the group experience. Participants can be encouraged to study the items in detail, since the items constitute a behavioral definition of the trait being measured. This process can result in their considering changing specific behaviors.

The facilitator may wish to use instrumented outcomes to manipulate group composition for brief, experimental demonstrations of the effects of group composition on task accomplishment. Long-term groups can also be built that offer promise of demonstrating group task competences. Extremes of both homogeneity and heterogeneity can be avoided if instrumented data are utilized.

If human relations training groups have as their *raison d'etre* the awareness of self and the resulting growth, evolution, and change in individuals' behavior, then it becomes clear that measuring these emerging human phenomena can be a needed, natural and realistic expectation of laboratory learning activity. Instruments can provide the method for assessing growth and change on both individual and group levels. Even scales with relatively low reliability can be effectively used to study group behavior patterns and attitudes on a pre, post, and post-post design. This measurement of outcome can provide some of the most crucial feedback for individuals in a laboratory setting and may help to validate the experience for themselves and for the group in general. In addition, instrumented research will provide feedback to the facilitator on the effectiveness of his own style and intervention skills and will aid him in designing laboratory experiences for other groups.

TRAITS

One given in the use of instrumentation is that you are dealing with outcomes based on visible elements of human behavior known as traits. We think that it is important for a facilitator who chooses to include instruments in a training design to work through his understanding of the nature of the traits upon which the instruments he is using are based, prior to the actual administration of the instruments. He needs to be able to ease the anxiety of his participants concerning what the instruments have "revealed" about them in a knowledgeable, nonthreatening way. This is important in terms of a learning theory presupposition that if a person is highly anxious, he will be largely incapable of hearing, seeing, and learning. The following discussion of traits is intended as a means of focusing the concept for the facilitator.

Behavioral scientists, like natural scientists, build taxonomies or ways of naming observable phenomena. The reason for naming is to provide a common ground for communication to take place regarding what may be experienced by individuals. The naming does not create the phenomena; it merely attempts to label, in some meaningful way, what already exists. Traits, then, are sets of categories invented by psychologists or behavioral scientists to permit the orderly description of behavior. This working definition of traits is illustrated by the following anecdote.

Three baseball umpires were involved in a heated discussion of what they considered to be strikes and balls.

First umpire: "Well, it's easy, fellahs. I call 'em as they *are*: If they're a strike, I call 'em a strike; if they're a ball, I call 'em a ball."

Second umpire: "Wait a minute! I see it different! I call 'em the way I *see* 'em. If I see 'em as a strike, I call 'em a strike, and if I see 'em as a ball, I call 'em a ball!"

Third umpire: "You're both wrong! They ain't *nothin'* 'til I call 'em! Nothin' but a baseball that got thrown 'til I holler 'Strike!' or 'Ball!'"

In the anecdote, we get to the heart of the issue. People do not "have" traits in themselves. They do not, for example, have a trait of inclusion or a trait of affection or a trait of control, per se. These are labels that are imposed upon people's behavior to add some order, understanding, and predictability to the behavior. One of the difficulties in using instrumentation is that many people tend to infer that the trait being measured is, in fact, an integral part of their psychological makeup or behavior pattern. It is important to stress the fact that these are simply imposed categories and that these behavior "traits" do not exist in themselves any more than a strike or ball exists before it is called by an umpire.

A related concept that may serve to help debunk the image of infallibility which participants often assume about instruments is the story about the Air Force way of dealing with things. It is said that the Air Force method is to measure it with a micrometer, mark it with a crayon, and then cut it with an axe. The final outcome of instrumentation is equally inexact, even though the intent has been to be as precise as humanly possible. The key word here is "humanly." At best, the outcomes merely suggest kinds of behavior. Yet, even this suggestion can be of great value if it is seen for what it really is—an indication.

It is not necessary to adopt a trait-factor theory of personality in order to employ instrumentation effectively in human relations training. It is possible to process instrumented feedback in terms of widely varying theoretical positions, from analytical to existential. Extreme positions related to instrumentation are illustrated by the following two attitudinal statements:

1. If a thing exists, it exists in some amount. If you haven't measured it, you don't know what you are talking about.

2. No number or combination of numbers can ever adequately describe a dynamic, emerging person. The important characteristics of humans are immeasurable.

In the context of one's own theoretical frame of reference, it is possible to incorporate "objective" data to good effect so long as one bears in mind that the process simply abstracts from the mass of information about an individual what is deemed to be important.

One of the most powerful learnings derived in human relations training is that people are far more alike than they are different. Participants discover that many of the differences among people are non-critical. Behavioral scientists have been so busy in developing a psychology of individual differences that we have neglected to explore a psychology of sameness. Instrumentation can demonstrate the large overlap across persons in a wide array of human traits. Outcomes can be interpreted in a perspective which acknowledges that, at a humanistic level, all differences do not necessarily make a difference. Ordinarily one uses inventories to discriminate among people, to spread them out for study or instruction. We are proposing that it is equally advantageous to use instrumentation to demonstrate graphically the common core of humanness that can bind us together.

DISADVANTAGES AND ADVANTAGES

It is important to recognize that there are both advantages and disadvantages to using instrumentation in human relations training. These can most appropriately be dealt with by acknowledging their existence and working on ways of minimizing the problems connected with their utilization and maximizing the advantages of the instruments. In this discussion, we will first approach the problematic elements of using instruments.

Disadvantages. One of the key disadvantages of using instruments is that the participant may fear that someone has obtained an indelible fingerprinting of him, that he has been exposed, that somebody has gotten into his mind and "psyched" him out. This fear may be accompanied by resentment and a loss of potential learning. An accompanying problem may be that participants can, in essence, accept their scores as unquestionably accurate descriptions of themselves: they *are* "assertive," "aggressive," or "withdrawn." Some participants may attach pathological or quasi-pathological definitions to these traits and turn them into a self-fulfilling prophecy. This labeling problem may also take place when participants are dealing with each other. They may still refer to Joe as "at the 98th percentile on control" after the laboratory experience in spite of the fact that Joe may have spent a great deal of energy during the laboratory in experimenting with new behaviors and may have modified his control pattern considerably. This problem of not allowing people out of their old "bags" is particularly counter-productive for intact groups. Joe may discover three years later that some individuals are still relating to him as "at the 98th percentile on control." It is extremely important that the facilitator make an effort to reduce this tendency to over-generalize the accuracy and stability of the instrument. To avoid having participants see instruments as a "God-directed opening of the soul to the world," the facilitator should discuss the margin of error and other factors which contribute to less-than-absolute results. The instrument can be seen as analagous to a thermometer—the reading would be expected to vary from time to time. Participants should be allowed and encouraged to explore the instrument thoroughly so that they can see how it was designed and how their scores were derived. They need to acknowledge the fact that all they have done is to give their answers to a lot of situations that were described in the instrument, and they added numbers denoting those answers to come up with a score. If they have trouble understanding where the score came from, they should be encouraged to go back to each item fed into the score, to examine how they responded to each item, to see how they scored them, and perhaps to compare their responses to other individuals' responses, item by item and situation by situation. It is also valuable to show participants how instrumentation is related to everyday, choice-making experiences which are fraught with inconsistency and are subject to influences of all kinds, such as one's psychological set of the moment, one's physical state, and so on. Hopefully, efforts such as these on the part of the facilitator will dispel the mysticism surrounding instrumentation and supply a realistic way of looking at "testing" outcomes. Participants need to understand that instrumented feedback, like other forms of feedback, can only *indicate* what *may* be true of the individual.

A second problem which may arise for the facilitator is that instruments sometimes promote flight from personal and interpersonal issues for the participants. This flight may be experienced in several ways. Instruments may generate a rash of nit-picking (inappropriate) responses. Participants sometimes question items, reliability, validity, or the value of the instrument. A lot of potential learning time can be wasted in arguing about the instrument itself. Nit-picking is often a result of the fact that a participant has received or is about to receive information that disturbs him. He has a tendency to fear that this profile is irrevocably him or that people are going to interpret his data in a negative fashion. This participant is likely to attack the value of instruments, turning the group process into a debate. Hostility may also be generated from another source. Some participants may see instruments as irrelevent, time-consuming, and diverting from the key issues of the workshop. This may, in part, be attributable to a preconceived notion that "structure" is not an appropriate part of group experience, particularly in a personal growth group. A non-hostile "flight" may involve a tendency to psychologize about the traits the instrument is measuring. Those in the helping professions particularly may become involved in a discussion of the pathological origins of the traits. Participants from other backgrounds may begin discussing the value of a particular trait. The facilitator can alleviate these flights if he has dealt thoroughly with the mysticism and reality of instruments.

It will also aid the situation to have made the expectation clear prior to the workshop that instrumentation will be a part of the design and to discuss why the facilitator believes instrumented feedback to be a valuable part of that particular laboratory for the specific group's needs and goals. The facilitator can intervene to refocus the group discussion on the data obtained from the instrument and away from the instrument itself so that participants become involved in the learning process once more.

The use of instruments can be a means of dissipating the tension of person-to-person encounter, especially in a personal growth workshop. Both the participant and the leader may be freed of some of the ambiguous but potentially growthful tension that face-to-face encountering and reacting to each other produces. It may also tend to pull an individual away from the interpersonal processes of the group if the data from the instrument have created an emotional overload for the individual. He may become too preoccupied integrating the data, and his behavior may become dysfunctional to the rest of the group. Some of this difficulty can be eased if the facilitator takes time to process the data from the instrument to the point where the participants can handle it and manage to integrate it without its interfering with the life of the group.

A balance must be maintained, consistent with the goals of the group, between instrumentation and the interpersonal learning needs of the participants. Processing the data can and should include more than the facilitator's interpretation of scores. Participants should be given an opportunity to talk through their scores and to compare their scores with the scores of others in the group and with appropriate norm groups if they are available. The facilitator should emphasize and legitimize the differing life perspectives and orientations among people and should encourage participants to explore why they see life from a different perspective than do some of the other participants. The facilitator may wish to use his scores to illustrate how his personal orientation governed his responses to the instrument and share with others what the personal impact of this feedback has been for him.

A third disadvantage of instrumentation which takes skillful handling on the part of the facilitator is the tendency for this activity to foster dependency of the participants on the facilitator. The administration of instruments and the accompanying feedback processing puts the facilitator into an expert role during these phases of the laboratory. It is easy for this to become a role-binding experience, since most facilitators operate from a process-consultation posture and eschew the expert role. Participants who initially find it anxiety-producing to be in a group situation where the "leader" does not assume traditional leadership responsibilities for the direction of the participants may find it hard to let the facilitator get out of the "authority" role. It is particularly important for the facilitator to shift the responsibility for learning during the feedback-processing stage as early as possible to the participants themselves and thereby aid the transition from a highly-structured experience to minimally-structured group processes. The responsibility for learning rests with the participant; the meaning is his, as he integrates these data with his understanding of himself.

Another disadvantage is that "taking a test" may provoke subtle anger or undue anxiety on the part of participants. Instruments can trigger unpleasant memories of school grading practices. It is important for the facilitator to avoid using the word "test" and to stress that the instrument is non-evaluative. There are no "right" or "wrong" answers.

Finally, there is the fact that instruments are subject to distortion, lying, and answering in a socially-desirable way and that virtually all instruments have a great deal of transparency. The more sophisticated the group is, in terms of test-taking, the more potential there is for them to distort the results by manipulating their scores. However, if the participants have a commitment to their own learning, the tendency to distort will be greatly lessened. If the participants have volunteered for the group experience, their level of commitment is generally high. If the group is an intact, non-voluntary one, the facilitator should attempt to inspire commitment to the learning goals of the experience since this commitment must exist if the experience is to be productive on any level.

Advantages. Given that there are problems in using instruments and that there are means of coping with or avoiding problems, the advantages become very clear. Hall conceptualizes the amount of learning as it relates to the amount of personal involvement along a continuum. Illustrating minimal involvement on the extreme left is lecture, followed by discussion, case study, instrumented workshop, T-group, and, on the extreme right, the personal growth group, having maximal involvement.

Learning Involvement Continuum

Lecture	Discussion	Case Study	Instrumented Workshops	T-group	Personal Growth Group
⊢——————⊥——————⊥——————⊥——————⊥——————⊣					

It is Hall's contention that involvement increases in going from the first to the last of these learning situations, so that the person is approaching the point at which learning becomes extremely relevant, important, and involving to him. It follows from this model that the person gets more learning from the kind of situation in which he is simultaneously highly involved. Note that the instrumented workshop (that is, a workshop in which *all* activity centers around instruments) is placed between the case study approach and the training group. It is more involving than the case study group because the person is working with information about himself. It is less involving than the T-group or the personal growth group, in which the information that one deals with is somewhat more personal, emotional, and perhaps somewhat more threatening.

Instrumented approaches give a recipient early opportunities to understand the theory involved in the dynamics of his own group situation, understanding that can increase his involvement. By judicious choice of an appropriate instrument during the first group session, the facilitator can quickly offer the participant a theory about personality style, group development, interpersonal relations, or leadership that he can use throughout the rest of the group experience.

If separate theory sessions are part of the laboratory design, participants will find them stimulating and meaningful if they are explaining a rationale for the instrumented feedback which they have received. Theory sessions without such previous experience with instrumented feedback, however, can be experienced by participants as a sudden thrusting from an active, involved situation into a passive listening situation.

A related advantage of using instruments is that it gives the person some constructs and terminology early in the group experience that he can use in looking at his and other people's behavior and categorizing and describing what goes on between individuals or within an individual. Another advantage of using instruments in human relations training is that the participant forms a commitment to the information, constructs, and theory that he has been given. This occurs because his instrumented feedback describes him in terms of these constructs. One way of tying a person's self to some useful theory about groups and interpersonal relations is to give the theory personal impact. The participant's learning is crystallized in this process.

Through instrumentation, a participant can be given feedback about his personal behavior early in a group experience. It often happens in a workshop that a person does not get feedback from other participants about his style or about the way he relates until the last day, the last meeting, or the last two or three hours of the workshop. It often takes that long before the other participants have developed the skills necessary to give effective feedback to someone, and it often takes that long before an atmosphere of trust has developed in the group so that members can feel comfortable in giving that kind of feedback to another member. Regardless of the reasons, the tragedy of this situation is that the person now has some information that he needs to know about himself with no time to work on new behavior that might modify the aspect of himself that has been described. Receiving periodic affirmation about one's effective behaviors can be experienced as supportive during a personal growth laboratory. Instruments administered early in the group experience help to compensate for the lack of feedback from others. A person can get some feedback about his style, his set toward other people, and the way others react to him. He can generate an agenda of behavior modification for himself on the characteristics uncovered by the instrument while he has the remainder of the workshop to work on it. The person can "contract" with the group to experiment with new behavior based on the clearer focus that the instrument gives. The instrumented feedback also increases the chances that the individual will form a commitment to personal change and growth that may not occur with feedback from a group member, which is sometimes easier to discount or "forget." This may generalize to the individual's interpersonal relationships in and outside the group, where commitment to changed behavior patterns may be essential to the life of the relationships.

Instruments give feedback to an individual or to an organization in a way that is characterized by relatively low threat. That is, when a person gets information from a questionnaire that he has filled out himself, he is more likely to trust that data as compared with data he receives from another individual on his personal style. At least he does not have the dilemma of trying to sort out whether the information is mostly a function of his behavior or of the set of the person who is giving him the feedback or of some chemistry that exists between the two of them. He can be fairly sure that the instrument holds no personal malevolence toward him; therefore, he can be freer to accept the information, understanding the fact that the information actually came from his own responses to descriptions of situations.

Another advantage is that instruments not only give feedback about the individual but also allow him to see himself as he compares with others. We all are aware that we may be more or less dominating than other people, that we may enjoy being with people more or less than others, that we may have a greater or lesser need for people to like us, and so on. However, it is often an eye-opening experience to find out that we are stronger in one or more of our characteristics than ninety-nine percent of the people in a certain norm group. This last piece of information, indicating that a person is not only high on a characteristic, but that he is *unusually* high on it, may cause a person to pause and to examine carefully whether this characteristic is becoming dysfunctional for him, *e.g.*, getting in the way of his performance on the job or at home.

An important advantage of instrumentation is that it can promote involvement with data of all kinds. Participants often come to a laboratory having never heard the word feedback, or, if they have heard it, it was in connection with computers. It provides a good learning flow to take participants from the concept of feedback as it applies to data processing to its relationship to instruments and finally to its application in interpersonal relationships. Their first experience with personal feedback can be the data derived from instrumentation provided early by the facilitator. They can be given an opportunity to practice giving and receiving feedback through a relatively non-threatening experience such as predicting other participants' scores. This process may allow participants to learn to give and receive constructive interpersonal feedback earlier in the life of the group and give the group experience a greater chance to impact the behavior of the participants. It may also facilitate a group which needs energizing by providing feedback which can be dealt with productively.

Instruments surface covert issues that could be dealt with in the group setting. This is true whether the issues and problems are within an individual, between individuals, or within an organization. By administering an instrument that uncovers these issues, the concerns are made public, *i.e.*, brought outside of the individual or the organization. They then become legitimate topics to deal with, to discuss, to try to correct or improve.

An advantage for the facilitator of small groups is that instruments allow him to focus the energies and time of the participants on the most appropriate material and also to control, to some extent, what things are dealt with in the workshop. In this way he is able to ensure that crucial, existing issues are worked on rather than less important ones that the members may use to avoid grappling with the more uncomfortable ones.

A final advantage is that instruments allow longitudinal assessment of change in a group, an organization, or an individual. This assessment can be useful in organization development for demonstrating that the group interventions in which the organization is involved are compatible with the goals that the consultant and the client have determined from sensing efforts and also with the stated goals of the organization. This advantage is valuable in terms of group research and also for personal goal feedback.

In summary, the following lists are offered:

THE USE OF INSTRUMENTATION IN SMALL GROUPS

Disadvantages

Engenders fear of exposure.

Encourages "labeling."

Promotes flight from confrontation.

Generates time-consuming nit-picking.

May be seen as diverting from key issues and arouse hostility.

Relieves potentially growthful tension

Can result in feedback overload.

Fosters dependency on the facilitator.

Makes the facilitator an "expert."

Triggers anger and anxiety from school connotation.

Makes possible feedback distortion by manipulation of scores.

Advantages

Enables early, easy theory learning.

Promotes personal involvement.

Develops early understanding of constructs and terminology.

Supplies personal feedback earlier than other participants are able to.

Produces personal commitment to information, theory and constructs.

Facilitates contracting for new behavior.

Fosters open reception of feedback through low threat.

Provides for comparisons of individuals with norm groups.

Promotes involvement with data and feedback process.

Surfaces latent issues.

Allows facilitator to focus and control group appropriately.

Facilitates longitudinal assessment of change.

AVOIDING THE DISADVANTAGES OF INSTRUMENTS

1. Legitimize with participants the use of instrumentation in the laboratory design.

   A. Make expectations concerning instruments and their value to the group experience clear prior to the beginning of the group's life.

   B. Be ready to intervene to refocus group discussion if participants use the instrument as a flight mechanism.

   C. Minimize anxieties so that more learning can occur.

2. Make a concerted effort to remove the mysticism surrounding instrumentation.

   A. Discuss the margin of error and other factors which contribute to less-than-absolute results.

   B. Allow and encourage participants to explore the instrument thoroughly so that they see how it was designed and how their scores were derived.

   C. Clarify the theoretical basis of the instrument.

3. Insure that sufficient time is made available for processing the data derived.

   A. Give them an opportunity to talk through their scores and compare their scores with others.

   B. Emphasize and legitimize the differing life perspectives and orientations among people.

4. Assure the participants that they have control over their own data.

   A. Define carefully the parameters within which scores are to be shared or not shared.

   B. Underscore the point that scores will not be reported to the participants' superiors (people frequently have a set that scores do get reported—like a report card).

ETHICAL CONSIDERATIONS

There is no commonly-accepted ethical code that binds users of training materials, but a number of practices in instrumentation raise concerns. It is not unusual to observe facilitators using materials which they have reproduced from copyrighted publications without permission. Occasionally scales are abstracted (borrowed?) from complex instruments, and many developers "steal" previously published items for inclusion in new scales. Scales are sometimes named to indicate more validity than has been demonstrated, norm groups are inadequately described; validity and reliability evidence is often missing. Users sometimes allow themselves to be overrepresented in terms of their qualifications, and they sometimes fail to ensure that participants are not harmed by the results of instrumentation. It is not uncommon for participants to be co-opted into revealing themselves through instrumentation. We stress the potential learning to be derived from participation, but we discourage the practice of "publishing" scores on scales that denote pathology.

Chapter Two

INSTRUMENTATION

There is, we believe, a sharp distinction between just "giving" an instrument and using it properly, *i.e.*, getting the most value out of it in terms of the goals of the experience and the needs of the participants. In this chapter we will deal with some specific dimensions of instrumentation by focusing on seven phases in presenting an instrument:

(1) Administration.

(2) Theory input.

(3) Prediction.

(4) Scoring.

(4) Interpretation.

(6) Posting.

(7) Processing.

Rather than discussing these seven phases in a general way, we will illustrate them by describing the manner in which we present an actual instrument in a group.

We have also included three examples of training designs in which instrumentation was a key element. One example is from a teacher training workshop, the second is a two-day, team-building session for senior managers in a manufacturing facility, and the third is a leadership development workshop.

SEVEN PHASES IN PRESENTING AN INSTRUMENT

For the illustration of instrument presentation, we have chosen *FIRO-B*, an instrument uniquely well-suited to provide meaningful feedback data and theory input for human relations groups. The *FIRO-B* was designed by William C. Schutz and was copyrighted in 1957. A complete discussion of this instrument appears in Section A.

1. *Administration*
   (10-15 minutes)

Once a non-threatening atmosphere is established, the purposes for taking the instrument are discussed. In administering the *FIRO-B*, it is important to avoid giving any clues as to the nature of the traits that are being measured. After we have distributed the instrument, we simply caution the participants on two points: 1) they will experience a sense of repetitiveness of items in the instrument. We explain that there is no check on internal consistency, and they are to consider and answer each item independently. 2) Some of the answers do not quite fit; we tell them that they just need to be a little creative in following the intention of the instrument.

A difficulty, particularly in larger groups, is that individuals in the group will finish the instrument at different times. In a non-authoritarian way, the administrator of the instrument can establish the expectation that as people finish the instrument they will wait quietly for the others to finish. When everyone has completed the instrument, we move to the second phase—theory.

2. *Theory input*
(10-12 minutes)

The theory behind *FIRO-B* is that all human interaction can be divided into three categories: issues surrounding inclusion, issues surrounding control, and issues surrounding affection. Schutz's theory of group development suggests that a group proceeds through inclusion issues into control issues and finally into affection issues and then recycles. To illustrate these categories, the facilitator can ask the participants to consider a group of people riding in a boat. The inclusion issue, with the boat, is whether or not individuals have come along for the ride. The issue of control with the boat is who is running the motor or operating the rudder. The affection issue concerns how closely people are seated together in the boat.

The facilitator can follow this discussion of categories with an explanation of the *FIRO-B* six-cell diagram.

	INCLUSION	CONTROL	AFFECTION
Expressed Behavior			
Wanted Behavior			

The two dimensions which the diagram illustrates are inclusion, control, and affection in terms of what the individual expresses to others and inclusion, control, and affection in terms of what the individual wants from others. It is important for participants to hear that the expressed is *their* behavior and the wanted is the behavior they wish from *others*. Once the participants understand the six-cell diagram, we move to the prediction phase.

3. *Prediction*
(2 minutes)

We ask participants to predict whether they will score high, medium, or low in each of those six cells and to write those predictions in a corner of each cell in the diagram on their copy of the instrument. When the predictions have been made, we move to the fourth phase—scoring.

4. *Scoring*
   (6-8 minutes)

There are a number of ways to score instruments. Sometimes they require templates, sometimes they are self-scoring, and sometimes the scores are called out or written on newsprint or handed out on a mimeographed sheet. It is important to gauge the sophistication of the particular group in selecting what is the most appropriate way to score an instrument. In many cases it is more efficient to do clerical scoring; that is, you or an assistant score them rather than to attempt to have participants score them. The obvious negative factor in that approach is that individuals cannot get instant feedback, but frequently this can be handled by administering the instrument before a meal break and having the results available immediately after. The guideline, as we see it, is that the scoring process should not detract from the data being generated by the instrument. Sometimes people can create such a task out of the scoring process that they lose or diminish the actual results of the instrument.

Our experience with the *FIRO-B* is that scoring is most profitably done by the use of a mimeographed handout on which participants can enter their scores at their own pace once the administrator has worked through the first scale with them. After the scoring has been completed and the scores have been posted in cells along with the predictions, we begin the interpretation phase.

5. *Interpretation*
   (5-7 minutes,
   per person)

The manner of interpretation may vary sharply depending upon the participant group and the style of the administrator of the instrument. We like to handle interpretation in two stages: the first stage is an interpretation of the administrator's own scores or another staff member's scores and the second stage is a dyadic interpretation between participants. It is our preference to interpret, through a six-step method, the scores of another staff member so that participants can begin to see how interpretations are made. Then, we have that staff member interpret our scores in front of the group so that the participants are afforded a second opportunity to see some variances in the style of interpretation. This modeling of interpretation is a very important defusing element. If the staff are willing to show their scores to individuals within the workshop, the individual participants find it easier and less threatening to share their scores with other members of the group. The following are the six steps of interpretation as we employ them for the *FIRO-B*:

A. Compare the actual score cell by cell with their predictions of high, medium, or low. The converter that is needed in this particular design is:

Prediction	Actual Score
High	7-9 points
Medium	3-6 points
Low	0-2 points

B. Compare actual scores to norm averages.

Average Scores of the FIRO-B Norm Group

	INCLUSION	CONTROL	AFFECTION	
Expressed Behavior	5.4	3.9	4.1	13.4
Wanted Behavior	6.5	4.6	4.8	15.9
	11.9	8.5	8.9	29.3

In this phase we consider scores which are discrepant from the norm by 2 or more points to be significant for purposes of discussion.

C. Examine column scores to see the significance of inclusion, control, and affection scores by their relative importance to each other. For example, if the highest score is on control, control issues are the most important to that individual, if the second highest is on inclusion, it is the second highest importance, and if the lowest score is on affection then affection is the least significant concern in that person's life. A second part of step three is to look at the column scores in relationship to the norm scores and compare the individual scores against the totals for each of the columns. If there are more that 3 points of discrepency, they are worthy of discussion.

D. Examine the scores by row—expressed and wanted. The first comparison to make is the relative importance of expressed behavior versus wanted behavior in terms of which is a more characteristic or logical pattern for the individual The second comparison to make is the actual score in relationship to the norm score totals for the two dimensions. This process allows individuals to see their scores in relation to other individual's scores. A discrepancy of more than 4 points is worthy of discussion.

E. This step has to do with an index we call the Social Interaction Index. This is derived from adding either the columns or the rows to arrive at the sum of all six cells. This trait is then viewed in relation to 29 points, which is the norm for the sum of the scores of that particular instrument. If the individual score is 5 points higher or lower, it is then significant for discussion.

F. An interpretation is made of the "fit" between the profiles of two participants. For example, the expressed control of one person is compared to the wanted control of the other, and the compatibility of their behavior is discussed.

In the second stage, dyadic interpretation, we ask individuals to form pairs. Once the dyads have been established, the method we have found to be most effective is to have them exchange scoring sheets so that they are interpreting each other's scores. A model for this activity might be to give the dyads five to seven minutes for A to interpret B's scores and while that interpretation is taking place, B "bites the bullet" as a stoic, non-informational, non-feedback stance in dealing with the interpreter. Once that interpretation has taken place, they exchange roles; B then interprets A's scores and A "bites the bullet." When the five to seven minute phase is through, they can move to a five to ten minute discussion of the instrument in which they share the personal impact of their scores.

6. *Posting*
(5-8 minutes)

The sixth phase is posting. It has been our experience that posting scores on newsprint or chalkboard has the potential to dissipate some of the concerns that people have about negative values and lack of social desirability attached to any particular score. At the same time, it can generate additional useful data for the group to process. This particular model of generating scores and then posting them for discussion can be particularly effective in dealing with sub-groups within a large workshop design.

7. *Processing*
(15-20 minutes)

The final and perhaps most crucial phase of instrumentation is processing. Group processing of the data generated by an instrument has the potential of simultaneously defusing negative affect and promoting integration of the concepts.

The optimal size of the group for the processing of data generated by instruments varies from six to twelve participants. In a stranger group, the smaller size maximizes the potential for individual "air space." In an intact group, the goal is to include as many people as possible in order to maximize the common exposure to the information being shared.

Some sample questions that we have found to be effective are:

(1) Which scale scores seem to fit your self-concept *most* accurately?

(2) Which scale scores seem to fit your self-concept *least* accurately?

(3) Based on the common history of the members of the group, which scale scores seem to be *most/least* like those that other group members would have predicted for the individual whose scores are being discussed?

(4) What value does each individual place on a high or low score on a particular trait? For example, the *Survey of Interpersonal Values* produces six scales:

   Support
   Conformity
   Recognition
   Independence
   Benevolence
   Leadership

Is a high score on conformity socially desirable (or undesirable)? This last question promotes a forum of value clarification that provides an opportunity for disclosure (what I hold as valuable) and awareness (what other members of the group see as valuable).

Potent Scores. Occasionally instruments produce feedback that may be simultaneously accurate and discrepant with self-concept. For example, a low benevolence score on the *SIV* may be disorienting for a minister, a low score on Time Competence on the *Personal Orientation Inventory* may be disorienting for an executive who sees himself as extremely competent, or a high expressed control score may be disconcerting for a teacher who sees himself as egalitarian. In leading a group processing phase, a facilitator must be tuned in to scores that are disorienting, i.e., not easily integrated. Frequently this situation can be handled most effectively by a one-to-one rap with the person after the group processing session.

It is our contention that it is the facilitator's responsibility to assist in the integration of all data generated by instrumented feedback. This responsibility may, in some cases, mean that you promote dealing with disconcerting feedback (as opposed to permitting a wholesale discounting). Frequently it takes days for individuals to "accept" dissonant feedback. Conversely, instruments can produce inaccurate data that should not be indiscriminately accepted.

NOTES ON FACILITATOR STYLE

It is important for the facilitator to develop a psychological atmosphere that is conducive to participants receiving instrumented feedback readily. The climate should be non-clinical, open, and experimental. The style which the facilitator exhibits when using instrumentation should be "light" rather than "heavy" should not convey the impression that this is a deadly serious business that is going to yield some delicate data. In a sense he "sells" the instrument to the participants by attempting to induce a psychological set toward frankness in responding to instrument items.

The Gestalt concept of *presence* may be useful to guide the facilitator's thinking about his style in relation to instrumentation. The facilitator who has presence exhibits confidence, demonstrates that he is "on top of" the situation, and exudes an aura of being organized and alert. People tend to follow his instructions without challenge, and in this sense he is somewhat charismatic. If the facilitator lacks presence, it often results in participants asking a great many questions, nit-picking about items, and casting aspersions about the validity of the procedure. Being present in this context presupposes that the facilitator is well prepared to use the instrument. He knows the procedure which he is about to direct, he is comfortable in explaining the theory related to the scales, and he is flexible in managing the learning situation.

In introducing an instrument the facilitator needs to be sensitive to the possible immediate emotional impact which "testing" may have on participants. He needs to defuse the experience by relating the instrument to the learning goals of the training event and by pointing out that the intent is to be instructive rather than diagnostic. He may model openness by interpreting his own scores and by soliciting feedback relative to them.

The following list is intended to enhance the effectiveness of the facilitator in using instrumentation.

DON'T'S AND DO'S OF INSTRUMENTATION

Don't use the word "test."

Don't give instructions while participants are reading.

Don't give too many instructions at once.

Don't put undue pressure on participants to publish scores that may make them appear "sick."

Don't diagnose participants' weaknesses for them.

Don't label participants.

Do take the instrument yourself first.

Do point out to participants how the instrument fits into the goals of training.

Do encourage participants to be open in describing themselves on the instrument.

Do plan plenty of processing time.

Do watch for participants who may be experiencing difficulty in integrating their scores with their conception of themselves.

Do solicit feedback on your style: particular things you do in instrumentation that helped and impeded learning.

LABORATORY/WORKSHOP DESIGNS

In designing laboratory experiences in which you plan to include instruments there are some issues to be examined. One major concern in using more than a single instrument in any training design is that the traits measured be supplementary. The choice of instruments should not include two which measure exactly the same characteristics since this adds little or no new information. Yet the traits measured should not be so diverse that the participants have a difficult time putting together a congruent picture of themselves. For example, we would not recommend using the *Personality Inventory* (Bernreuter) and the *Eysenck Personality Inventory* in the same design, since the data would tend to be repetitive. On the other hand, the choice of *Personality Research Form* and *Val-Ed* in the same group experience would tend to provide a disconcertingly diverse focus to the feedback.

A second concern is that the facilitator anticipate the type of interaction affect the instrumented feedback will produce. He should avoid overloading the participants with data which will generate a heavy emotional atmosphere and perhaps move the interaction to a non-productive level. It is equally important to avoid instruments which may produce feedback that the participants are not at a level of sophistication to handle well or to use instrumented feedback which is inappropriate to the goals of the experience which may create a shut-down of interaction. It would not be productive to administer the *MMPI* to a group of managers during a team-building workshop.

The key to managing the integration of data in productive ways when incorporating instrumentation in a training design is in the careful selection of instruments and the consciousness of the processing issues as they relate to the interaction in the group. If the decision is to use the *FIRO-B* and the *FIRO-F*, the design must include time to process each of the instruments and time to process the relationship of the two sets of scores produced.

There are a number of instruments that have "Natural" pairings with structured experiences, for example, *Supervisory Attitudes: The X-Y- Scale (1972 Annual Handbook for Group Facilitators)* and "Win as Much as You Can" (Volume II, *A Handbook of Structured Experiences for Human Relations Training*), or Bass' *Ori* with any intergroup task such as "Towers" (Volume III) or making a checkerboard ("Group Tasks," Volume II). The integrated use of instruments and structured experiences tends to reinforce learnings and crystallize concepts since they both supplement and complement each other.

Chapter Three

TECHNICAL CONSIDERATIONS

In this chapter we will explore a number of technical topics related to instrumentation. The purpose of this treatment is to provide a basic framework for studying instruments for possible use in training settings. The following list includes the major categories of concerns which the user needs to take into account when choosing an instrument:

Validity.   What does the instrument measure? Will the data be useful?

Reliability.   How accurate or stable are the scores derived from the measurement?

Objectivity.   Can the instrument be scored by untrained judges, such as participants?

Availability.   Can the instrument be obtained easily for use in a particular training event?

Cost.   How expensive are the materials?

Time.   How much time is required in using the instrument?

Sophistication. What background is required to use the instrument?
At what reading level is it written?

Complexity.   What kinds of feedback can be derived from the items?
How complicated is the interpretation?

Supplementation. Will the instrument yield data that add to what participants already know?

The most critical considerations are validity and reliability, and they are discussed in more detail below.

VALIDITY

The basic validity questions center around what traits are being measured, what the scores mean, and how useful the data are. Six types of considerations about validity are commonly made, and these are outlined briefly below.

Content Validity. Content validity, or face validity, refers to the first impressions which the user has of the instrument. Does the scale appear to be measuring the characteristic it is supposed to measure? We would caution the user not to put a lot of confidence in or make important decisions on the basis of instruments that do not appear to have content validity. You will never be happy using a scale that does not look like it measures what its author claims it measures. Furthermore, you will probably be questioned about it by respondents and anyone to whom you have to report results for making decisions. In general, it *is* possible for an instrument to measure something it does not appear to be measuring or fail to measure something it appears to measure, but such occurrences (especially the former) are notable by their rarity.

Predictive Validity. In addition to studying content or face validity, there are some other ways of checking on whether an instrument measures what it claims to measure. One of these is predictive validity. If it is a measure of the ability to learn to fly, people who score high on it should learn faster and fly with more skill when they subsequently begin flying lessons. If they do not live up to this prediction, there is a question of the validity of the measure. There are a number of instruments used to select people for occupational potentials, ranging from electronics technicians to foresters. However, there are a large number of instruments for which the concept of selection or prediction is less appropriate. Scales to measure introversion-extraversion, dominance needs, style of relating to other people, and personal temperament, for example, are not intended to predict any performance (although predictions are often made using them). For these instruments (and for instruments that are used in prediction) there are other criteria for determining validity. One of these methods is concurrent validity.

Concurrent Validity. As the name implies, concurrent validity is established by showing that there is a relationship with a present criterion. For example, those who are presently engaged in an occupation and are doing well should score higher on an aptitude measure than those who are doing poorly. Student members of the Young Republicans should score higher than student members of the Young Democrats on a scale of political conservatism.

Convergent Validity. If an instrument is measuring what it is supposed to measure, then it should relate positively to other measures of the same thing, since they should all be "converging" on the same trait. The idea is that they are all sampling from the same behavioral domain, (for example, neuroticism) from slightly different angles and should, therefore, have substantial overlap.

Discriminant Validity. The other side of the coin from convergent validity is, "Is it unrelated to scales that measure traits it is not supposed to be measuring?" The usual "other scales" that are investigated are likely alternative explanations of the scores on the instrument being examined, such as intelligence, need for approval, authoritarianism, socio-economic status, or education. These traits may affect test-taking style and ability and could raise or lower scores on, for example, a neuroticism scale.

Construct Validity. Many instruments that measure personal or group characteristics are related to, issue from, or are the basis for a theory. The scale measures a concept or construct, such as achievement motivation, which takes on its full meaning through the theory. The theory attempts to explain what kinds of childhood experiences lead to high achievement motivation, what the preferred leisure time activities of the person with a high need for achievement should be, the kinds of situations in which he will do well, the kinds in which he will do poorly, and so on. If the scale is measuring the kind of achievement motivation the theory explicates, then high scorers will report these predicted childhood experiences more than low scorers, perform better in some situations than low scorers, or perform less well than low scorers in other situations. If the predicted pattern of relationships is found, then both the instrument and the construct will have been validated simultaneously. If the predicted pattern is not found, then the tester has the problem of determining whether the fault was in the instrument, in the theory, or in his testing of the instrument and theory. Usually *some* hypotheses are confirmed, so that clues are available as to what may be right and what may be wrong with both the theory and the instrument.

Validity is not inherent in instruments. The user must validate the instrument himself for the specific uses for which he will employ it. This means that he will study the validity evidence available in the manual or other supporting documents, and he will carry out his own evaluation of the usefulness of the instrument. Using the same instrument in a variety of ways with different people can build experience and supply data that can add validity to an instrument. In this sense, validity resides in the user rather than in the items.

RELIABILITY

There is a basic question which you must ask of any measuring device. "Is it consistent?" Imagine a ruler made of taffy. Each time the person measures something with the ruler, the ruler has become shorter or longer through handling. The person cannot decide the effect of different kinds of fertilizer on the height of his African violets because he cannot measure the height in a reliable or consistent way using the taffy ruler. Thus, low reliability means that scores are due to something other than the trait you wanted to measure, or there is a lack of consistency in the measuring. These factors we put into one container we call "error," or "error of measurement."

Reliability indices give scores that range between 0.00 and 1.00. A reliability of 0.00 means there is nothing consistent being measured and that scores are being determined by error, chance, or random fluctuations in conditions. A score of 1.00 means that error, chance, or other extraneous conditions have no effect on the measurement procedure, as shown in the following table.

Appropriateness of Use
Related to Reliability of the Scale

RELIABILITY	USES	SOME EXAMPLES
over .85	Counseling Group Averages Research	*Omnibus Inventory* *MMPI*, a few scales *NOTE: Few personality instruments have many scales over .85*
.60 - .85	Counseling* Group Averages Research	*FIRO-B* *Ori* *Involvement Inventory*
Under .60 or unknown	Group Averages* Research*	*HIM-B* all scores *ACL* subscales *EPPS*, some scales

*uses are questionable

A reliability index of .85 or higher is generally considered to be effective for all purposes, including individual counseling. An index of between .60 and .85 indicates reliability that is effective for measuring and talking about groups of people and in doing research but may be too low for placing high confidence in an individual's score. Reliabilities below .60 indicate that the variability due to extraneous factors is so great that the instrument should probably not be used for an individual's diagnosis, that it should be used to talk about groups of individuals with caution, and that, even though it may be useful in research, the error in the instrument may hide or mask significant differences or changes that exist.

The idea behind requiring higher reliability of an instrument before it is used in a personal growth activity is that as reliability goes down, error of measurement goes up. Error of measurement is an index of how close a person's hypothetical "real" score is to the one he received on the instrument. A large error of measurement means that scores would vary widely if you gave him the instrument a number of times; a small error of measurement means that scores would be very similar over a number of administration times for the same person.

An important consideration which the user of instruments needs to make is that measures that have relatively low precision can be utilized to study group phenomena. Averages of groups have more stability than do individual scores. An instrument used to measure employee morale over time need not be so accurate as an inventory intended for career development counseling. A comparatively crude index of the level of interpersonal trust in a group or team can be employed if the interest is in studying how the average changes as the group develops.

Reliability is used to refer to whatever is left after the error of measurement has affected the scores. Reliability has been used to describe two rather different elements—homogeneity of the statements and stability of the scores. The following discussion is an attempt to clarify these two meanings of the term.

Reliability/Homogeneity. Most indices of reliability measure the extent to which statements in a scale are measuring the same characteristic. If two statements are measuring the same thing, then as scores go up on one, they go up on the other; as they go down on one, they go down on the other. They vary together, or they are said to "covary." Homogeneity (all the same) is a characteristic of a good measure; if an instrument is purporting to measure a certain trait, all of the parts should be measuring facets of that trait. It is like an army that claims to be "marching to Pretoria" and yet begins with the soldiers marching off in different directions at the same time. An observer might legitimately ask, "How can you say your army is marching any place?" Scores of the various statements on the scale should vary together, although they should not vary together perfectly, because then we would have duplicate measures of exactly the same thing, and that would add no new information. At the other extreme, we would not want statements that are unrelated (not measuring the same general thing) because it is impossible to say what a score measures, and responses might be due to guessing or chance. The ideal of homogeneity is a scale with statements correlated on the average between .15 and .50. Such statements can then be viewed as measuring various aspects or facets of the same thing.

Reliability/Stability. The aspect of reliability measured by the test-retest method is stability. The idea behind this technique is that if you are measuring something reliably, you should get the same score on repeated measures (a steel ruler rather than a taffy ruler). If scores are due to guessing, chance, momentary reaction to ambiguous wording, or other extraneous factors, scores will vary from taking to taking. The correlation coefficient is used to calculate test-retest reliability.

Reliability and validity are closely related considerations. An instrument cannot be valid without some precision, but a highly stable measure may not necessarily be useful. Reliability is necessary but not sufficient. The overriding concern is the utility of the outcomes from the use of the instrument.

MEANINGS OF NUMBERS

Scores derived from instruments do not have meaning except as they are related to both the content of the items and the method of deriving numbers. Interpreting an index of anxiety based on counting how many items a respondent marked as true for himself is different from determining the meaning of a score in a forced-choice inventory.

The basic number systems relevant to instrumentation are as follows:

Nominal. Numbers are used to "name" things and are arbitrarily assigned. No "greater than" is implied. Example: the numbers on football jerseys.

Ordinal. Numbers represent ranks. There is the notion of "greater than" but not "how much greater." Example: rank in graduating class.

Interval. Numbers denote how many units greater one score is than another. There is no true zero point, however. Example: a Fahrenheit thermometer.

Ratio. Numbers indicate positions on a scale with a true zero point, such as weight. Comparisons such as "twice as much" are permissible. Example: a bathroom scale.

In practice the instruments reviewed in this book are assumed to generate ordinal and interval data. When the group facilitator collects ordinal data, however, he is restricted in the types of statements which he can make. For example, if participants are asked to rank-order the other member of the group on some characteristic, they must be reminded not to interpret such *rankings* (ordinal) as though they were *ratings* (interval).

NORMS

Norms are descriptive statistics—average scores, or percentiles of various groups of people. These descriptions give the respondant a framework which he may use to compare his scores with those of various groups of people. They are not standards, but they are often misinterpreted as such. Normative data need to be used as non-evaluatively as possible so as to avoid any implication that there are "right" ways of responding or that there is a profile that the participant "should" have.

The major concern related to norms is that they be based on a relevant reference group. Usually this means that norms of locally-based groups are most meaningful to participants, but tables included in instrument manuals may be useful if the groups represent participants in some way. For example, the *FIRO-B* development group is not described in the manual, but there are averages available for members of twelve occupational groups, ranging from traveling pencil salesmen to teachers.

Summary

The technical considerations about instrumentation are intended to ensure that the data to be used in human relations training are not misleading. The overriding concerns are validity and reliability, and information on these characteristics is often missing or inadequate. It is encumbent on the facilitator to explore the technical characteristics of an instrument which he is considering. He needs to be prepared to answer technical questions straightforwardly, and he needs to determine for himself the validity of the instrument for his particular purposes.

Chapter Four

INSTRUMENT DEVELOPMENT

When an instrument cannot be located that meets the special needs of the group with which the facilitator will be working, an instrument can be developed. The purpose of this chapter is to outline the considerations and steps in creating scales for the measurement of training-related traits. The intent is to provide a resource of ideas for building instruments that will satisfy requirements for instrumented feedback for the personal use of a facilitator and his participants. The time span under consideration is in terms of hours or perhaps a day. This chapter is not intended to describe the formal procedures for developing instruments of established reliability and validity for wide-spread psychometric application.

A DEVELOPMENTAL SEQUENCE

A number of steps are taken in generating numerical data that can be useful in personal growth, leadership development, and organization development interventions. We wish to present what we consider to be a functional sequence in the development and administration of a new instrument.

Definition. The trait to be measured is defined. Presumably the characteristic is directly related to the goals of the training.

Specification. Behavioral instances of the trait are specified and are written as items for a questionnaire, or they are in some manner incorporated into the instrument, depending on the style of instrument the developer has chosen.

Scaling. A response format is devised that will yield numbers for interpretation. (Various scaling options will be discussed later in this chapter.)

Keying. A scoring procedure is selected, *e.g.*, weighting response numbers. The developer examines the key as it applies to the instrument to ensure that it will be functional.

Duplication. The scale is published in a mimeographed pencil-and-paper format or through some other device to make it available to the participants.

Administration. The administrator facilitates the understanding of the instructions for completing the instrument.

Scoring. The key is applied.

Interpretation. Participants are instructed on what high and low scores presumably mean. Limitations on validity and reliability are specified.

Norming.   Frequency distributions and averages are developed for the participants and are posted. The administrator may ask participants to post their own scores to indicate the group "photograph" and to facilitate discussion.

Critiquing.   The instrument can be refined by studying its utility in the training setting. Participants can be encouraged to share what they have learned.

SCALING

After the content of the instrument has been specified, the facilitator devises a scaling procedure. Several uncomplicated, "portable," and useful strategies are discussed below.

Summative Scale. The summative scale, developed by Likert, is constructed by first devising statements that a person might use to describe himself, *e.g.*, "I am nervous right now," or "I generally let other people decide what we will do together." Some reasonable categories are then developed for the respondent to use to indicate his feelings. The most usual response categories are 1) yes, unsure, and no; 2) true, unsure, and false; or 3) strongly agree, agree, slightly agree, uncertain, slightly disagree, disagree, and strongly disagree. Example:

Circle the response that most clearly reflects your feelings.
   SA = Strongly Agree
    A = Agree
  SLA = Slightly Agree
    U = Uncertain
  SLD = Slightly Disagree
    D = Disagree
   SD = Strongly Disagree
1. I am a very persistent and steady worker. SA A SLA U SLD D SD.

Researchers have moved away from the seven-point Likert scale because they feel there is ambiguity in it. (The meaning of "agree" seems very similar to the meaning of "Slightly disagree." If you have only some slight disagreement with a position, that means you basically agree with it). Others have moved away from the use of the middle "Uncertain" or "unsure" category because it allows the respondent to avoid committing himself. Thus, we would like to propose an alternative set of four responses: "Disagree; Unsure, probably disagree; Unsure, probably agree; Agree." This acknowledges that a respondent may be unsure about his reactions, and at the same time it measures the intensity of his feelings. Even though his uncertainty is acknowledged, the respondent is asked to indicate which way he tips slightly. On the other hand, if he is sure of his reaction, he can indicate that his conviction is sure.

Circle the response that most clearly reflects your feelings.
    A = Agree
   UA = Unsure, probably agree
   UD = Unsure, probably disagree
    D = Disagree
1. I find it easy to influence people. A UA UD D.

A score for a person is obtained by assigning a number to each of the response categories and then adding up the numbers for each response he used.

The number can be assigned before the person is administered the instrument so that the respondent places a number in the response space, *e.g.,* 1 for disagree; 2 for unsure, probably disagree; 3 for unsure, probably agree; and 4 for agree. The person's score would be the sum of the scores he wrote down responding to the statements. If a statement is worded in opposition to the characteristic being measured, then the scoring key is reversed so that a response of "1" is counted as "4," "2" is counted as "3," "3" as "2," and "4" as "1." Suppose you wished to devise an instrument which measures need for interaction with others. Let us assume that you have four statements, with a person's responses recorded in front of them.

3   1. I enjoy being with a lot of people.

3   2. I often organize parties or get-togethers.

1   3. I prefer reading to talking with people.

4. 4. The good life is the life of friendship, wine, and song.

Statement number 3 is reverse-worded, so the response of 1 will be counted as 4. Thus, the person's score on the four-item scale is $3+3+4+4=14$ out of a possible range of from 4 to 16 (*i.e.,* he appears to be socially extroverted). This person might have responded with an "agree" (4) to statement 1 if it had not had the words "a lot" in it. It is desirable to have some statements that are more extreme than others to help separate those individuals who are high on a characteristic from those who are *very* high on it.

Rating Scales (Semantic Differential). The semantic differential approach is the most well-known use of the rating scale. In the use made by Osgood, Succi, and Tannenbaum (1957), objects (groups, organizations, practices, people, countries) are rated on a series of bi-polar scales, such as the following:

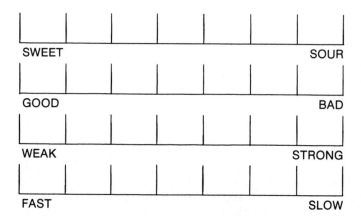

SWEET   SOUR

GOOD   BAD

WEAK   STRONG

FAST   SLOW

Sometimes the spaces are numbered 1 to 7, and sometimes they are numbered from -3 to +3. The first system gets rid of minus signs; the second system indicates clearly whether an attitude is positive or negative. Osgood and his colleagues analyzed their data to try to reduce the number of measures to a few broad ones that seemed to indicate how people react to social objects. They found that there were three basic dimensions that accounted for much of the way people understood or reacted to things. They are: evaluation (whether he likes it), potency (whether he thinks it is powerful), and activity (whether he thinks it is moving).

Scales that measure the evaluation dimension are:

1. Sweet-sour
2. Beautiful-ugly
3. Tasteful-distasteful
4. Kind-cruel
5. Pleasant-unpleasant
6. Bitter-sweet
7. Happy-sad
8. Sacred-profane
9. Nice-awful
10. Good-bad
11. Clean-dirty
12. Valuable-worthless
13. Fragrant-foul
14. Honest-dishonest
15. Fair-unfair

Scales that measure the potency dimensions are:

16. Large-small
17. Strong-weak
18. Heavy-light

Scales that measure the activity dimension are:

19. Active-passive
20. Fast-slow
21. Hot-cold

More of the evaluative adjectives were given in the above tabulation because it is the strongest factor in people's reactions, and it is most often used (it seems to be an effective measure of pure attitude or pure affect).

The basic technique can be expanded in two ways. First, the number of rating scales can be varied. The instrument developer can add bi-polar labels that fit his interest, *e.g.*, open-closed, risky-cautious, demanding-yielding, colorful-drab, deep-shallow. Second, the social objects that can be rated are limited only by the time, energy, and creativity of the developer. Examples of objects to be rated may include: this organization, this organization ten years from now, me, my ideal self, me as others see me, our relationship, this apple, the person in this group I admire the most, Fred, Ed, etc. Example:

Place a check in the space that indicates your reaction to the object.
Object: The organization

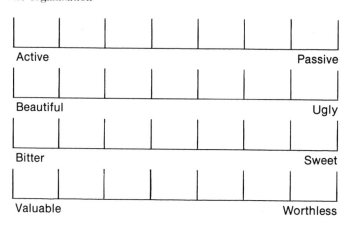

Object: My boss

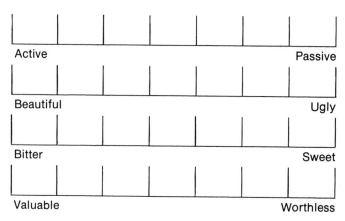

As with the summative scales, numbers are assigned to ratings, *e.g.*, the spaces from left to right are 7, 6, 5, 4, 3, 2, and, 1, with the exception of the number 6, Bitter-Sweet, which has response numbers of 1, 2, 3, 4, 5, 6, and 7. The user adds the responses to all of the bi-polar scales that are getting at the same characteristic (*e.g.*, goodness or potency). The total is that person's score, rating that specific object on that specific characteristic.

Forced-Choice Scales. One of the problems with most scale techniques is that the respondent can work at making himself look good rather than describing what he is really like. The forced-choice technique presents him with two alternatives and asks him to choose which one he prefers. He may hate them both. He may think that both are excellent. Regardless, he must choose one and reject one. Example:

Choose the activity you prefer by placing a check in front of it. You may check only one; be sure to respond to each pair.

1.   ____ Walking through the woods on a cool, sunny day.
      ____ Attending a football game on a cool, sunny day.

2.   ____ Lying on a beach talking to a member of the opposite sex.
      ____ Reading a good novel at home.

The advantages of the forced-choice approach are: 1) the respondent is forced to choose among alternatives, a behavior that is part of life (*i.e.*, given limitations in time and energy we cannot do everything; therefore, we must choose), and 2) the choices are usually equated in their social desirability so that neither choice makes the respondent who chooses it appear healthier, more motivated, more moral, or more intelligent than the other choice.

One of the advantages of the forced-choice method—the difficulty for the respondent to shade his answers in a socially desirable way—also leads to a disadvantage. With forced-choice techniques all respondents get the same total score, *i.e.*, if you sum their scores on scales A, B, and C, they will always equal the same number. Thus, a person whose total involvement in the three areas measured is extremely high will obtain the same total score as the person whose total involvement in the three areas is near zero. This is represented by such forced-choice instruments as Bass's Orientation Inventory. A second disadvantage of the forced-choice method is that it irritates respondents by requiring them to choose between two equally attractive (or equally unattractive) alternatives. For example, participants sometimes complain about the Personal Orientation Inventory in this regard.

There are three modifications you can make on the simple "pick one" forced-choice approach. One thing you might do is follow the method used in Bass's Orientation Inventory and in the Strong Vocational Interest Blank: present the respondent with three or four alternatives and have him select the one he likes least. This approach gives him a little more flexibility than just two alternatives. A second method you could use is that adopted by Jay Hall in his Teleometrics series: the respondent is given just two alternatives, but instead of choosing one of them he is asked to allocate five points between the two choices. Thus, he may give alternative A a rating of 5 and alternative B a rating of 0, or he may give A a 4 and B a 1, and so on. This approach gets away from forcing an artificial choice. Hall also does not count all responses, *i.e.*, some alternatives are used to indicate neither (or none) of the scales being studied. If a person responds to an alternative that is irrelevant to the characteristics being measured, it reduces his scores on the scale being assessed and lowers his total score.

Sociometric Ratings. One application of the rating scale technique is the rating of members in a group (department, family, office, etc.). Ratings can then be summed two ways as shown in the following figure (assuming that people are using a 7-point rating scale on some dimension, for example, commitment to the group). One can see at a glance on the matrix whether person A rated person B in a way that is discrepant from the way B was rated by the others in the group, whether person A rated person B in a way that is discrepant from A's usual rating scale, who received the highest total rating (Joe), who received the lowest (Zelda), who tended to rate everybody up (Marsha), and who rated everybody down (Joe). It is also possible to look at people's self-ratings (diagonal cells) to see if some are unusually hard or easy on themselves.

Matrix of ratings given and received

		RATEE					Ratings Given To Others	
		Bill	Joe	Marsha	Nancy	Zelda	Total	Mean
	Bill	4	6	2	5	1	18	3.6
	Joe	2	4	1	3	1	11	2.2
	Marsha	6	7	5	5	4	27	5.4
RATER	Nancy	5	7	2	4	1	19	3.8
	Zelda	3	5	1	2	1	12	2.4
Ratings Received from Others	Total	20	29	11	19	8	87	17.4
	Mean	4.0	5.8	2.2	3.8	1.6	17.4	3.5

In general, the sociometric technique is one that can be done on the spur-of-the-moment, does not need any forms, allows open discussion right in the group (this should be agreed upon before they do it), and gives a number of informative and discussable indices.

GENERATING CONTENT WITHIN THE GROUP ITSELF

One of the most effective and unique uses of instrument development is that of generating the instruments "on the spot" with the participants when the facilitator identifies a need which cannot be met by any of the instruments he may have brought to the design. Items that may be used to form an instrument can be developed quickly with the assistance of participants. This approach has the advantage of developing a sense of ownership, commitment, and relevance. If the recipients of instrumented feedback are involved in specifying what is to be measured, they are more likely to learn from the process and less likely to reject the data.

You can create an instrument that can generate intensive discussion by the following procedure. In a leadership workshop, have the participants brainstorm the qualities of a good leader. Then have each rank the list from first to last in order of importance. A large group may be broken into small groups for discussion. Participants compare their rankings, get a group average, discuss differences and similarities of their biases, and attempt consensus. A crude measure of influence can be obtained by summing differences between the group consensus ranking and the original points of view of individuals. Presumably those with low scores would be influential.

Adjective checklists can be developed by asking that the participants write down two or three adjectives that describe his best friend and two or three that describe the one person with whom he has had the least satisfactory relationship. Attitude scales can be derived from declarative sentences about issues facing members of the group or the organization. A trait can be defined and group members can brainstorm behavioral instances of high and low values of the characteristic. Traits can be selected from an adjective checklist to form the basis of a rating scale. Group process phenomena can be identified that can become the content of reaction instruments; such dimensions of group development as trust and openness can be further differentiated into behavioral referents.

In duplicating an instrument such as the adjective checklist, it is not necessary to go through a mimeographing process. It can be written on a chalkboard or newsprint for the participants to see, or they can make their own copies on blank sheets of paper. Oral instructions can be given in a two-way communication mode.

CONCLUSION

It is possible for a facilitator to develop instruments that measure exactly the characteristics he is interested in, and he should feel free to use his creativity to get at those characteristics in whatever way seems most appropriate. However, beware of over-interpreting the results. Homemade tests tend to be unreliable, yielding scores that are unstable. The results should be viewed by the participants as suggestive, not conclusive.

Chapter Five

RESEARCH USES OF INSTRUMENTATION
IN HUMAN RELATIONS TRAINING

The use of instruments in research appears to be deceptively easy. In simplistic terms, all you have to do is have people fill out an instrument and see if their scores relate to some group or individual goal criterion. The deceptiveness lies in the number of problems that can arise in using instruments in research or, for that matter, in doing research of any kind. These problems can make doing research very difficult. However, this difficulty can be diminished if the researcher remembers that the vast majority of problems are avoidable if some advanced planning is used, and many problems are not really problems if you understand their nature.

The purpose of this chapter is to help you to anticipate factors that cause you to fail in finding significant differences or make the results you do find open to several different explanations. The major problems areas are reliability, validity, pretesting and posttesting, transparency and social desirability, management, and human concerns. The discussion that follows centers on each of these difficulties. An example of a research design is briefly outlined.

THE RELIABILITY PROBLEM

The term "reliability" has become one that strikes terror in the hearts of users of instruments. People are not sure what "reliability" means and, therefore, are never sure whether or not their instrument has a sufficient amount of it.

Test reliability means that the instrument is measuring something other than chance responses, guesses, or some characteristic that comes and goes. One way in which this is demonstrated is by showing that people respond about the same way the second time an instrument is administered as they did the first time (usually an interval of about two weeks). This is termed test-retest reliability. If their responses had been guesses, it is highly unlikely that they would guess the same way again. A second way of demonstrating reliability is to examine the extent to which responses to two halves of an instrument or two different forms of an instrument are correlated, i.e., measuring the same thing. High correlations indicate that all of the individual questions are getting at the same general attitude and that some actual characteristics are being measured. (See "Chapter Three. Technical Considerations.")

The importance of reliability is that it determines the error of measurement. The higher the error of measurement, the less sure you are that the score a person obtained is near what they would obtain if they took a parallel form of the test or the same test again after a waiting period.

How much is enough reliability? This is a more important question for the counselor than it is for the researcher. A counselor may be trying to draw conclusions and pose alternatives based on scores. If an instrument is unreliable and he does not know it, it is possible that he may offer an erroneous alternative, e.g., that a student not bother to apply for a certain college or that he seek out a field that requires interaction with a large number of people. A researcher, on the other hand, has a built-in check that prevents him from drawing conclusions based on unreliable instruments—statistics. Statistics allow a comparison of the amount of change in a person's responses against the amount of random change in scores or the difference between two or more groups of people against the variation in scores within the group. Unreliable instruments show an excess of random variation in scores. The greater the error in the instrument the less likely it is that the differences between average group scores will appear statistically significant (so large a difference between groups that it is unlikely to have occurred by chance). See the figure below. If you are using an unreliable instrument, you are not likely to find a difference between groups or conditions that is greater than the large error of measurement, and you will not be likely to be uncovering significant findings using that instrument.

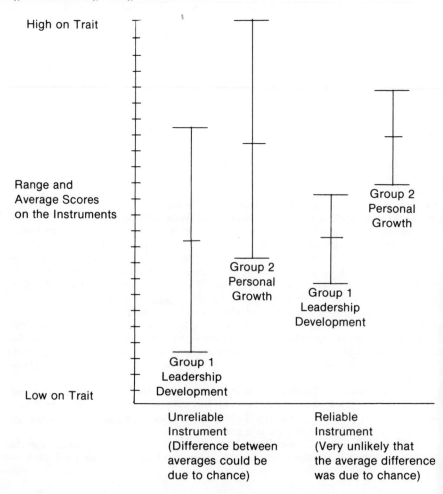

Non-significant results do not permit you to say "there is no difference between the groups," or "there was no change." All you can say is that you were not able to demonstrate that there is a difference. You are not likely to get into trouble with an unreliable instrument, but you will be frustrated because you cannot draw any conclusions about what you have studied.

Unreliable instruments lead to conservative, non-risk errors. Later in this section, we will discuss other kinds of problems (validity, control groups, pretest, posttest problems, and transparency of the instrument) which can lead to risky errors in which the researcher has found a significant difference but for the wrong reasons. This is not to say that the conservative errors of an unreliable instrument are not something to be concerned about. Science proceeds by the gradual accumulation of confidence or disenchantment with a theory, procedure, or test. If people test a valid theory or procedure with an unreliable instrument and find no support for it, they have done a disservice to the theory, the theorist, and the quest for "truth." They have also wasted their own time and effort.

THE VALIDITY PROBLEM

The validity of an instrument is the degree to which it measures what the publisher and author say it measures. An instrument can be reliable, yet be invalid. It may be measuring an undetermined entity consistently. On the other hand, a very unreliable instrument cannot be valid because it is not measuring much of anything but random responses and guesses.

One way in which validity is usually demonstrated is by showing that an instrument correlates positively with another instrument that is measuring the same general characteristic (convergent validity). A high positive correlation (+ .50 or better) means that high scores on instrument A were obtained by people who got high scores on instrument B, and low scores on instrument A were obtained by people who got low scores on instrument B. Another method used to determine the validity of an instrument is to show whether people who should score in a predicted way on a certain characteristic do, in fact, score that way on the instrument; for example, William F. Buckley, Jr. should score nearer the conservative end of a liberalism—conservatism scale than should Edward Kennedy. There are other ways to validate instruments, but the above two approaches should give you an indication of how it is done. (See Chapter Three.)

Even if an instrument has substantial reliability and validity co-efficients as reported in its manual or in published research, you cannot automatically proceed with the confidence that you have a good instrument. You must first examine the instrument very carefully to try to cut through the use of labels, psychological jargon, and general descriptions so that you can find out exactly what it measures. This is done in the following way.

(1) Examine the questions in the instrument and ask yourself, "Are these questions really able to reflect what the author says the instrument is measuring? If not, what are they measuring? If so, are they measuring other characteristics as well?"

(2) Examine the correlations with other instruments and ask yourself, "What are all of the factors which could cause a person who scores high on this instrument to score high on the other instrument?"

(3) Look at the differences between norm groups (*e.g.*, men versus women, college students versus construction workers) and ask "In how many other ways do these groups differ? Could this instrument be measuring one (or more) of these factors instead of, or in addition to, what it purports to measure?"

(4) Complete the instrument yourself and think through your personal experience with it before deciding whether it is a valid measure of what it claims to be.

We believe the most serious occurrence of invalidity is in using good instruments to measure what they have not claimed to measure. A researcher wants to investigate the effect of loving attention from members of the opposite sex on individuals' perceptions of their own sexual attractiveness. He cannot locate a measure of perceived sexual attractiveness, so instead, he uses a previously validated measure of self-esteem. Although the instrument has some questions relevant to sexual attractiveness, most of them measure other aspects of self-esteem. He finds that his experimental situation had no significant effect on the scores he obtained. He did not get his results because the instrument was not valid as a measure of perceived sexual attractiveness. In his case, it would probably have been preferable for him to write his own instrument with questions that related exactly to what he was expecting to measure. In that way, if he found significant results, he would have some confidence that he had tested the characteristic in which he was actually interested. *Even if he had obtained significant results* with the self-esteem scale, he would be faced with the fact that he had not tested his predictions in a valid way and really did not know the effect of having attention from someone of the opposite sex on a person's perceived sexual attractiveness.

The point is that a reliable and valid instrument that does not really measure the trait which you are researching is almost useless. A compromise approach would be to use an instrument or two that come as close as possible to measuring what you want and then add your own instrument to the research. It is well to remember that the majority of theory-testing articles published in social psychology use only one, or at most, three questions to measure the effect obtained in their experiment. They get their results because they use strong experimental manipulations, and their few questions are aimed *exactly* at the effect they expect.

PRETEST, POSTTEST PROBLEMS

One of the most useful ways to do research from both a common sense and a statistical viewpoint is to use a pretest before the participants begin an experience and a posttest after they have completed the experience. The logical way to measure change is to evaluate a group of people on a characteristic prior to an experience and then evaluate them again on that characteristic after the experience that was supposed to change them. If the scores are the same or close enough that error of measurement could account for the difference, then the people did not change. If the group average shifted significantly in the expected direction between the first evaluation and the second evaluation, then they did change. Using a pretest–posttest design makes more intuitive sense than using a "posttest only" approach in which you do not measure the experimental group initially but compare their scores at the end of an experience with the scores of a group that did not go through the experience. No matter what the outcomes are, it is often hard to convince others, or even yourself, that the two groups were the same except for the experience.

The statistical advantage of the pretest–posttest approach is that it allows you to use a form of analysis which ignores differences between people and measures only how much change occurred within people. This means that you may need a smaller change to have occurred in the group than with the posttest-only approach in order to have a statistically significant difference, since differences between members of two separate groups would not be the prime concern.

One argument against a pre-post approach is that participants may remember how they responded the first time. This may make their responses the second time open to conscious comparison by them. A second problem is that completing the instrument before the experience may sensitize them to how they are expected to change, and they may simulate change rather than actually changing because of the experience. One solution is to "bury" the research question(s) in a larger questionnaire given before the experience. In this way, the participant responds to so much material that he is less likely to remember how he filled out any specific question the first time when he takes it the second time. He is also kept in the dark until the end of the experience as to which parts of the pre-group questionnaire were important. A second solution to the problem of the respondent remembering his first response is to use a line scale to measure his attitude or characterization of himself. The respondent strikes a slash along a line that has few "anchoring" terms or descriptions (at most, three: both ends and the middle). For example:

Right now I am feeling:

| L_____|_____J |

High	Usual	Very
Anxiety,	Anxiety	Relaxed,
Heavy Sweating	or	Good
	Concern	

A variation on this approach would be to use a line response format in place of the usual five-category response format placed after a number of statements. There is a delay imposed by the necessity to measure the position of the slash with a ruler before scores can be calculated. The line technique tends to increase the error of measurement somewhat because every muscular quiver shifts the responder's arm and hand to the right or left, and the respondent may use shifting definitions of the meaning of various locations on the minimally anchored scale.

Another technique is to divide an instrument into two parts, giving half of the group the first part and the other half of the group the last part. After the experience, each half of the group takes the part of the instrument that they did not take the first time. Group scores for the pretest and, later, the posttest equal the sum of the scores across the two halves.

Another problem with pretest–posttest format that may be endemic to human relations settings is the commitment to providing "learning experiences" and to giving people feedback about themselves. There is social pressure to have people score and interpret their scores and score patterns. If that is done, then they have been sensitized to the dimensions being assessed and may modify their behavior in a way they would not have if they had not taken the instrument. Even if a person does not change because he took the instrument, the others around him may change because they took the instrument and present him with a group experience that is different from what it would have been if the instrument had not been given.

There is a conflict between giving participants useful feedback to help them set up personal agendas for a workshop versus withholding all instrument data from the participants so that they will not be affected by knowledge of their scores. One control group is needed to discover if pretesting generates behavior or reactions which differ from the behavior and reactions of people who did not take a pretest. Another possible control would be to administer the pretest to a group and not give participants the feedback. The difference between the experimental group (scored and discussed pretest scores) and control group one (only took the pretest) and control group two (did not take the pretest) on the posttest will tell if taking a pretest causes changes in posttest behavior and whether taking a pretest and discussing one's own scores causes even greater changes.

TRANSPARENCY/SOCIAL DESIRABILITY PROBLEMS

Instruments vary in how obvious they are. Some of them measure one variable, and the respondent is virtually certain that he knows what the variable is by the time he reads the fifth statement. At the other extreme are the instruments that measure twelve or more different characteristics. These also sometimes contain distractors, or checks, such as, "I breathe air." The person has so many plausible guesses about what the questionnaire is measuring that theoretically he stops trying to figure out what it is attempting to measure and starts responding to each statement at face value.

An important thing to remember is that transparency is not necessarily problematic. It causes trouble primarily when the instrument is being used to *evaluate* people (they are described as experiencing "evaluation apprehension") or when the way in which it is being used lets the respondent decide whether or not he wants to "help" the researcher. However, when a person is filling out an instrument for his own use, transparency becomes more of an annoyance than a real difficulty. The transparency is an annoyance because the person is trying to remember how he has reacted to each situation described or how he feels about some statement. His awareness that he can move his score at will up or down some obvious dimension may be a temptation. This becomes a distraction since he may then "lean over backwards" to avoid "cheating," thereby depressing his score artificially.

It has been found that when people are put in a situation which arouses evaluation apprehension, they present themselves in a way that will make them appear more "socially desirable". If you suspect that the situation in which you are using instruments may make some of your respondents so strongly motivated to appear healthy, competent, tolerant, etc., that they may distort their answers in a socially desirable direction, then you should take steps to make it difficult for them to distort, or you should "correct" for this distortion.

There are a number of ways you can do this. First, you can bury the real intent of your instrument among a number of distractor questions. However, if the questions you are interested in have a "look good" answer, your respondents will still distort. Thus, you may have to rewrite your questions. The second approach is to structure your questions so that there is no obvious "healthy" response. For example, the question, "Do you ever have erotic fantasies of yourself with a famous actress?" might elicit a less guarded response if it were changed to something like, "Men tend to have erotic fantasies of themselves with famous actresses. Circle how often you have such fantasies."

A third way of creating minimal distortion is by first asking respondents to check the statements that would make them "look good" if they agreed with them. Then have them check the statements that would make them "look good" if they *disagreed* with them. After examining the statements that received a lot of checks, you could either rewrite the instrument (perhaps reversing the wording of some statements) so that a high score (or a low score) could *not* be obtained by giving "look good" responses or develop a social desirability key. A social desirability key includes all the responses that are "look good" responses. A person gets a score on the key whenever he gives a "look good" response. If a respondent gets a high score on social desirability (in the upper ten to fifteen per cent of respondents) you may wish to exclude him from the analysis since there is a good chance that he is more concerned with looking good than being honest.

MANAGEMENT PROBLEMS

A major concern in doing research in human relations training is the effect of administrative timing on participant responses. Timing of measurement phases becomes important because participants in human relations training experiences are often at high emotional levels at the beginning and end of workshops. We will first examine using instruments at the beginning of an experience.

Pretests. The first day or first few hours of a laboratory workshop are usually marked by feelings of anxiety and general excitement. In many ways, the opening hour of the workshop is a poor time to administer a questionnaire. Often it is the facilitator's only opportunity to do pretesting, however, so he must live with the problematic elements of this timing. To help alleviate some of the concern, a facilitator can reassure the participants that he will give them as much feedback about their performance as possible and that the scores, although not anonymous, will be kept confidential.

One way of eliminating the difficulties involved in first-day administration of instruments is to mail the pretests to the participants a week or two before the training experience begins. This is a viable alternative, and a number of facilitators use it. The difficulty with this approach is that there are always a few people who signed up for the workshop after the mailing of the questionnaires, some who do not receive the questionnaires, or others who leave them at home. A second way of avoiding measuring at the height of "opening night" tension is to wait to give your pretest until after a session or two. The participants have had an opportunity to become familiar with the training conditions and have put their irrational fears to rest somewhat; however, they are also somewhat different from the way they were before the first one or two sessions. As with many of the issues discussed in this book, the user is faced with compensating, counter-balancing factors. He must choose those alternatives that he considers most relevant to the situation at hand and those most important to the intent of the research design.

Posttests. Just as the beginning of a laboratory experience has its unique set of problems, so the closing of an experience carries with it its special concerns. At the end of a personal growth laboratory, people tend to be happy, sentimental, euphoric, and perhaps even mystical. They are not usually in a mood to fill out questionnaires. There is a legitimate question about the value of their responses if they had been forced to fill out a questionnaire right after the workshop. One solution is to give them the questionnaires and ask them to mail them to you within three days. You may also mail the questionnaires to them with the same instructions. The problem with these solutions is that some people will neglect to return them. Gathering research data through a mailing process has its own inherent problems centering around a human reluctance to interrupt personal priorities to respond to another's priorities when the other person is not present. Your success in mailing questionnaires depends on the amount of patience and energy you are willing to expend to get your research data.

HUMAN PROBLEMS

One of the underlying premises of human relations training is the assumption that people should be open and honest with each other and that such behavior leads to the most productive outcomes of training. The tendency of researchers to avoid telling participants what they are attempting to accomplish by failing to give them feedback about their scores on pretests and not processing data during the experience violates this pervasive assumption about openness. Participant hostility and resentment is a common result of researcher standoffishness. Hostile participants can give invalid results. The researcher must choose between withholding feedback versus running the risk of participants knowing "too much," between a clean research design versus a contaminated design, and between risking nonvalidity through insignificant results versus invalidity through biased results.

SAMPLE RESEARCH DESIGN

When you are concerned with studying the comparative outcomes of various training designs, you must also be interested in training versus no training. Control groups (members receive no "treatment" or simply are brought together with no training intent) are used to compare the effects of experimental conditions with the absence of treatment. An effort must be made to keep all groups equal except for the specific training interventions to be tested.

For example, let us assume that you want to explore the differential effects of a personal growth laboratory which has a theory-centered design (a heavy focus on lecture material) and a laboratory that is saturated with structured experiences. It is conceivable that neither laboratory will be found to produce lasting, observable changes in the behavior of participants, and this possibility must be taken into account in the research design. You might take applications for a laboratory experience and randomly assign persons to one of three groups:

(1) Experimental Group I. These persons will participate in the laboratory that focuses on theory.

(2) Experimental Group II. These applicants will attend the laboratory built around structured experiences.

(3) Control Group I. These applicants will be excluded from the laboratory experience. (Alternatives: they may be asked to wait until later to attend a laboratory, or they may be brought together for informal discussions or seminars.)

Ideally you would have 30-40 persons in each of the two experimental groups and more in the control group. In addition, you may wish to establish other control groups such as the following:

(4) Control Group II. Non-volunteers, drawn from the same population from which laboratory applicants are drawn, e.g., middle-management.

(5) Control Group III. A representative sample of people in general. (Sometimes these data can be found in manuals of instruments.)

You might use a variety of instruments to assess outcomes. These should be selected to measure variables directly related to the goals of the laboratory training. The scales can be given on a pretest, posttest, and followup basis to determine which changes are temporary and which are lasting. One may also discover "delayed reactions." Data could be collected from the participants themselves, from their associates, and from fellow participants and facilitators during the training.

The references section of this book (Appendix E) contains a listing of books dealing with research design and statistical analysis of results. An example of a well-constructed study of effects of human relations training is an article by Yalom and Lieberman. (A Study of Encounter Group Casualties. *Archives of General Psychiatry*, 1971, 25, 16-30.)

PART II
Instruments

INTRODUCTION TO PART II
ORGANIZATION OF THE
INSTRUMENT ANNOTATIONS

The organization of this part of *Instrumentation in Human Relations Training* will be described by using the outline format followed in annotating the instruments in the section. We will discuss what is included in each portion of the format. This outline contains the following sub-section titles: Description, Ordering, Administering, Scoring and Interpreting, and References.

DESCRIPTION

This sub-section includes the information which we consider important for you to know in making the decision about whether the instrument meets your needs. We consider length of the instrument, time estimates for administering and scoring, descriptions of scales, specific uses, positive features of the instrument, and concerns in using the instrument to be the major factors upon which the decision to order the instrument is made. In each description we examine only those factors which are crucial to the individual instrument being considered. This means that for some instruments, all six factors are discussed and for others fewer are discussed. For example, with some instruments, there are no special concerns about their use.

Length: The number of statements is the index of length most often used. We attempt to indicate when the response format is such that the number of statements is an overestimate or an underestimate of the length of the instrument.

Time: Estimates of time have come from a number of sources. For many of the instruments, the time needed to administer the instrument is given in the manual. For many of those for which there is no time estimate given in the manual, we time our own groups to obtain an estimate. In some cases, we complete the instrument ourselves, keeping track of the time as we take the instrument. Timing of the scoring is figured by the same methods we use to estimate administration time.

Scales: In most cases, the material for the description of the scales comes from the manual. We often include sample statements, but typically we limit the sample statements to only a few of the scales on a particular instrument. We think that this is sufficient to give the reader a clear impression of the item format.

Uses: Under the following subtitles, we discuss uses that can be made of instruments in general. For a more inclusive discussion of uses see Chapters One and Two. The "Uses" section in the instrument descriptions supplements the general discussion of the two chapters.

Generating Personal Agendas. An instrument can be used to confront an individual with his personal and interpersonal style and allow him to consider whether or not he is currently actualizing his full potential. If he decides that he is not, he can make plans to work on some aspects of his style or make some decisions about his life while he is in the relative safety and experimental environment of the laboratory setting.

Bringing Covert Issues to the Surface. Often an organization has issues regarding leadership, interpersonal style, interpersonal relations, trust, and cooperativeness. Members may sense these concerns, but they may not have been dealing with them in the work setting. Instruments can be used to surface these covert issues and may provide a structure for working with them productively.

Instruction. Instruments can be used to teach people concepts and theories relevant to human relations by making them aware of terminology, categories, and dimensions along which people's behavior can be plotted. In addition, instrumentation can teach the value and use of feedback in gaining self awareness.

Monitoring the Group. Instruments can be used to focus the group on the here-and-now issues of its own internal functioning. The facilitator can use the data to create new groups (homogeneous, heterogeneous) to illustrate how the working patterns differ with various types of groups.

Positive Features: Positive features may include such elements as interesting format, comfortable length, well-documented validity, good method of illustrating a meaningful theory or way of categorizing interpersonal relations, ease in scoring, or low cost.

Concerns: Concerns may include such elements as low face validity, extensive length or complexity considering the amount of useful data obtained, boring or frustrating format, difficulty in scoring, questionable reliability and/or validity, or inordinately high cost.

ORDERING THE INSTRUMENT

Assuming you are still interested in the instrument after reading the previous section, you are now given information for obtaining the instrument and price data.

Where To Order: The name, address, and telephone number of the publisher is listed here. The Index of Publishers (Appendix D) also includes this information.

Cost: Under this sub-heading are the costs of specimen sets and other materials. Ordinarily specimen sets contain test booklets, answer sheets, manuals, profile sheets, and scoring keys. Information is always geared toward hand-scored answer sheets and keys.

ADMINISTERING, SCORING, AND INTERPRETING

A detailed example of these procedures in Chapter Two focuses on the *FIRO-B*. In general, the following illustrates these three activities. The information given in the individual instrument descriptions supplements these guidelines.

Administering: The following general procedure is recommended for administering an instrument:

1. Distribute the instrument and tell the participants that you will read the instructions to them.

2. Read the instructions while the participants read along with you.

3. When the participants have finished completing the instrument, discuss the theory or dimensions measured by the instrument.

4. It is often useful to ask participants to estimate the scales on which they scored low (first quartile) and high (fourth quartile).

Scoring: There are a number of ways to score an instrument, depending on time, the number of people involved, the scoring format proposed by the author-publisher, and the intent of the facilitator in using the instrument. One way of scoring an instrument with a group is to read the correct answers to the group, tell them how to combine the numbers, and, in general, talk them through the scoring procedure. A second approach is to reproduce the steps the facilitator would have used to talk the participants through the scoring procedure and distribute them to participants or post them on newsprint or chalkboard. They will then have these steps in front of them as they score their own instrument. A third approach is to pass around scoring stencils to participants or have scoring stencils available at four or five locations. A fourth approach is to use clerical assistance to score the questionnaires during a meal break or while attention is focused on some other aspect of the workshop.

Interpreting: Depending upon the nature of the group, it is generally effective to have participants post their scores on newsprint or chalkboard. Post your own first to legitimize this activity and to indicate what their scoring sheet should look like. If estimates were made, they should appear next to the actual scores in parentheses. Form the participants into small groups or dyads to discuss their scores. Each participant should have the opportunity to discuss his personal score pattern in detail, recognizing high and low scores and discrepancies between estimates and obtained scores. Other members of the interpretation group should tell whether they are surprised by the individual's scores or feel that the scores were predictable (i.e., indicate the nature of the individual as they see him) as a method of personal feedback. The members of the interpretation groups should return to the total group to discuss the experience which the instrumentation has given them.

In addition to the above procedures, participants can generate some local norms on the instrument so that they can compare their scores with those of others in the group (rather than "undergraduates at a large midwestern university"). Local norms are developed by obtaining a frequency distribution.

1. List the scores down the left hand side of the newsprint or chalkboard.

2. Use tally marks next to the scores to represent the number of participants who obtained each score.

3. Divide the number of participants into 100. In the following example, fifty people took the instrument.

4. Multiply the cumulative frequency by the number obtained in the above step (in this example, 2) to obtain the cumulative percentages or percentiles.

Score	Tally	Cumulative Frequency	Percentile
20	I	50	100%
19	II	49	98
17	JHT III	47	94
16	JHT JHT	39	78
15	JHT JHT IIII	29	58
12	JHT	15	30
11	IIII	10	20
10	III	6	12
9	II	3	6
7	I	1	2

Often such local norms are more meaningful than those in the manual.

A way of demonstrating the meaning of the scores is to form groups of homogeneous participants using the local norms and give them some task to perform while the other participants observe. This may require that participants not be informed of their scores until after the exercise, although their knowledge of their scores may not affect the dynamics of the group interaction once they are involved in the task.

REFERENCES

We include references only when you need them to locate an instrument for which there is not a manual or for further understanding of an instrument. The publishers of testing materials provide lists of references in manuals and in separate bibliographies. For further reference, Buros (1970) lists studies that have been conducted on the instruments or studies which have employed the instruments. Buros also lists articles that critically evaluate the instruments. General reference materials will be found in Appendix E.

CHOICE OF MATERIALS TO BE INCLUDED

Since the focus of this book was mainly on instruments available through publishers, we decided to describe rather than to reproduce instruments in order to include as many instruments as possible in the format we have chosen. If we had decided to reproduce instruments, less than ten per cent of the instruments in this book would have qualified because of copyright prohibitions.

We also decided to leave out any kind of discussion of the reliability and validity data on the scales in each of the instruments. This information is almost always available in the manual or in the reviews or references cited in Buros (1970).

We would like to point out that the inclusion of an instrument in this book should not be considered to be an endorsement of it by us, and exclusion of an instrument should not be considered an indication that we consider it to be poor. The two major considerations involved in selecting instruments were relevance to human relations groups and general availability. In the last weeks before the book went to press, we were still discovering good instruments that could have been included if we had come upon them earlier. This experience serves to reinforce the idea of publishing a supplement to this volume.

SECTION A
Instruments with a Personal Focus

Short and Uni-Scaled Instruments

SURVEY OF PERSONAL VALUES

Leonard V. Gordon

DESCRIPTION

Length: thirty sets of three statements.

Time: *Administering* fifteen minutes
Scoring five to ten minutes

Scales:

> *Practical Mindedness*
> *Achievement*
> *Variety*
> *Decisiveness*
> *Orderliness*
> *Goal Orientation*

The scales are designed to measure certain critical values that help determine the manner in which an individual copes with the problems of everyday living. The scales are defined by the values of high-scoring individuals. There are no separate descriptions for low-scoring individuals; they simply do not value what is defined by the particular scale. The respondent chooses the statements most like him and least like him for each set of statements.

Practical Mindedness. To always get one's money's worth, to take good care of one's property, to get full use out of one's possessions, to do things that will pay off, to be very careful with one's money.

Sample statement:
A. *To do things that will pay off.*
B. *To be a very orderly person.*
C. *To take a definite stand on issues.*
(Practical Mindedness response: *A—Most*)

Achievement. To work on difficult problems, to have a challenging job to tackle, to strive to accomplish something significant, to set the highest standards of accomplishment for oneself, to do an outstanding job in anything one tries.

Sample statement:
A. *To have an objective in mind and work toward it.*
B. *To do things that are highly profitable.*
C. *To accomplish something important.*
(Achievement response: *A—Most*)

59

Variety. To do things that are new and different, to have a variety of experiences, to be able to travel a great deal, to go to strange or unusual places, to experience an element of danger.

Decisiveness. To have strong and firm convictions, to make decisions quickly, to always come directly to the point, to make one's position on matters very clear, to come to a decision and stick to it.

Orderliness. To have well-organized work habits, to keep things in their proper place, to be a very orderly person, to follow a systematic approach in doing things, to do things according to a schedule.

Goal Orientation. To have a definite goal toward which to work, to stick to a problem until it is solved, to direct one's efforts toward clear-cut objectives, to know precisely where one is headed, to keep one's goals clearly in mind.

Uses: Given within a group, the SPV can give insight into personality and individual differences of group members. Scores on various scales of the SPV might be referred to as illustrating the possibility that the disagreements between two (or more) individuals might derive from individual differences in their personal values.

Positive Features: The best feature of the SPV is that it measures six values which may determine to a large degree what a person does or how well he performs.

The SPV employs the forced-choice format, which has been found to be minimally susceptible to manipulation in the measurement of personality traits. Another positive feature of the SPV is that it is short, self-administering (all directions required are given in full on the title page of the booklet), easy to score, and fairly simple to interpret using the information provided in the test manual.

ORDERING

Where To Order: Science Research Associates, Inc.
259 East Erie Street
Chicago, Illinois 60611
Phone (312) 944-7552

Cost:		
Specimen Set	$ 2.10	
Manual	$ .64	
Scoring Stencil	$ .90	
Package of 20 test booklets	$ 4.75	

ADMINISTERING, SCORING, AND INTERPRETING

Scoring: Scoring is done through the use of an overlay stencil. The number of responses showing through the holes are counted for each scale separately and recorded at the bottom of the page in the appropriate box. After scoring each of the scales, add them together. If the SPV has been correctly marked, the number attained will be 90. For incorrectly marked papers where the check scores fall between 85 and 95 and no more than two sets have been mismarked or omitted, the obtained scores may be used.

Scoring could be done by one or more persons depending upon the number of hand overlay stencils available. It would be preferable if enough stencils were available so as to allow each person to score his own *SPV*, because it allows for quick feedback.

Interpreting: The scales are interpreted in terms of the items they contain as determined by factor analytic methods. The first step in the interpretation of the scores is converting the raw scores into percentiles. The test manual presents national percentile norms for college students and regional norms for high school students for both male and female students.

Example: Sue is a female college student who took the *SPV*. Following are her scores:

	P	A	V	D	O	G
Raw Score	5	21	26	17	13	8

Referring to the national percentile norms for female college students given in the manual, Sue's percentiles are found to be:

	P	A	V	D	O	G
Percentile	11	83	93	64	48	4

The next step in the interpretation of the scores is the interpretation of the percentiles. For convenience the range can be divided into five levels of equal standard score magnitude.

Very High (VHi) - 94th to 99th percentile
High (Hi) - 70th to 93rd
Average (Av) - 31st to 69th percentile
Low (L) - 8th to 30th percentile
Very Low (VL) - 1st to 7th percentile

For Sue, the interpretations would be:

	P	A	V	D	O	G
Raw Score	5	21	26	17	13	8
Percentile	11	83	93	64	48	4
Interpretation	L	Hi	VHi	Av	Av	VL

STUDY OF VALUES

**Gordon W. Allport, Philip E. Vernon,
Gardner Lindzey**

DESCRIPTION

Length: Thirty two-choice statements, plus fifteen statements in which the respondent ranks four alternatives

Time: *Administering* fifteen to twenty-five minutes
Scoring   about ten minutes

Scales:

Theoretical
Economic
Aesthetic
Social
Political
Religious

Theoretical. Interested in the discovery of *truth;* observes and reasons.

> Sample statement:
> *If you had some time to spend in a waiting room and there were only two magazines to choose from, would you prefer:*
> *(a) Scientific Age*
> *(b) Arts and Decorations*
> (Theoretical response: *a*)

Economic. Interested in what is useful, practical; accumulation of wealth and luxury.

> Sample statement:
> *Do you prefer a friend (of your own sex) who:*
> *(a) is efficient, industrious and of a practical turn of mind,*
> *(b) is seriously interested in thinking out his attitude toward life as a whole,*
> *(c) possesses qualities of leadership and organizing ability,*
> *(d) shows artistic and emotional sensitivity.*
> (Economic response: *a*)

Aesthetic. Values *form* and *harmony;* that things be fitting, charming, beautiful.

> Sample statement:
> *If you were a university professor and had the necessary ability, would you prefer to teach:*

(a) poetry
(b) chemistry and physics?
(Aesthetic response: a)

Social. Values love of people; altruism and philanthropism, kindness and unselfishness.

Political. Interested primarily in *power;* desires influence and renown.

Religious. Values *unity;* tends to be mystical, to see something divine in life or seeks higher reality by withdrawing from life.

Uses: The *Study of Values* can be used in the following ways: (1) comparing a person's scores with his guesses of high, medium, or low scores, (2) comparing the scores of any pair or group of people who must get along with each other, and (3) encouraging people to examine how their life situation fits into their value system.

Positive Features: The instrument measures six important values that motivate many of life's activities. The instrument has been widely used, and there is a large amount of validational data on it. It is easy to administer, easy to score, and it gives results that are clearly understandable.

ORDERING

Where To Order: Houghton Mifflin Company
53 West 43rd Street
New York, N.Y. 10036
Phone (212) 867-8050

Cost: *Specimen Set* $ .96
Manual $ .60
Packages of Tests 35-Hand-Scorable Tests $4.50

GORDON PERSONAL INVENTORY

Leonard V. Gordon

DESCRIPTION

Length: Twenty sets of four statements, two responses for each set

Time: *Administering* ten to fifteen minutes
      Scoring   two to four minutes

Scales:

> *Cautiousness*
> *Original Thinking*
> *Personal Relations*
> *Vigor*

The respondent chooses the statements *most* like him and *least* like him for each set of statements.

Cautiousness. High scorers consider matters very carefully before making decisions and do not take chances or run risks. Low scorers are impulsive, act on the spur of the moment, make hurried or snap decisions, enjoy taking chances, and seek excitement.

Sample of scored statements:
   A. *Very cautious before proceeding*
   B. *Enjoys taking chances just for the excitement*
(Cautiousness responses: A. = Most *like me*
                          B. = Least *like me*)

Original Thinking. High scorers like to work on difficult problems, are intellectually curious, enjoy thought-provoking questions and discussions, and like to think about new ideas. Low scorers dislike working on difficult or complicated problems, do not care about acquiring knowledge, and are not interested in thought-provoking questions or discussions.

Sample of scored statements:
   A. *Tends to be creative and original*
   B. *Dislikes working on complex and difficult problems*
(Original Thinking responses: A. = Most *like me*
                               B. = Least *like me*)

Personal Relations. High scorers have great faith and trust in people and are tolerant, patient, and understanding. Low scorers reflect a lack of trust or confi-

64

dence in people and a tendency to be critical of others and to become annoyed or irritated by what others do.

Vigor. High scorers are vigorous and energetic: they like to work and move rapidly, and they are able to accomplish more than the average person. Low scorers have low vitality or energy level, prefer a slow pace, and tend to tire easily and be below average in productivity.

Uses: The four scales measured by the *Gordon Personal Inventory* represent a person's self-perception when he is forced to choose among four statements. Comparison of his self-description through the instrument with the way he would describe himself using global, general terms, such as the names of the scales in the instrument, can be informative and give him reason to re-examine his self concept. Furthermore, comparison of both of these sources of information with the perceptions of others is valuable.

Positive Features: It is easy to administer and score and has a wide sampling of normative populations for a person to use to obtain a percentile rank for each of the scales. Gordon has matched response alternatives on social desirability so that it is difficult for a person to select his answers just to make himself "look good."

Concerns: Because the statements have been grouped so that "looking good" is not a major consideration in the responses made, and perhaps because of the nature of the scales being used, the respondent has to make some choices from alternatives that seem nearly alike. These similar alternatives may cause the respondent to guess out of frustration or spend a lot of time puzzling over his decision.

ORDERING

Where To Order: Test Department
Harcourt, Brace & World, Inc.
757 Third Avenue
New York, N.Y.
Phone (212) 572-5000

Cost: *Specimen Set* $2.00
Packages of Tests 35 tests $4.80

ADMINISTERING, SCORING AND INTERPRETING

Scoring: Scoring is accomplished by either machine or hand stencils. There is a hand scoring stencil provided which can be cut into four strips or used as one stencil and slid into position four times.

Interpreting: Fred's scores will be used as an example. He obtained the following scores with their associated percentile ranks:

Scale	Score	Percentile Rank
Cautiousness	21	9
Original Thinking	30	70
Personal Relations	23	23
Vigor	20	8

In interpreting a score pattern, two comparisons must be kept in mind. First, the person is choosing that characteristic in comparison with the other three characteristics measured by the instrument. Secondly, he is basing his self-judgment on his associates and those he uses as his comparison people. Respondents should be reminded that their scores are affected by such comparisons when you are interpreting their scores with them.

Fred is slightly above average in Original Thinking, slightly below average in Personal Relations and low in Cautiousness and Vigor. Focussing on the two scales in which his scores deviate most from average (C and V), Fred describes himself as a person who is not highly cautious, as a person who does not like to consider matters carefully before making decisions. He is more likely to enjoy taking chances and seeking excitement; he is more impulsive. Fred's low score on vigor indicates that he describes himself as someone who sets a slow pace and is below average in sheer output.

GORDON PERSONAL PROFILE

Leonard V. Gordon

DESCRIPTION

Length: eighteen sets of four statements, two responses for each set

Time: *Administering* seven to fifteen minutes
       Scoring   five minutes

Scales:

> *Ascendancy*
> *Responsibility*
> *Emotional Stability*
> *Sociability*

Ascendancy. High scorers on this scale are verbally ascendant, adopt an active role in a group, are self-assured and assertive. They tend to make independent decisions. Low scorers tend to play a passive role in a group and listen rather than talk.

Sample of scored statements:
+ *Assured in relationships with others*
- *Prefers not to argue with other people*

Responsibility High scorers on this scale are able to stay with any job assigned them, are perservering and determined, and can be relied on. Low scorers are unable to stay with tasks that do not interest them and tend to be flighty and irresponsible.

Sample of scored statements:
+ *Follows well-developed work habits*
- *Unable to keep a fixed schedule*

Emotional Stability. High scorers on this scale are well-balanced, emotionally stable, and relatively free from anxieties and nervous tension. Low scorers have excessive anxiety, hypersensitivity, nervousness, and low frustration tolerance.

Sample of scored statements:
+ *A calm and unexcited person*
- *Feelings are rather easily hurt*

Sociability. High scorers on this scale like to be with and work with people and are gregarious and sociable. Low scorers restrict their social contacts and, in the extreme, actually avoid social relationships.

Sample of scored statements:
+ *Inclined to be highly sociable*
- *Would rather keep to a small group of friends*

Uses: Three of the scales measured by the *Profile* are directly relevant to human relations (Ascendancy, Emotional Stability, and Sociability), and the fourth is relevant to organizational behavior (Responsibility). As such, they make the *Personal Profile* useful for motivating people to examine aspects of themselves relevant to their interpersonal relations.

Positive Features: The *Profile* is well-designed for administering and scoring, so that scores are obtained easily. Substantial information on the scales is given in the forms of case studies, differences between groups of people, and relations between scores on each scale and scores on other scales.

Concerns: The pairings of items in terms of social desirability and the forced-choice "most like you, least like you" format slows the administration time even though there are only 18 groups of 4 statements. Furthermore, Gordon's use of negatively-worded descriptions complicates the decision of which characteristic is least like you.

ORDERING

Where To Order: Harcourt, Brace, and Jovanovich, Inc.
757 Third Avenue
New York, N.Y.
Phone (212) 572-5000

Cost: *Specimen Set* $2.00 (includes both *Personal Profile* and *Personal Inventory*)
Packages of Tests 35 tests $4.80

PERSONAL VALUE SCALES

William A. Scott

DESCRIPTION

Length: sixty-item version
240-item version

Time: *Administering* thirty minutes (sixty-item version)
sixty to seventy minutes (240-item version)
Scoring five to eight minutes (sixty-item version)
ten to twelve minutes (240-item version)

Scales:

> Intellectualism
> Kindness
> Social Skills
> Loyalty
> Academic Achievement
> Physical Development
> Status
> Honesty
> Religiousness
> Self-Control
> Creativity (Originality)
> Independence

Intellectualism. High scorers are interested in world affairs, curious, and take an active interest in all things scholarly. Low scorers have narrow interests and little knowledge, if any, of current events.

Sample statements:
+ *Striving to gain new knowledge about the world.*
- *Being non-interested in one's work.*

Kindness. High scorers are kind to people, helpful, and considerate. Low scorers are not interested in anyone but themselves first, hurt others' feelings, and ignore the needs of others.

Sample statements:
+ *Being concerned about the happiness of other people.*
- *Letting each person go it alone, without offering help.*

69

Social Skills. High scorers are well-mannered, poised, gracious, and charming. Low scorers dress sloppily, have bad manners, and are discourteous.

Sample statements:
+ *Being able to get others to cooperate with him.*
- *Being unable to act in a way that will please others.*

Loyalty. High scorers work hard to improve the prestige and status of their groups and help organize group activities. Low scorers let other people do all the work for the group and are uncooperative.

Academic Achievement. High scorers study hard, work hard, and strive to get the highest grades. Low scorers are content with average grades, do not do their work well, and pay no attention to lectures and textbooks.

Physical Development. High scorers are graceful and well coordinated, take good care of themselves, and are good in some form of sport. Low scorers are physically weak and puny, indoor types, and poorly proportioned physically.

Status. High scorers are respected, gain recognition for achievements, and do what they are told. Low scorers act in an undignified manner and do not take pride in their achievements.

Honesty. High scorers never cheat, always tell the truth, and support honesty in all things. Low scorers take things that don't belong to them, deceive others, and tell falsehoods.

Religiousness. High scorers are devout in their religion, always attend religious services, and encourage others to attend religious services. Low scorers are atheists and pay little attention to religion.

Self-control. High scorers practice self-control, reply to anger with gentleness, and never lose their temper. Low scorers lose their temper easily and express their anger.

Creativity (originality). High scorers are able to create beautiful and artistic objects, develop new and different ways of doing things, and constantly experiment with new ways of approaching life. Low scorers are involved in ordinary activities, never have new ideas, and enjoy a routine.

Independence. High scorers are outspoken and frank, stand up for what they think is right, and are independent. Low scorers are crowd pleasers, keep their opinions to themselves, and act in ways that parallel other people's ways of doing things.

Concerns: Scott defines a value as something a person regards as absolutely, and universally good, whatever it might be. In keeping with this definition, the only response that he counts in his *Personal Value Scales* is "Always Admire." "Depends on Situation" and "Always Dislike" are not counted. The problem with this approach is that it can antagonize people who believe that they must know the situation before they can decide whether or not a given behavior is admirable and depress the score of the person who avoids responding at the extreme of any scale. One solution is to use the response categories as described by Scott, but instead of weighting them 1 for "always" and 0 for the other two responses, weight them 2 for "always," 1 for "depends" and 0 for "never." To get away from the existing format, you could use the four-response format described in the section on developing your own instrument:

Agree
Unsure, probably agree
Unsure, probably disagree
Disagree.

ORDERING

Where To Order: The instrument is located in W.A. Scott, *Values and Organizations*, Chicago, 1965.

        Rand McNally
        Box 7600
        Chicago, Illinois 60600
        Phone (312) 267-6868

Cost: $8.95

THE PERSONALITY INVENTORY

Robert G. Bernreuter

DESCRIPTION

Length: 125 questions; yes-no format

Time: *Administering* fifteen to twenty minutes

       Scoring   forty-two minutes (seven minutes per scale)

Scales:

> *Neurotic Tendency*
> *Self Sufficiency*
> *Introversion-Extroversion*
> *Dominance-Submission*
> *Confidence*
> *Sociable*

Since the scales were based on factor analytic techniques, all statements are in all scales. We shall indicate some of the statements that are heavily weighed in the different scales.

Neurotic Tendency (B1-N). Emotional instability versus emotional well-balance.

> Sample statement:
> *Do your feelings alternate between happiness and sadness without apparent reason?*
> (Neurotic response: *Yes*)

Self sufficiency (B2-S). Prefer to be alone, rarely ask for sympathy or encouragement, ignore the advice of others versus dislike of solitude.

> Sample statement:
> *Do you usually enjoy spending an evening alone?*
> (Self Sufficient response: *Yes*)

Introversion (B3-I). Live within self, imaginative versus few emotional upsets or worries.

> Sample statement:
> *Are your feelings easily hurt?*
> (Introversion response: *Yes*)

Dominance (B4-D). Ascendance versus submission.

Confidence (F1-C). Feel inferior and be self-conscious versus well-adjusted and wholesome self-confidence.

72

Sociable (F2-S). Independent and non-social versus gregarious and sociable.

Uses: As with almost all personality instruments, the results may prove confrontive, *i.e.*, they make the respondent pause and deal with information about himself. Selection of two scales (see below) should give the person some idea of where he stands on the two main characteristics measured by the scales which may be termed personal adjustment and sociability.

Positive Features: Since the scales have high reliability, we can have confidence in their homogeneity, *i.e.*, all of the weighted items in a scale are measuring the same thing.

Concerns: The scoring for all six scales takes a very long time (approximately 40 minutes). Furthermore, the use of all six yields highly redundant information, *i.e.*, some of the scales are measuring almost exactly the same thing. The correlation of B1 with B3 is .95, B1 with B4 is -.80, B1 with F1 is .95, B2 with F2 is .60, B3 with B4 is -.69, B3 with F1 is .90, and B4 with F1 is -.88. Thus, there is a cluster of B1, B3, B4, and F1, all measuring approximately the same thing. B2 and F2 are unrelated to the first cluster but relate well enough to each other that they form a cluster. It is recommended that the most reliable scale from each cluster (B1 and B2) be scored and the other scales ignored.

The *Bernreuter Personality Inventory* has a flavor of psychopathology: scale 1 is called "neurotic tendency" and, on the individual's report sheet, it states "Those scoring above the 98 percentile (on scale B1-N) would probably benefit from psychiatric or medical advice." The same indication is made for scales B3 and F1.

ORDERING

Where To Order: Consulting Psychologists Press, Inc.
577 College Avenue
Palo Alto, California 94306
Phone (415) 326-4448

Cost: *Specimen Set* $ .75
Manual and Norm $ .35
Scoring Stencils $2.50
Packages of tests   25 tests $ 3.50
                    100 tests $13.00
Packages of Answers Sheets   50 sheets $ 3.00
                                    250 sheets $13.50
Packages of Profiles   25 profiles $1.25
                       100 profiles $6.00

PERSONAL GROWTH INVENTORY

Michael G. Blansfield
Gordon L. Lippitt

DESCRIPTION

Length: twenty-three pairs of rating scales with labels at the ends, six open-ended questions

Time: *Administering* five to ten minutes

Scales:

> *Personal Growth (Self-Estimation)*
> *Personal Growth (Estimation of Another Person)*

There are twenty-one described traits which the respondent rates on 9-point line scales from low to high. In addition, one other person also rates the respondent on these twenty-one traits using the line scales. These twenty-one traits are as follows: Self Understanding, Self Esteem, Courage to Fail, Giving Love, Accepting Love, Openness, Peace of Mind, Tendency to Trust Others, Level of Aspiration, Physical Energy, Versatility, Innovativeness, Expressing Anger, Receiving Hostility, Clarity in Expressing My Thoughts, Ability to Listen in an Alert and Understanding Way, Reactions to Comments About or Evaluations of My Behavior, Tolerance of Differences in Others, Interest in Learning, Independence, and Vision of the Future.

Self Understanding

    SAMPLE SCALE:

            SELF-ESTIMATION

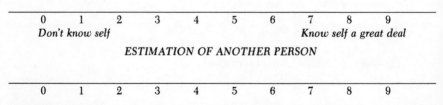

    0   1   2   3   4   5   6   7   8   9
    Don't know self   Know self a great deal
        ESTIMATION OF ANOTHER PERSON

    0   1   2   3   4   5   6   7   8   9

In addition to the twenty-one prescribed items, two blank "scales" are provided for the respondent to fill in with important dimensions relevant to his personal growth. Space is also provided for the respondent to indicate factors in himself, others, and his work situation that support his personal growth goals and those that tend to block his growth.

74

Uses: The respondent describes his current situation through the scales and gets feedback from others in the group (both from ratings and orally) about his behavior. He makes plans to reduce the blocking factors and to strengthen and use the supporting factors to carry out his personal growth goals.

Positive Features: It is brief and measures a number of characteristics important to human relations training.

Concerns: Because it is brief and composed of line rating scales, it is not very impressive. Furthermore, there are no suggestions in the manual about how to reduce the number of dimensions considered. Since the "scales" consist of a single rating, they can be assumed to be fairly unreliable; that is, scores may shift two or three points fairly readily.

ORDERING

Where To Order: Leadership Resources, Inc.
1750 Pennsylvania Avenue, N.W.
Washington, D.C. 20006
Phone (202) 298-7092

Cost: *Per copy* 1-99 $ .25
100 or more $ .20

EYSENCK PERSONALITY INVENTORY

H. J. Eysenck
Sybil B. G. Eysenck

DESCRIPTION

Length: fifty-seven questions, yes/no format

Time: *Administering* seven to ten minutes
      Scoring   two to five minutes

Scales:

> *Extraversion-Introversion*
> *Neuroticism*
> *(Lie Scale)*

Extraversion-Introversion. High scorers tend to be outgoing, impulsive, and uninhibited, have many social contacts and frequently take part in group activities. Low scorers are quiet, retiring, introspective, fond of books rather than people, reserved, and distant except to intimate friends.

Sample of scored statements:
+ *Do you nearly always have a "ready answer" when people talk to you?*
- *Do you like working alone?*

Neuroticism. High scorers are emotionally labile and over-reactive. They tend to be emotionally over-responsive and to have difficulties in returning to a normal state after emotional experiences.

Sample of scored statements:
+ *Have you often got a restless feeling that you want something but do not know what?*

Lie Scale. Eighteen statements that have been used in lie scales in other instruments such as the *MMPI* were modified and included. High scorers try to appear in a socially desirable light.

Sample of scored statements:
+ *As a child did you always do as you were told immediately and without grumbling?*
- *Do you sometimes get cross?*

Positive Features: It is brief and has been used extensively in research.

Concerns: The term "Neuroticism" is guaranteed to make high scorers defensive and may inhibit the goal of constructive self-examination.

ORDERING

Where To Order: Educational and Industrial Testing Service
Box 7234
San Diego , California 92107
Phone (714) 488-1666

Cost: *Specimen Set* $2. 25
Manual $1.25
Scoring Stencils $1.50
25 Tests $3.50

HOW WELL DO YOU KNOW YOURSELF?

Thomas N. Jenkins

DESCRIPTION

Length: 120 statements

Time: *Administering* thirty-five to forty-five minutes
        Scoring   fifteen to twenty minutes

Scales:

Irritability	*General Morale*
Practicality	*Persistence*
Punctuality	*Nervousness*
Novelty-Loving	*Seriousness*
Vocational Assurance	*Submissiveness*
Cooperativeness	*Impulsiveness*
Ambitiousness	*Dynamism*
Hypercriticalness	*Emotional Control*
Dejection	

Irritability. Tendency to feel annoyed.

> Sample statement:
> *When I'm sick, I feel cranky.*

Practicality. Tendency to do or think about that which is useful.

> Sample statement:
> *I would rather do problems than think up new problems.*

Punctuality. Tendency toward promptness or timeliness.

Novelty-loving. Tendency to like what is new, such as new decisions or activities.

Vocational Assurance. Tendency to feel confident about earning a living.

Cooperativeness. Tendency to feel like joining or sharing in united action.

Ambitiousness. Tendency to desire and to strive for prestige.

Hypercriticalness. Tendency toward fault-finding.

Dejection. Tendency to feel downcast, sad, or gloomy.

General Morale. Tendency to feel optimistic.

Persistence. Tendency to strive in the face of internal or external obstacles.

Nervousness. Tendency to feel tense or jumpy.

Seriousness. Tendency to be earnest.

Submissiveness. Tendency to yield and comply.

Impulsiveness. Tendency to decide or act without deliberation.

Dynamism. Tendency to feel active or energetic.

Emotional Control. Inhibition of socially disapproved emotional manifestations.

ORDERING

Where To Order: Executive Analysis Corporation
76 Beaver Street
New York, N.Y. 10017
Phone (212) 867-0471

Costs: *Specimen Set* $2.50
30 Tests $6.50
Set of Scoring Stencils $2.00
Manual $1.10

SELF-ACTUALIZATION TEST

W. J. Reddin
J. Brian Sullivan

DESCRIPTION

Length: twenty-eight sets of three statements, respondent distributes a total of three points among each set (e.g., 3,0,0; 1,1,1; 0,2,1; 0,1,2)

Time: *Administering* eight to ten minutes
       Scoring   three to four minutes

Scales:

> *Physical Needs*
> *Security Needs*
> *Relationships Needs*
> *Respect Needs*
> *Independence Needs*
> *Self-Actualization Needs*

Physical Needs. Unfulfilled needs concerned with filling biological appetites.

> Sample statement:
> *I wish that I had more good meals.*

Security Needs. Unfulfilled needs concerned with maintaining safety and security.

> Sample statement:
> *I wish that I could buy a bigger insurance policy.*

Relationships Needs. Unfulfilled needs concerned with obtaining love, affection, and a feeling of belongingness with others.

> Sample statements:
> *I wish that I had more friends.*

Respect Needs. Unfulfilled needs concerned with obtaining self-respect and the esteem of others.

Independence Needs. Unfulfilled needs concerned with obtaining autonomy.

Self-Actualization Needs. Unfulfilled needs concerned with attaining self-fulfillment.

ORDERING

Where To Order: Organizational Tests, Ltd.
Box 324
Fredericton, N.B. Canada
Phone (506) 455-8366

Costs: *Test Booklet* $3.00

THE INVOLVEMENT INVENTORY

Richard Heslin
Brian Blake

DESCRIPTION

Length: 102 statements

Time: *Administering* eight to fifteen minutes
Scoring five to fifteen minutes

Scales:

> *Affective Involvement*
> *Behavioral Involvement*
> *Cognitive Involvement*
> *Total Involvement*

The scales measure involvement levels with people, objects, and ideas respectively.

Affective Involvement. Measures the extent to which a person is openly, actively involved with people. A high scorer is expressive, emotional, and extroverted.

Sample of scored statements:
+ *I like to get close to people.*
- *When I am angry, I become quiet.*

Behavioral Involvement. A high scorer is project-oriented and enjoys task accomplishment.

Sample of scored statements:
+ *I always have at least four projects going at once.*
- *I prefer to follow and let someone else take the lead.*

Cognitive Involvement. A high scorer is analytic, questioning, and critical.

Sample of scored statements:
+ *I love to try to spot the logical flaws in TV commercials.*
- *I have trouble finding things to criticize in something I read.*

Total Involvement. A high total score (sum of the other three scales) indicates a person who generally "pushes out" against the world, has high energy, and is active.

Uses: The *Involvement Inventory* can be used at the beginning of a workshop to show a participant the domains (people, objects, ideas) where he functions best, and how he compares in energy expenditures beyond the everyday maintenance levels. If there is asymmetry between a person's involvement scores and his self concept or his job situation, the person can take steps to try to change himself, to modify or change his job, or to live with the asymmetry realizing that he has made that choice. A group or organization that is heavily involved on one of the three dimensions should be aware that it has potential blind spots and vulnerability to some kinds of contingencies.

Positive Features: The theory behind the ABC scales is one of the strong points of the instrument. The concept that people not only vary in how active or passive they are but that some people may be active in one area, *e.g.*, behavior, but passive in another area, *e.g.*, cognition, is an important element in describing human interaction. The second positive feature is that the sum of the three scales yield an overall involvement score which can be useful in further interpretation. The scales have good reliability, are easy to administer, score, and interpret.

Concerns: The *Involvement Inventory* is somewhat long. However, the response format allows for rapid completion.

ORDERING
Where To Order: University Associates
Box 615
Iowa City, Iowa 52240
Phone (319) 351-7322

Cost: *25 tests* $3.50
25 Answer sheets and scoring sheets $2.00

ADMINISTERING, SCORING, AND INTERPRETING
Scoring: Participants total the number of checks in each of twenty-four sub-columns, multiply the totals by a weight, and add the resulting four products to obtain six sums that give both directions of the three scales. They then sum the two directions of each scale to yield each scale score. Finally, they sum the three scale scores to arrive at the total involvement score.

Interpreting: Given below are the Interquartile ranges (approximately 50% of the respondents scored within this range) for each scale. The scores in Table 1 are based on eighteen people involved in various phases of human relations work (e.g., career counselor for clergymen, director and staff of a growth center, psychologist involved in drug abuse therapy, university counselors, members of a training staff of a large corporation, etc.)

		Affect	Behavior	Cognition	Total	
Median		*116*	*100*	*86*	*300*	
Interquartile Range		*107-122*	*88-109*	*78-92*	*289-320*	
Percentiles:	90	*130*	*113*	*94*	*328*	*Very High*
	70	*122*	*110*	*93*	*320*	*High*
	50	*116*	*100*	*86*	*300*	*Average*
	30	*112*	*90*	*83*	*292*	*Low*
	10	*92*	*85*	*76*	*260*	*Very Low*

Table 1. Median, Interquartile Ranges, and Selected Percentile Scores for the four scales.

For example, we will compare Bob's scores with the figures in Table 1 (see Table 2).

	Affect	Behavior	Cognition	Total
Score	130	79	88	297
Designation	Very High	Very Low	Average	Average

Table 2. Bob's Scores and Description of Their Meaning.

In general, Bob's scores indicate that his overall level of activity or involvement in life is about average with that of his peers. However, he distributes this energy to a much greater proportion in being expressive and open with people and to a lesser proportion than most in initiating projects, especially those involving working with objects. He does not fear getting close to people and letting them get close to him, but he probably breaks out in a cold sweat at the thought of paneling his basement.

The scores in a workshop or group will take on meaning within the context of the workshop range and averages. One procedure is to ask the members to post their scores on newsprint and place them on the walls around the room using masking tape. The facilitator asks participants to call out their A scores, and he makes a frequency distribution (see Introduction to Section Two to see how to make a frequency distribution). As in Tabel 1, the top 10 per cent of scores are designated "Very High," the next 20 per cent "High," the next 40 per cent "Average," the next 20 per cent "Low," and the bottom 10 per cent "Very Low." Repeat the process with the other two scales and the total score.

An alternative way of demonstrating the involvement styles is to construct small homogeneous groups based on the obtained scores in the total group and ask them to discuss and come to a decision about some topic while the rest of the participants observe each group. Observers can rate the groups on interpersonal style (e.g., open, task-oriented, confrontive, involved) and discuss whether they reflect their scale scores.

REFERENCE

Heslin, R. and Blake, B. The Involvement Inventory. Jones, J.E. and Pfeiffer, J.W. (Eds.) *The 1973 Annual Handbook for Group Facilitators,* Iowa City: University Associates Press, 1973.

COPING OPERATIONS PREFERENCE ENQUIRY

William C. Schutz

Length: thirty responses required (five responses to each of six situations)

Time: *Administering* five to ten minutes
      Scoring   five to ten minutes

Scales:

> *Denial*
> *Isolation*
> *Projection*
> *Regression*
> *Turning Against the Self*

COPE measures a person's preference for defense or coping mechanisms. Situations are described that contain anxiety-producing potential because the person described has tendencies toward either *too much or not enough* of: a) being with people, b) taking charge and making decisions, and c) being close and personal with people. Thus, six situations are described.

For example, "In a group meeting yesterday, Sam, who rarely takes charge of things even when it might be appropriate, appeared to be very disturbed." Thus, Sam's usual behavior is described and the fact that there is a problem is established.

"When a request was made for volunteers for the chairmanship, Sam suddenly seemed to realize that he might like the job." A discrepancy between his usual behavior and behavior that meets his needs is indicated.

"He appeared to feel that he might enjoy his relations with people more if he were not so reluctant to be more assertive." Here a dissatisfaction with the discrepancy is indicated.

"Today he appears to be still concerned. How would you guess he really feels now?" Finally, the problem is presented to the respondent.

To each of the 6 situations described in the *COPE* instrument, the respondent ranks five ways that "Submissive Sam" or "Personal Paul" could be reacting. Each of the five reactions represents a defense style.

Sample statement:
DENIAL   *He feels this isn't a very important problem. He isn't worried.*

85

ISOLATION	*He may be cool toward others, but he doesn't feel this has much to do with how much he enjoys people.*
PROJECTION	*Although he may be too domineering, he feels that this is because other people expect this of him.*
REGRESSION	*He feels that he may be too personal with others but that with help from someone more experienced, he could change.*
TURNING AGAINST THE SELF	*He realizes that the fault for taking too little respon- sibility lies completely with himself and with no one else.*

Uses: *COPE* can be used to identify preferred styles of dealing with interpersonal anxiety early in a human relations group. Getting *COPE* scores accomplishes three objectives early in the life of the group:

1. Having each person discuss his characteristic ways of reacting to inter-personal situations, as evidenced by his scores, legitimizes talking about such material in the group.

2. Early discussion of possible disfunctional aspects of over-dependency on any one of the five styles can be used to help members form a personal agenda in which they will work at reducing the tendency to use one type of defense all of the time.

3. Discussion and posting of people's scores can help other members realize that the cause of their conflicts with the respondent may be due to different approaches to interpersonal problems as indicated by scores on *COPE*.

Positive Features: The translation of the scores on the five defenses into *decile scores* tells a respondent not only that he uses "turning against the self" as a characteristic defense but that he uses it more than, perhaps, 90% of the people who have been administered the instrument (based upon a normative sample of almost 6000 persons). This is a useful piece of information to have. You may suspect that you are high or low in use of a defense, but it often comes as a shock to find that you are *that* different from most people.

A second positive feature of *COPE* is its simplicity. A respondent can quite easily re-examine the responses that led to an unusually high use of a defense mechanism, thereby seeing specifically when he reacted the way he did. For ex-ample, a high score on projection means that a person is shifting the lines of causality for his behavior from himself to others. "Other people expect this of him" is the phrase that recurs in the projection responses. Whether or not one wants to label this as "projection" is immaterial. It may also reflect that such a person is living his life primarily to meet others' expectations. Such a style is not conducive to his being aware of his own feelings or to his knowing what *he* wants. Thus, the specific feeling ascribed to the people in the stories can be ex-amined in detail for what they mean about the respondent.

Concerns: The primary concern with *COPE* is that there is no way of obtaining a nonpathological score. The use of clinical terminology (denial, projection, etc.) coupled with the absence of a healthy response category makes it likely that people may become somewhat upset and defensive about their scores. The facilitator can avoid the problem by pointing out that there is no possibility of obtaining a "healthy" score on *COPE* and that any of the alternatives can represent a reasonable and defensible way of handling some of these situations.

Some less pathological names that a facilitator could assign to the five behavioral styles are:

Old Name	New Name
Denial	*Ignores the problem*
Isolation	*Questions the generality of the problem*
Projection	*Lives up to other's expectations*
Regression	*Seeks help*
Turning against self	*Takes responsibility for the problem*

There is an optimum amount of tension and anxiety that fosters self-examination and commitment to change. If anxiety is too low, we feel no need to bestir outselves from other concerns; if anxiety is too high, self-examination is too threatening and we use a defense such as those measured by *COPE*. One way of using the old and new names listed above is to begin with the old names and use the new names for persons who seem to be reacting so negatively to the old labels that they are rejecting the information it conveys.

A second problem with *COPE* is that the five response categories are very similar from situation to situation (in the case of Denial, the five response categories are identical), so that a respondent knows if he is assigning the same feelings to all of the story characters. It is simple to obtain the same rank ordering of defenses to each situation because of the transparency of the responses. One saving aspect of this problem of obviousness of response categories is that the respondent usually perceives of them as varying responses to situations rather than as indicators of a defense style. Another aspect of the instrument that alleviates or at least reduces the problem of respondents recognizing the same response alternative to each situation is the fact that there is no "socially desirable" response. Thus, one of the problems with *COPE*—the fact that all categories are defenses—turns out to be an asset, because it prevents respondents, consciously or unconsciously, from being able to make themselves "look good."

ORDERING

Where To Order: Consulting Psychologists Press
577 College Ave.
Palo Alto, CA 94306
Phone (415) 326-4448

Cost: *Specimen Set* $3.25
Packages of Tests 25 tests $ 3.25

ADMINISTERING, SCORING, AND INTERPRETING

Administering:

1. Distribute the *COPE* question and answer booklets.

2. Read the instructions aloud. Ask the participants to stop after they are finished and not score their answers.

3. When they are finished, give a short lecture on the meaning of the *COPE* defense styles.

4. Have the participants guess which one they use the most and the least.

5. Have them score their booklets, using the form on the back page of the test booklet.

6. Read the decile equivalents from the manual.

Scoring: In contrast to the other FIRO tests, *COPE* does not yield scores related to inclusion, control, and affection, nor does it use intensity response categories such as "strongly agree, agree, etc.," or "most people, some people, etc." Respondents rank the five response statements in terms of how likely it is that each describes how the person in the story feels.

On the back of the instrument, the respondent can calculate his own raw score (total rank) for each of the five coping mechanisms by means of an easy-to-use table. Caution them to be careful when copying responses from the inside of the booklet to the back page. Scores for the left-hand column come from the right hand page and vice versa. The totals are useful in their own right: low total ranks indicate preferred styles for handling anxiety about interpersonal relations. However, since the total ranks for each defense mechanism vary widely (denial = 24, turning against self = 13), Schutz provides a conversion table from total rank to decile score in the FIRO manual.

Interpreting: Focus attention on the one or two extremely high or low defenses which indicate an over- or underuse of that method of coping with interpersonal problems. If 80 or 90% of the population use that defense more or less than the participant does, it should be mentioned. Encourage the participants to explore 1) how they use their preferred style in other situations, 2) how overuse of any one style may be maladaptive, and 3) why other participants prefer styles different from theirs.

INVENTORY OF AFFECTIVE TOLERANCE

V. E. Fisher
Robert I. Watson

DESCRIPTION

Length: sixty-one statements

Time: *Administering* fifteen minutes
Scoring three minutes

Scale:

Affective Tolerance

Affective tolerance. This is the capacity to deal with excitement or tension, the capacity to withstand emotional disturbance, the ability to discharge emotional tension in an appropriate way.

Sample statement:
I am embarrassed at my blunders.

Positive Features: The *IAT* attempts to measure a composite of traits that is thematic in human relations training. The instrument can produce a discussion that promotes the expansion of the norm for expressing affect in a group.

Concerns: Even though the instrument takes only 18 minutes to administer and score, it is a great deal of time for only one scale. Furthermore, the instrument suggests pathology: it contains words such as nightmares, blues, anxiety, unpleasant dreams, useless thoughts, and buzzing or roaring sounds in the ears. Finally, the statements can clearly be manipulated for a "look good" result, and there is no Lie or Social Desirability scale to measure the honesty of the responses. Thus high affective tolerance scores could be obtained by non-tolerant individuals who are trying to present themselves in a socially desirable light.

ORDERING

Where To Order: Sheridan Supply Company
Box 837
Beverly Hills, California 90213
Phone (213) 474-1744

Cost: *Specimen Set* (complete test not included) $ .40
25 tests $2.50
Scoring key $ .35
Manual $ .25

MULTIPLE AFFECT ADJECTIVE CHECK LIST

Marvin Zuckerman
Bernard Lubin

DESCRIPTION

Length: 132 Adjectives

Time: *Administering* three to six minutes
     Scoring   three to five minutes

Scales:

> Anxiety
> Depression
> Hostility

Anxiety consists of 21 adjectives.

Sample of scored adjectives:
+ afraid   + fearful   + nervous   + shaky
- calm   - contented   - joyful   - pleasant

Depression consists of 40 adjectives.

Sample of scored adjectives:
+ alone   + blue   + discouraged   + gloomy   + lost
- active   - clean   - fine   - free   - glad

Hostility is a scale consisting of 28 adjectives.

Sample of scored adjectives:
+ angry   + cruel   + discontented   + furious   + mad
- agreeable   - cooperative   - friendly   - kindly   - sympathetic

There is a "Today" form and an "In General" form. They are identical excep for the instructions.

Uses: Having members discuss their scores and their responses to individua adjectives has the potential of moving people quickly toward an orientation whe they are willing and ready to talk about things that are bothering them as a pr cursor to doing something about them. *MAACL* can be used as a monitor of grou feelings. It could be used to establish that there is a thematic feeling in the grou (say, hostility) as a result of some event or decision.

Positive Features: *MAACL* is fast to administer and score. It yields three usefu non-overlapping scales that describe unhappiness in its various manifestations.

indicates to some people that they may overwork one manifestation of unhappiness. For example, it may never occur to a depressive that he could react with hostility or to a hostile person that he is placing all of the cause outside himself and that a mixture of hostility and anxiety would probably be more appropriate. This insight could result in some motivation to change.

Concerns: *MAACL* has a flavor of psychopathology, *i.e.*, one has to be willing to describe himself in troubled ways (*shaky, terrified, tormented, panicky*) to score high. This characteristic suggests that *MAACL* may be more appropriate for therapy groups than for human relations training groups.

It is fairly easy to err in scoring *MAACL*. When the person lays the stencil on his answer sheet, the first response he is likely to make is to count the number of marks that show through the punched-out holes. However, such a procedure will give an incorrect total. He must rather examine the plus or zero next to the hole. If it is a plus and there is a mark showing through the hole he counts "one." However, if the indication next to the hole is a zero, then there must be *no* mark showing through the hole for him to count "one." If he has a plus with no mark or a zero with a mark, he counts "zero" (*i.e.*, no count).

ORDERING

Where To Order: Educational and Industrial Testing Service
P. O. Box 7234
San Diego, CA 92107
Phone (714) 488-1666

Cost: *Specimen Set* $2.25
Packages of Forms   25 MAACL forms $ 3.50
100 MAACL forms $12.50
500 MAACL forms $49.50

ADMINISTERING, SCORING, AND INTERPRETING

Administering: Distribute the form. Read the instructions aloud. You may wish to modify "Today" to be interpreted as "during the last 2 hours," "during the last 10 minutes," or "right now."

Scoring: Distribute stencils. (You do not need as many stencils as forms because many people can share one set of three stencils.) Remind participants that even non-checks are counted if they are in a hole with a zero beside it. See the manual for details. You may wish to use the brief scales described on page 21 of the manual for measures of anxiety, depression and hostility that are more independent of each other.

Interpreting: A T-score conversion table (average of 50 and standard deviation of 10) for MAACL is on page 7 of the manual. Have the participants post their T-scores on newsprint around the room. They can form dyads or small groups to discuss the meaning of their pattern of scores, reconvening in moderate size groups to share the experience and work on what has been highlighted by the instrument.

CALIFORNIA F SCALE

**T. W. Adorno, Else Frenkel-Brunswik,
D. J. Levinson and R. N. Sanford**

DESCRIPTION

Length: thirty statements

Time: *Administering* four minutes
      Scoring   three minutes

Scale:

> *Authoritarianism*

The *California F Scale* is a measure of tendency toward *authoritarianism* or espousing anti-democratic attitudes. Although the *F Scale* is a single scale it is made up of statements that measure nine orientations that describe the authoritarian personality. The person rates each statement with the following responses: 1) agree 2) unsure, probably agree 3) unsure, probably disagree 4) disagree.

Conventionalism. Rigid adherence to conventional middle-class values.

> Sample statement:
> *A person who has bad manners, habits, and breeding can hardly expect to get along with decent people.*

Authoritarian Submission. A submissive, uncritical attitude toward idealized moral authorities of the in-group.

> Sample statement:
> *Science has its place but there are many important things that can never possibly be understood by the human mind.*

Authoritarian Aggression. A tendency to condemn people who violate conventional values.

> Sample statement:
> *What youth needs most is strict discipline, rugged determination, and the will to work and fight for family and country.*

Anti-intraception. Opposition to self-examination in understanding oneself or trying to understand others.

Superstition and Stereotype. Belief in mystical determinants of fate; tendency to think in rigid categories.

Power and Toughness. Preoccupation with dominance-submission and identification with power figures.

Destructiveness and Cynicism. Low estimation of human nature.

Projectivity. The tendency to believe that wild and dangerous things go on in the world; the outward projection of unconscious motivation.

Sex. Exaggerated concern with sexual "goings-on."

Uses: The *F Scale* is of less immediate use for human relations training or interpersonal relations. However, it can give the respondent some insight into himself.

Positive Features: The *F Scale* is brief and is easy to administer and score. It is one of the most heavily researched instruments in existence.

Concerns: In its original form, all statements are worded to relate positively to the trait being measured so that a person who has a tendency to agree with all statements will get a high score whether or not he is authoritarian. A second concern with the *F Scale* is its high relationship to amount of education: the less educated a person is, the higher his F score tends to be. A third concern with the scale is the heavy "good people-bad people" tone of the instrument. Finally, the *F Scale* does not measure a pure personality syndrome but a politically-modified one, *i.e.*, high *F Scale* scorers espouse right-wing types of rigidity.

ORDERING

Where To Order: The instrument is located in J.W. Adorno, Else Frenkel-Brunswik, D.J. Levinson, and R.N. Sanford, *The Authoritarian Personality*, New York: Norton, 1969.

> W.W. Norton Co., Inc.
> 55 5th Avenue
> New York, New York 10003
> Phone (212) 255-9210

Cost: $4.95

DOGMATISM SCALE

Milton Rokeach

DESCRIPTION

Length: forty statements

Time: *Administering* five to eight minutes
 Scoring five to six minutes

Scale:

Dogmatism

The dogmatism scale was designed to measure mental rigidity, intolerance, and authoritariansim in a way that did not limit the applicability to only right-wing authoritarians in the way that the *California F Scale* does.

Sample of scored statements:
> *The highest form of government is a democracy, and the highest form of democracy is a government run by those who are most intelligent.*
> *Once I get wound up in a heated discussion, I just can't stop.*
> *A man who does not believe in some great cause has not really lived.*

Concerns: All of the statements are worded to relate positively to the trait so that a person who tends to agree with all statements will score high on dogmatism whether he is dogmatic or not. Second, there is a good-person-versus-bad-person flavor to the instrument. Closed-minded (dogmatic) persons are not as "good" as open-minded persons.

ORDERING

Where To Order: The scale is located in M. Rokeach, *The Open and Closed Mind*, New York: Basic Books, 1960.

> Basic Books, Inc.
> 10 East 53rd Street
> New York, New York 10022
> Phone: (212) 593-7057

Cost: $8.50 (hardcover); $3.95 (paperback)

SOCIAL DESIRABILITY SCALE

D. Marlowe
D. Crowne

DESCRIPTION

Length: thirty-three statements

Time: *Administering* eight to ten minutes
      Scoring   ten to twelve minutes

Scale:

> *Need For Approval*

When a person always responds to statements that carry a strong evaluative tone with them in a way that indicates that he is thorough, neat, kind, loyal, energetic, and courageous, it is assumed that he wants people to approve of him.

Sample Statement:
> *I investigate the qualifications of all of the candidates before I vote in an election.*
> *My table manners at home are the same as when I dine out.*

Concerns: It is assumed by the developers of this instrument that a high scorer has a high need for approval and that is why he is responding in a socially desirable way. We see two alternative explanations of a very high score on this scale. First, the respondent may not need people's approval, but he consciously manipulates people's perceptions of him for his own self-serving goals. Second, it is also possible that the person may be a genuinely thorough, kind, conscientious, perseverent, neat person. Of course he may have as high a need to look good as those who distort their responses in that direction.

ORDERING

Where To Order: The scale is located in D. Crowne and D. Marlowe, *The Approval Motive*, New York, Wiley, 1964.
        John Wiley & Sons, Inc.
        605 Third Avenue
        New York, New York 10016
        Phone: (212) 867-9800

Cost: $7.50

REPRESSION-SENSITIZATION SCALE

Donn Byrne

DESCRIPTION

Length: 127 statements

Time: *Administering* fifteen to twenty minutes
Scoring ten to fifteen minutes

Scale:

Repression-Sensitization

The *R-S Scale* measures a person's characteristic way of responding to a threat. A person who scores at the high or sensitization end of the scale uses approach defenses such as intellectualization: a low scorer (repressor) uses avoidance defenses such as denial.

Uses: The *R-S Scale* has been used to form groups with particular characteristics. LeBlanc (1966) found that a group composed of medium repressers was most effective in finding a solution to social problems that were presented to the group for discussion and solution. The group composed of a combination of very high repressers and very high sensitizers was least effective. The facilitator might ask participants identified as high and low repressers to discuss how they handle frustration or threat situations. The functions and dysfunctions of each style of responding to threat could be described by each subgroup.

Concerns: The *R-S Scale* was taken from the *MMPI* and therefore has a strong flavor of pathology. For example some statements read, "At times I have fits of laughing and crying that I cannot control," and "I have strange and peculiar thoughts." There is no control for or measure of the respondent's attempt to present himself in a way that makes him appear socially desirable.

ORDERING

Where To Order: The *R-S Scale* is really only a key for scoring a new scale on the *MMPI*. To use the instrument effectively, you need three items: 1) the *Minnesota Multiphasic Personality Inventory (MMPI)* described in this section, 2) the original R-S key and details on the scale, Byrne, D. "The repression-sensitization scale: rationale, reliability and validity," *Journal of Personality*, 1961, 29, 334-349, and 3) the new, revised scale, Byrne, D., Barry, J., and Nelson, D., "Relation of the revised repression-sensitization scale to measures of self-description," *Psychological Reports*, 1963, 13, 323-334.

SECTION A
Instruments with a Personal Focus

Long, Multiple-Scaled Instruments

PERSONAL ORIENTATION INVENTORY

Everett L. Shostrom

DESCRIPTION

Length: 150 pairs of numbered statements, respondent chooses one from each pair

Time: *Administering* thirty minutes
Scoring twenty to thirty minutes

Scales:

> *Time Competent/Time Incompetent*
> *Inner Directed/Other Directed*
> *Self-Actualizing Value*
>
> | | |
> |---|---|
> | *Existentiality* | *Feeling Reactivity* |
> | *Spontaneity* | *Self - Regard* |
> | *Self - Acceptance* | *Nature of Man* |
> | *Synergy* | *Acceptance of Aggression* |
>
> *Capacity for Intimate Contact*

Time Competent/Time Incompetent. Measures the ability to live fully in the here-and-now. This includes the capacity to tie the past and the future to the present in a meaningful continuity. The time-incompetent person can be characterized by either an *excessive post-orientation* (guilt, regrets, and resentments) or *an excessive future-orientation* (life begins tomorrow).

Inner Directed/Other Directed. Measures whether the source of feeling about the individual's own worth comes from inside the person or from the perceptions of other people. High scorers are independent, have low fear of rejection, and low need for approval from others.

Self-Actualizing Value Measures affirmation of the primary value of self-actualizing people.

Existentiality. Measures the ability to situationally or existentially react without rigid adherence to principles.

Feeling Reactivity. Measures sensitivity of responsiveness to one's own needs and feelings.

Spontaneity. Measures freedom to react spontaneously or to be oneself.

Self - Regard. Measures affirmation of self because of worth or strength.

Self - Acceptance. Measure affirmation or acceptance of self in spite of weaknesses or deficiencies.

Nature of Man. Measures degree of the constructive view of the nature of man, masculinity, femininity.

Synergy. Measures ability to be synergistic, to transcend dichotomies.

Acceptance of Aggression. Measures ability to accept one's natural aggressiveness as opposed to defensiveness, denial, and repression of aggression.

Capacity for Intimate Contact. Measures ability to develop contactful, intimate relationships with other human beings, unencumbered by expectations and obligations.

Positive Features: The *POI*, perhaps more than any other instrument described in this book, measures the things talked about by people in human relations training. For this reason it is an excellent teaching device. It awakens people to important dimensions of life and ways of viewing the world and themselves that they may well not have considered previously. It is a confrontive, potent instrument *i.e.*, it is likely to present the participant with information about himself that may be affirming or upsetting, but either way, informative.

Concerns: The instrument is quite transparent to anyone who has some familiarity with human relations training or, for that matter, with anyone who is experienced in taking objective tests. In most cases, the "right answer" in each pair is fairly obvious.

ORDERING

Where To Order: Educational and Industrial Testing Service
Post Office Box 7234
San Diego, California 92107
Phone: (714) 222-1666

Cost: *Specimen set* $2.25
Manual $1.75
Packages of Materials
   25 Test Booklets (Reusable) $9.50
   50 Hand scoring answer sheets $3.75
   50 Profile sheets $3.75

ADMINISTERING, SCORING, AND INTERPRETING

Interpreting: An awareness that we have developed over the past few years is that the time and support ratios are exceptionally potent measures. It is important to recognize that while inner-directedness is valued by the instrument, it is possible to be *too* inner-directed. The extreme of inner-directedness would be manifest as an unwillingness to hear or accept feedback. Similarly, the extreme of time competence would truncate the awareness of previous "errors" and eliminate all future-oriented planning.

MYERS-BRIGGS TYPE INDICATOR

Katharine C. Briggs
Isabel Briggs Myers

DESCRIPTION

Length: Part I: seventy questions with a choice of two answers and one question with a choice of five answers

Part II: fifty-two pairs of words from which to choose the most appealing

Part III: forty-three questions with a choice of two answers

Time: *Administering* fifty to sixty minutes

Scoring twenty to thirty minutes

Scales: The type indicator yields four scores (sixteen combinations)

> *Introverts-Extraverts*
> *Feeling Types-Thinking Types*
> *Intuitives-Sensing Types*
> *Perceptives-Judging Types*

Introverts-Extraverts. Introverts like quiet for concentration, uninterrupted work on one subject, have some problems communicating, and work contentedly alone. Extraverts like variety and action, are impatient with long, slow jobs, usually communicate well, like to have people around, and are good at greeting people.

Feeling Types-Thinking Types. Feeling types are aware of other people and their feelings, like harmony, need occasional praise, dislike telling people unpleasant things, tend to be sympathetic, and relate well to most people. Thinking types are unemotional and uninterested in people's feelings, like analysis and putting things into logical order, are able to reprimand people or fire them when necessary, may seem hard-hearted, and tend to relate well only to other thinking types.

Intuitives-Sensing Types. Intuitives like solving new problems, dislike doing the same thing over and over again, jump to conclusions, are impatient with routine details, and dislike taking time for precision. Sensing types dislike new problems unless there are standard ways to solve them, like an established routine, must usually work all the way through to reach a conclusion, show patience with routine details, and tend to be good at precise work.

Perceptives-Judging Types. Perceptives tend to be good at adapting to changing situations; may have trouble making decisions; may postpone unpleasant jobs; and tend to be curious; and welcome new light on an idea, situation, or person. Judging types are best when they can plan their work and follow the plan, may decide things too quickly; may not notice new things that need to be done; and tend to be satisfied once they reach a judgment on an idea, situation,or person.

Positive Features: The traits measured are relatively value-free. There is an emphasis on the importance of the compatibility of co-workers' profiles rather than the implicit valuing of any individual profile.

Concerns: As shown by the example below, the descriptions of the scales tend to be excessive and very general.

EXTRAVERTED INTUITIVE TYPES
ENTP and ENFP

The extraverted intuitive is the enthusiastic innovator. He is always seeing new possibilities—new ways of doing things, or quite new and fascinating things that might be done—and he goes all out in pursuit of them. He has a lot of imagination and initiative for originating projects, and a lot of impulsive energy for carrying them out. He is wholly confident of the worth of his inspirations, tireless with the problems involved, and ingenious with the difficulties. He gets so interested in the current project that he thinks of little else.

He gets other people interested too. Being a perceptive type, he aims to understand people rather than to judge them; often, by putting his mind to it, he achieves an uncanny knowledge of what makes them tick, and uses this to win support for his project. He adapts to other people in the way he presents his objective, but never to the point of giving it up. His faith in his intuition makes him too independent and individualistic to be a conformist, but he keeps a lively circle of contacts through his versatility and his easy interest in almost everything.

In his quieter moments, his auxiliary gives him some balancing introversion and adds depth to the insights supplied by his intuition. At its best, his insight, tempered by judgment, may amount to wisdom.

His trouble is that he hates uninspired routine and finds it remarkably hard to apply himself to humdrum detail unconnected with any major interest. Worse yet, even his projects begin to seem routine and lose their attraction as soon as he has solved the problems and reached plain sailing. He may discipline himself to carry through, but he is happiest and most effective in jobs that permit one project after another, with somebody else taking over as soon as the situation is well in hand.

If his judgment and self-discipline are undeveloped, he will immerse himself in ill-chosen projects, fail to finish them, and squander his inspirations, abilities and energies in irrelevant and half-done jobs. At his worst, he will be unstable, undependable, fickle, and easily discouraged.

ENTP	ENFP
With thinking as auxiliary	**With feeling as auxiliary**
More independent, more analytical and critical of his inspirations, more impersonal in his relations to people, more apt to consider their effect on his project rather than their feelings. May be an inventor, scientist, trouble-shooter, promoter, or almost anything that it interests him to be.	More enthusiastic, more concerned with people and skilful in handling them. Has remarkable insight into their possibilities and interest in their development. May be inspired and inspiring teacher, scientist, artist, advertising man, salesman, or almost anything it interests him to be.

ORDERING

Where To Order: Educational Testing Service
Princeton, New Jersey 08540
Phone: (609) 921-9000

Cost: *Specimen Set*, including manual $3.00
    Per test $ .30
    Set of Scoring Stencils $7.50
    25 Answer Sheets $1.00

SELF-DISCLOSURE QUESTIONNAIRE

Sidney Jourard

DESCRIPTION

Length: sixty statements, respondent makes five responses to each statement

Time: *Administering* fifteen to twenty minutes
      Scoring   ten to fifteen minutes

Scale:

Self-Disclosure

Thirty scores can be obtained from the instrument. There is one overall scale—self-disclosure—which is the extent to which the person talks freely about himself: his attitudes and opinions, his tastes and interests, his work, his money situation, his personality, and his body. Each of these six areas is measured by ten statements dealing with various aspects of that area.

Answer sheets have numbers down the left hand side to correspond with the numbers in front of the statements; to the right of the numbers are five columns headed by "Mother," "Father," "Male Friend," "Female Friend," and "Spouse." Respondents are to write in five numbers (or letters) next to each topic, one in each column from the following four alternatives:

X - Have lied or misrepresented myself to the other person so that he has a false picture of me.

0 - Have told the other person nothing about this aspect of me.

1 - Have talked in general terms about this item...

2 - Have talked in full and complete detail about this item to the other person.

Attitudes and Opinions.

    Sample statement:
      My personal views on drinking.

Tastes and Interests.

    Sample statement:
      My likes and dislikes in music.

Work (or studies).

    Sample statement:
      My feelings about the salary or rewards that I get for my work.

Money.

   Sample statement:
   My most pressing need for money right now, e.g., outstanding bills, some major purchase that is desired or needed.

Personality.

   Sample statement:
   Whether or not I feel that I am attractive to the opposite sex; my problems, if any, about getting favorable attention from the opposite sex.

Body.

   Sample statement:
   My past record of illness and treatment.

   Scores can also be obtained for the target person as follows: Self-Disclosure: Mother, Self-Disclosure: Father, Self-Disclosure: Spouse, Self-Disclosure: Male Friend, Self-Disclosure: Female Friend.

ORDERING

Where To Order: The scale is located in Sidney Jourard's *The Transparent Self.* Princeton: Van Nostrand, 1964.

   Van Nostrand Reinhold Co.
   450 W. 33rd Street
   New York, New York 10001
   Phone: (212) 594-8660

Cost: $5.75

ADMINISTERING, SCORING AND INTERPRETING

Scoring: X's are counted as zeroes. Scores for all subcategories, *e.g.,* Attitudes and Opinions-Father, Attitudes and Opinions-Mother, can be obtained by simply adding the numbers in that subcategory. Column and row totals can be obtained to discover level of self-disclosure for Mother, for Father, and level of disclosure on each of the six categories. Finally, the person's overall level of self-disclosure is obtained by summing the column totals.

TAYLOR-JOHNSON TEMPERAMENT ANALYSIS

Roswell H. Johnson
(Revised by Robert M. Taylor and Lucile P. Morrison)

DESCRIPTION

Length: 180 questions, one response to each question

Time: *Administering* thirty to forty-five minutes
      Scoring   five to eight minutes

Scales:

> *Nervous vs. Composed*
> *Depressive vs. Lighthearted*
> *Active-Social vs. Quiet*
> *Expressive-Responsive vs. Inhibited*
> *Sympathetic vs. Indifferent*
> *Subjective vs. Objective*
> *Dominant vs. Submissive*
> *Hostile vs. Tolerant*
> *Self-Disciplined vs. Impulsive*

Nervous versus Composed. High scorers are tense, high-strung, or apprehensive. Low scorers are calm, relaxed and tranquil. High scorers are unable to concentrate, have undue worry or anxiety, have excessive concern about health or well being, engage in excessive smoking, eating, drinking. Low scorers are characterized by serenity, ability to recover composure quickly, and the absence of external nervous mannerisms.

> Sample of scored statements:
> + *Is...more excitable than most people?*
> - *Is...relatively calm when others are upset or emotionally disturbed?*

Depressive versus Lighthearted. High scorers feel pessimistic, discouraged, dejected, apathetic, disillusioned, emotionally exhausted, unwanted, fearful, and tend to be easily disheartened by criticism. Low scorers are happy, cheerful, and have a sense of well-being and optimism, a conviction that life is worthwhile, and the tendency to laugh and smile readily.

Active-Social versus Quiet. High scorers are energetic, enthusiastic, actively social, have a feeling of energy and vitality, briskness of movement, and are tireless and industrious workers. Low scorers are socially inactive, lethargic, withdrawn, prefer an inactive, restful, quiet life, and prefer being alone rather than with people.

Expressive-Responsive versus Inhibited. High scorers are spontaneous, affectionate, demonstrative, warm, friendly, cordial, personal, talkative, animated, enthusiastic, and outgoing. Low scorers are restrained, unresponsive, repressed, unable to express tender feelings, reserved, and self-conscious.

Sympathetic versus Indifferent. High scorers tend to be kind, understanding, compassionate, sympathetic, concerned for the weak, and helpful. Low scorers tend to be unsympathetic, insensitive, unfeeling, strict, thoughtlessly inconsiderate, and slow to recognize the needs of family and friends.

Subjective versus Objective. High scorers tend to be emotional, illogical, self-absorbed, overly sensitive, introspective, jealous, self-conscious, and hold grudges. Low scorers tend to be fair-minded, reasonable, logical, analytic, impartial, dispassionate, and not plagued by internal doubts and fears.

Dominant versus Submissive. High scorers tend to be confident, assertive, competitive, influential, self-assured, have leadership characteristics, show initiative, be firm, emphatic, and enjoy speaking in public. Low scorers tend to be passive, compliant, dependent, followers, avoid complaining, and taken advantage of by others.

Hostile versus Tolerant. High scorers are critical, argumentative, punitive, superior-acting, overbearing, impatient, sarcastic, and have a quick temper. Low scorers tend to be accepting, patient, humane, have respect for other human beings, are free from racial and religious prejudice, and have a disinclination to complain or criticize.

Self-Disciplined versus Impulsive. High scorers tend to be controlled, methodical, persevering, neat, orderly, set goals, budget, and have high self-control. Low scorers tend to be uncontrolled, disorganized, changeable, hasty in making decisions, vacillating, take chances, easily tempted, as well as unable to break bad habits.

ORDERING

Where To Order: Psychological Publications, Inc.
5300 Hollywood Boulevard
Los Angeles, California 90027
Phone (213) 465-4163

Cost: *Counselor's Kit*	$25.00
Six plastic scoring stencils	$12.50
25 Question Booklets	$10.00
50 Answer Sheets	$ 4.50
50 Profile Sheets	$ 4.50

THE SIXTEEN PERSONALITY FACTOR TEST

Raymond B. Cattell
Herbert W. Eber

DESCRIPTION

Length: Forms A and B: 187 three-response questions
Forms C and D: 105 three-response questions

Time: *Administering* Forms A and B: forty-five to sixty minutes
Forms C and D: twenty-five to forty minutes
Scoring Forms A and B: ten to fifteen minutes
Forms C and D: seven to ten minutes

Scales:

Reserved vs. Outgoing	*Trusting vs. Suspicious*
Less Intelligent vs. More Intelligent	*Practical vs. Imaginative*
Affected by Feelings vs.	*Forthright vs. Shrewd*
Emotionally Stable	*Placid vs. Apprehensive*
Humble vs. Assertive	*Conservative vs. Experimenting*
Sober vs. Happy-Go-Lucky	*Group-Dependent vs. Self-Sufficient*
Expedient vs. Conscientious	*Undisciplined Self-Conflict vs.*
Shy vs. Venturesome	*Control*
Tough-Minded vs. Tender-Minded	*Relaxed vs. Tense*

Reserved versus Outgoing. High scorers are good-natured, easygoing, and emotionally expressive. Low scorers tend to be stiff, cool, and skeptical.

Less Intelligent versus More Intelligent. High scorers tend to be quick to grasp ideas and are intelligent. Low scorers tend to be slow to learn, dull, and given to concrete and literal interpretations.

Affected by Feelings versus Emotionally Stable. High scorers tend to be emotionally mature, stable, and realistic about life. Low scorers tend to be low in frustration tolerance for unsatisfactory conditions, changeable and plastic, and evade necessary reality demands.

Humble versus Assertive. High scorers tend to be self-assured, independent-minded, and austere. Low scorers tend to be docile, conforming, and accommodating.

Sober versus Happy-Go-Lucky. High scorers tend to be impulsively lively, enthusiastic, and cheerful. Low scorers tend to be prudent, serious, and taciturn.

Expedient versus Conscientious. High scorers tend to be persevering, staid, and rule-bound. Low scorers tend to evade rules, feel few obligations and be unsteady in purpose.

Shy versus Venturesome. High scorers tend to be socially bold, uninhibited, and spontaneous. Low scorers tend to be restrained, diffident, and timid.

Tough-Minded versus Tender-Minded. High scorers tend to be dependent, over-protected, and sensitive. Low scorers tend to be self-reliant, realistic, and no-nonsense.

Trusting versus Suspicious. High scorers tend to be self-opinionated, hard to fool, and mistrusting. Low scorers tend to be adaptable, free of jealousy, and easy to get on with.

Practical versus Imaginative. High scorers tend to be wrapped up in inner urgencies, careless of practical matters, and absent-minded. Low scorers tend to be careful, conventional, and regulated by external realities.

Forthright versus Shrewd. High scorers tend to be calculating, worldly, and penetrating. Low scorers tend to be natural, artless, and sentimental.

Placid versus Apprehensive. High scorers tend to worry and be depressed and troubled. Low scorers tend to be self-assured, confident, and serene.

Conservative versus Experimenting. High scorers tend to be critical, liberal, and analytic. Low scorers tend to respect established ideas, be tolerant of traditional difficulties, and be confident in what they have been taught to believe.

Group-Dependent versus Self-Sufficient. High scorers tend to prefer their own decisions, be resourceful, and prefer to go their own way. Low scorers tend to be "joiners," crowd followers, and prefer to work and make decisions with other people.

Undisciplined Self-Conflict versus Controlled. High scorers tend to be socially precise, have strong control of their emotions and general behavior, and are socially aware and careful. Low scorers tend to be careless of protocol, follow their own urges, and are not overly considerate.

Relaxed versus Tense. High scorers tend to be frustrated, driven, and over-wrought. Low scorers tend to be tranquil, torpid, and unfrustrated.

ORDERING

Where To Order: Institute for Personality and Ability Testing
1602 Coronado Drive
Champaign, Illinois 61820
Phone: (217) 352-4739

Cost: Forms A and B

Specimen Set	$ 5.00
Scoring Stencils	$ 2.25
25 Tests	$12.50
50 Hand Score Answer Sheets	$ 4.50

Forms C and D

Specimen Set	$ 4.30
Scoring Stencils	$ 2.00
25 Tests	$12.50
50 Hand Score Answer Sheets	$ 4.50

THE ADJUSTMENT INVENTORY

Hugh M. Bell

DESCRIPTION

Length: 160 questions answered by circling "Yes," "No," or "?"

Time: *Administering* thirty minutes
       Scoring   four minutes

Scales:

> *Home Adjustment*
> *Health Adjustment*
> *Social Adjustment*
> *Emotional Adjustment*
> *Occupational Adjustment*
> *General Adjustment*

Home Adjustment. High scorers tend to be unsatisfactorily adjusted to their home surroundings. Low scorers indicate satisfactory home adjustment.

> Sample statement:
> *Is any member of your present home very nervous?*

Health Adjustment. High scorers indicate unsatisfactory health adjustment. Low scorers indicate satisfactory adjustment.

Social Adjustment. High scorers tend to be submissive and retiring in their social contacts. Low scorers are aggressive in social contacts.

Emotional Adjustment. High scorers tend to be emotionally unstable. Low scorers are aggressive in social contacts.

Occupational Adjustment. High scorers tend to be dissatisfied with their present occupations. Low scorers tend to be well-pleased with their present jobs.

General Adjustment. Derived from the total score. High scorers tend to be unsatisfactory in their adjustment to life in general. Low scorers tend to be adjusting well to life in general.

ORDERING

Where To Order: Consulting Psychologists Press, Inc.
                577 College Avenue
                Palo Alto, California 94306
                Phone: (415) 326-4448

Cost: *Specimen Set* $1.00
    25 Test Booklets $3.25
    Hand Scoring Stencil and Manual $ .75

THURSTONE TEMPERAMENT SCHEDULE

L. L. Thurstone

DESCRIPTION

Length: 140 items, one response to each question

Time: *Administering* fifteen to twenty minutes
Scoring two to three minutes

Scales:

Active
Vigorous
Impulsive
Dominant
Stable
Sociable
Reflective

Active. A person who scores high usually works and moves rapidly. He is restless whenever he is in a situation in which he must be quiet. He likes to be "on the go" and tends to hurry even when there is no rush.

Sample of scored statements:
+ *Are you more restless and fidgety than most people?*
- *Do people consider you to be rather quiet?*

Vigorous. A person with a high score in this area participates in physical sports, work requiring the use of his hands and the use of tools, and outdoor occupations. The vigorous scale emphasizes physical activity using large muscle groups and great expenditure of energy. This trait is often described as "masculine," but many women score high in this area.

Sample of scored statements:
+ *Do you enjoy having a good physical workout?*
+ *Do you have a low-pitched voice?*

Impulsive. High scores in this category indicate a happy-go-lucky, daredevil, carefree, acting-on-the-spur-of-the-moment disposition. The person makes decisions quickly, enjoys competition, and changes easily from one task to another. The decision to act or change is made quickly, regardless of whether the person moves slowly or rapidly (Active), or enjoys or dislikes strenuous projects (Vigorous). A person who doggedly "hangs on" when acting or thinking is typically low in this area.

Dominant. People scoring high on this factor think of themselves as leaders, capable of taking initiative and responsibility. They are not domineering, even though they have leadership ability. They enjoy public speaking, organizing social activities, promoting new projects, and persuading others. They are the ones who would probably take charge of the situation in case of an accident.

Stable. Persons who have high Stable scores usually are cheerful and have an even disposition. They can relax in a noisy room, and they remain calm in crisis. They claim that they can disregard distractions while studying. They are not irritated if interrupted when concentrating, and they do not fret about daily chores. They are not annoyed by leaving a task unfinished or by having to finish it by a deadline.

Sociable. Persons with high scores in this area enjoy the company of others, make friends easily, and are sympathetic, cooperative, and agreeable in their relations with people. Strangers readily tell them about personal troubles.

Reflective. High scores in this area indicate that a person likes meditative and reflective thinking and enjoys dealing with theoretical rather than practical problems. Self-examination is characteristic of reflective persons. They are usually quiet, work alone, and enjoy work that requires accuracy and fine detail. They often take on more than they can finish, and they would rather plan a job than carry it out.

Positive Features: The *Thurstone Temperament Schedule* is easy to administer, very easy to score, and free of implications of psychological abnormality.

ORDERING

Where To Order: Science Research Associates, Inc.
259 East Erie Street
Chicago, Ill. 60611
Phone (312) 944-7552

Cost:	*Specimen Set*	$1.15
	25 Test Booklets	$5.95
	Manual	$ .43

THE ADJECTIVE CHECK LIST

Harrison G. Gough
Alfred B. Heilbrun, Jr.

DESCRIPTION

Length: three hundred adjectives listed, the respondent marks those considered
to be self-descriptive

Time: *Administering* ten to fifteen minutes
Scoring   twenty to thirty minutes

Scales:

Total Number of	Lability	Heterosexuality
Adjectives Checked	Personal Adjustment	Exhibition
Defensiveness	Achievement	Autonomy
Number of Favorable	Dominance	Aggression
Adjectives Checked	Endurance	Change
Number of Unfavorable	Order	Succorance
Adjectives Checked	Intraception	Abasement
Self-Confidence	Nurturance	Deference
Self-Control	Affiliation	Counseling Readiness

Total Number of Adjectives Checked. High scorer has surgency and drive, an
a relative absence of repressive tendencies. He is emotional, adverturous, whole
some, unintelligent, and frank. Low scorer is quiet, tentative, cautious, and pe.
haps taciturn and aloof.

Defensiveness. High scorer is apt to be self-controlled, resolute, insisten
and even stubborn. Low scorer tends to be anxious and apprehensive, critical c
himself and others, and given to complaining.

Number of Favorable Adjectives Checked. High scorer has a strong desire t
do well and to impress others, but always by virtue of hard work and conventiona
endeavor. Low scorer is much much more of an individualist, seen as clever
sharp-witted, headstrong, pleasure-seeking, and original. He more often exper:
ences anxiety, self-doubts, and perplexities.

Number of Unfavorable Adjectives Checked. High scorer appears to have a
impulsive lack of control over the hostile and unattractive aspects of his person
ality; others perceive him as rebellious, arrogant, careless, conceited, and cynica
and he tends to be a skeptic and threat to the complacent beliefs and attitudes o
his fellows. Low scorer is more placid, obliging, mannerly, tactful, and probabl
less intelligent.

Self-confidence. High scorer is assertive, affiliative, persistent, and concerne
about creating a good impression; others perceive of him as forceful, self-confi

dent, determined, ambitious, and opportunistic. Low scorer is a much less effective person, inactive and contemplative. Others perceive of him as unassuming, forgetful, preoccupied, reserved, and retiring.

Self-control. High scorers tend to be serious, sober individuals, interested in and responsive to their obligations. Low scorers seem to be inadequately socialized, headstrong, irresponsible, complaining, disorderly, narcissistic, impulsive, and even obnoxious, autocratic, and thankless.

Lability. High scorer is spontaneous but also excitable, temperamental, restless, nervous, and high-strung. The balance of forces is an uneasy one and change and new experiences seem impelling. Low scorer is more phlegmatic, routinized, and conventional; others perceive of him as thorough, organized, steady, and unemotional.

Personal Adjustment. High scorer is seen as dependable, peaceable, trusting, friendly, practical, loyal, and wholesome. He fits in well, asks for little, treats others with courtesy, and works enterprisingly toward his own goals. Low scorer sees himself as at odds with other people and is moody and dissatisfied. This view is reciprocated by observers, who describe him as aloof, defensive, anxious, inhibited, worrying, and withdrawn.

Achievement. High scorer is usually seen as intelligent, hard-working determined to do well, and successful. His motives are internal and goal-centered rather than competitive. Low scorer is more skeptical, more dubious about the rewards which might come from effort and involvement, and uncertain about risking his labors. He tends to be somewhat withdrawn and dissatisfied with his current status.

Dominance. High scorer is forceful, strong-willed, persevering, self-confident, direct, and forthright. Low scorer is unsure of himself and indifferent to both the demands and challenges of interpersonal life. He stays out of the limelight and avoids situations calling for choice and decision-making.

Endurance. High scorer is self-controlled, responsible, idealistic, and concerned about truth and justice. Low scorer is erratic and impatient, intolerant of prolonged effort or attention, and changeable in an abrupt and quixotic manner.

Order. High scorer is usually sincere and dependable at the cost of individuality and spontaneity. Low scorer is quicker in temperament and reaction. They prefer complexity and variety and dislike delay, caution, and deliberation.

Intraception. High scorer is reflective, serious, capable, conscientious, and knowledgeable. Low scorer, though talented, tends toward profligacy and intemperateness in its use. He is aggressive and quickly becomes bored where direct action is not possible. He is a doer, not a thinker.

Nurturance. High scorer is helpful and has a nurturant disposition but is sometimes too bland and self-disciplined; he may be too conventional and solicitous of other people. Low scorer is skeptical, clever, acute, self-centered, and less attentive to the feelings and wishes of others.

Affiliation. High scorer is adaptable and anxious to please, but not necessarily because of altruistic motives. Low scorer is more individualistic and strong-willed and tends to be less trusting, more pessimistic about life, and restless in prolonged situations with others.

Heterosexuality. High scorer is interested in the opposite sex, life, experience, and most of his environment in a healthy, direct, and outgoing manner. Low scorer thinks too much and dampens his vitality; he tends to be dispirited, inhibited, shrewd, and calculating in his interpersonal relationships.

Exhibition. High scorers tend to be self-centered and even narcissistic. They are poised, self-assured and, at the same time, quick-tempered and irritable. Low scorers tend toward apathy, self-doubt, and undue inhibition of impulse.

Autonomy. High scorer is independent, autonomous, assertive, self-willed, and fairly indifferent to the feelings of others. Low scorers are of moderate or subdued disposition, hesitating to take the initiative and follow the dictates of others.

Aggression. High scorer is competitive and views others as rivals. Impulses are strong and often under-controlled. Low scorers tend to be patiently diligent and sincere in their relationships with others.

Change. High scorers are perceptive, alert, spontaneous, comprehend problems and situations rapidly and incisively, and take pleasure in change and variety. They are self-confident and welcome challenges found in disorder and complexity. Low scorers seek stability and continuity in environment, are apprehensive of risk-involving situations, and are temperamentally patient and obliging. They are concerned about others but lacking in verve and energy.

Succorance. High scorer is dependent on others, seeks support, and expects to find it. Low scorer is independent, resourceful, and self-sufficient while being prudent and circumspect.

Abasement. High scorers see themselves as weak and undeserving, face the world with anxiety and foreboding, and are often self-punishing. Low scorers are optimistic, poised, productive, decisive, and do not fear others. Their tempo is brisk, manner confident, and behavior effective.

Deference. High scorers are conscientious, dependable, and persevering, self-denying out of a preference for anonymity, and free from stress and external demands. Low scorers are more energetic, spontaneous, and independent; they like attention, to supervise and direct others, and to express their will.

Counseling Readiness. High scorers are predominantly worried about themselves, feel left out of things, are unable to enjoy life to the full, and are unduly anxious. Low scorers are self-confident, poised, sure of themselves, and outgoing. They seek the company of others, like activity, and enjoy life in an uncomplicated way.

Concerns: Stencils for hand scoring the *ACL* are not provided by the publisher, and it is very slow and laborious to score the large number of scales from the manual without them.

ORDERING

Where To Order: Consulting Psychologists Press, Inc.
577 College Avenue
Palo Alto, California 94306
Phone: (415) 326-4448

Cost: *Specimen Set* $3.00
      25 Adjective Check Lists $2.75
      25 Profile Sheets $1.25
      Manual $2.50

PROFILE OF MOOD STATES

Douglas M. McNair
Maurice Lorr
Leo F. Droppleman

DESCRIPTION

Length: sixty-five adjectives, each is rated on a category scale

Time: *Administering* three to five minutes
  Scoring   five to six minutes

Scales:

> *Tension-Anxiety*
> *Depression-Dejection*
> *Anger-Hostility*
> *Vigor-Activity*
> *Fatigue-Inertia*
> *Confusion-Bewilderment*

Tension-Anxiety (T). Factor T is defined by adjective scales descriptive of heightened musculoskeletal tension.

> Sample of adjectives:
> *Tense, shaky*

Depression-Dejection (D). Factor D represents a mood of depression accompanied by a sense of personal inadequacy.

> Sample of adjectives:
> *Unhappy, sorry for things done*

Anger-Hostility (A). Factor A represents a mood of anger and antipathy towards others.

Vigor-Activity (V). Factor V is defined by adjectives suggesting a mood of vigorousness, ebullience, and high energy.

Fatigue-Inertia (F). Factor F represents a mood of weariness, inertia, and low energy level.

Confusion-Bewilderment (C). Factor C is characterized by bewilderment and muddleheadedness. It appears to measure aspects of both congnitive inefficiency and a disorienting mood state.

118

Concerns: *The Profile of Mood States* has a fairly strong pathological overtone to it that may be inappropriate for many human relations uses.

ORDERING

Where To Order: Educational and Industrial Testing Service
Post Office Box 7234
San Diego, California 92107
Phone: (714) 222-1666

Cost: *Specimen Set* $3.00
Manual $2.50
25 POMS Forms $3.50
25 Profile Sheets $2.50
6 Hand Scoring Keys $3.00

DIMENSIONS OF TEMPERAMENT

Robert L. Thorndike

DESCRIPTION

Length: twenty sets of ten statements, six responses to each set

Time: *Administering* thirty-five to forty-five minutes
       Scoring   eight to twelve minutes

Scales:

> *Sociable vs. Solitary*
> *Ascendant vs. Withdrawing*
> *Cheerful (Objective) vs. Gloomy (Sensitive)*
> *Placid vs. Irritable*
> *Accepting vs. Critical*
> *Tough-Minded (Masculine) vs. Tender-Minded (Feminine)*
> *Reflective vs. Practical*
> *Impulsive vs. Planful*
> *Active vs. Lethargic*
> *Responsible vs. Casual*

Sociable versus Solitary. Likes to be with other people, to do things in groups, and to go to parties rather than liking to be by himself, doing things by himself, and reading or engaging in other kinds of solitary activities.

    Sample of scored statements:
      You make friends easily.
    (Sociable response: *Like (for "most like you")*)
      You are something of a "lone wolf."
    (Sociable response: *Different (for "most different from you")*)

Ascendant versus Withdrawing. Likes to be in the center of the stage, to speak in public, to "sell" things or ideas, and to meet important people rather than tending to avoid personal conflict, disliking being in the public eye, and avoiding taking the initiative in relation to others.

    Sample statements:
      You usually argue a point when you think you are right.
    (Ascendant response: *Like*)
      You hate to make yourself conspicuous.
    (Ascendant response: *Different*)

Cheerful, Objective versus Gloomy, Sensitive. Seems to feel generally well and happy, satisfied with his relations with others, accepted by others rather than feeling moody, depressed, at odds with himself, and sensitive to the criticisms of others.

Placid versus Irritable. Even-tempered, easygoing, not easily ruffled or annoyed rather than being short-tempered, annoyed or irked by many things, and inclined to "blow his top."

Accepting versus Critical. Tends to think the best of people, to accept them at face value, to expect altruism to prevail rather than tending to question people's motives, expecting self-interest, and being conscious of the need for each to look out for himself.

Tough-Minded (Masculine) versus Tender-Minded (Feminine). Tolerant of dirt, bugs, and profanity; enjoys sports, roughing it, and the out-of-doors; uninterested in clothes or personal appearance as opposed to sensitive to dirt, both physical and verbal; concerned with personal appearance; intuitive rather than rational.

Reflective versus Practical. Interested in ideas, in abstractions, in discussion and speculation, in knowledge for its own sake rather than interested in doing and in using knowledge for practical ends, impatient with speculation and theorizing.

Impulsive versus Planful. Carefree, happy-go-lucky, ready to act at a moment's notice as opposed to being careful to plan life out in advance, systematic, orderly, and foresighted.

Active versus Lethargic. Full of energy, quick to complete tasks, able to accomplish a great deal rather than being slow, easily tired, less productive than others, and liking to move at a leisurely pace.

Responsible versus Casual. Dependable, reliable, certain to complete tasks on time, and somewhat compulsive as opposed to being often late with commitments, rushing to meet deadlines, and having difficulty getting things done.

ORDERING

Where To Order: The Psychological Corporation
304 East Forty-fifth Street
New York, N.Y. 10017
Phone: (212) 679-7070

Cost:
Specimen Set	$2.50
Manual and Hand Scoring Keys	$2.00
25 Booklets	$3.80
50 Answer Sheets	$3.00

EDWARDS PERSONAL PREFERENCE SCHEDULE

Allen L. Edwards

DESCRIPTION

Length: 225 pairs of statements

Time: *Administering* thirty-five to fifty minutes
     Scoring   twelve to fifteen minutes

Scales:

Achievement	Succorance
Deference	Dominance
Order	Abasement
Exhibition	Nurturance
Autonomy	Change
Affiliation	Endurance
Intraception	Heterosexuality
Aggression	

Description of Scales. The fifteen scales of the *EPPS* measure the primary needs proposed by Henry Murray. Each scale represents something the person wants, desires, or needs, *i.e.*, something that motivates him.

Achievement. To do one's best, to be successful, to do a difficult job well.

Sample statement:
A. *I would like to accomplish something of great significance.*
B. *I like to tell amusing stories and jokes at parties.*
(Achievement response: *A*)

Deference. To get suggestions from others, to find out what others think, to accept the leadership of others.

Sample statement:
A. *I like to plan and organize the details of any work that I have to undertake.*
B. *I like to follow instruction and do what is expected of me.*
(Deference response: *B*)

Order. To have written work neat and organized, to keep living and working environments neat and orderly, to organize details of work.

Exhibition. To say witty and clever things, to talk about personal adventures and experiences, to have others notice and comment upon one's appearance.

Autonomy. To be able to come and go as desired, to say what one thinks, to be independent of others in making decisions.

Affiliation. To be loyal to friends, to participate in friendly groups, to be helpful to friends.

Intraception. To analyze one's motives and feelings, to observe others, to understand how others feel about problems.

Succorance. To have others provide help when in trouble, to seek encouragement from others, to have others be kindly.

Dominance. To argue for one's point of view, to be a leader in groups to which one belongs, to be regarded by others as a leader.

Abasement. To feel guilty when one does something wrong, to accept blame for errors made, to feel that personal pain and misery suffered does more good than harm.

Nurturance. To help friends when they are in trouble, to assist others less fortunate, to treat others with kindness and sympathy.

Change. To do new and different things, to travel, to meet new people.

Endurance. To keep at a job until it is finished, to complete any job undertaken, to work hard at a task.

Heterosexuality. To spend time with members of the opposite sex, to engage in social activities with the opposite sex, to be in love with someone of the opposite sex.

Aggression. To attack contrary points of view, to make fun of others, to criticize others publicly.

    Sample statement:
      A. *I like to read newspaper accounts of murders and other forms of violence.*
      B. *I would like to write a great novel or play.*
    (Aggression response: A)

Positive Features: The *EPPS* is a widely-used instrument, and, even though it is moderately long, it does yield a large amount of information for the time spent. Also, the majority of the needs measured are inter-personal and thus quite relevant to human relations concerns. The needs are fairly low in social desirability overtones: there are no obviously good or "healthy" responses. Finally, there is very little overlap among the scales.

ORDERING

Where To Order: The Psychological Corporation
                  304 East 45th Street
                  New York, N.Y. 10017
                  Phone: (212) 679-7070

Cost: *Specimen Set* $ .75
      Manual with Stencils $ .60
      25 Tests $4.00
      50 Hand scoring answer sheets $2.70

CALIFORNIA TEST OF PERSONALITY

Ernest W. Tiegs
Willis W. Clark
Louis P. Thorpe

DESCRIPTION

Length: 180 Yes or No questions (five forms)

Time: *Administering* forty-five minutes
      Scoring   fifteen to twenty minutes

Scales:

Personal Adjustment Scales	Social Adjustment Scales
Self-Reliance	*Social Standards*
Sense of Personal Worth	*Social Skills*
Sense of Personal Freedom	*Anti-Social Tendencies*
Feeling of Belonging	*Family Relations*
Withdrawing Tendencies	*Occupation Relations*
Nervous Symptoms	*Community Relations*

Personal Adjustment Scales:

Self-Reliance. Overt actions indicate independence of others. Emotionally stable and responsible in behavior.

> Sample statement:
> *Can you work alone as well as with others?*
> (Self-Reliance response: *Yes*)

Sense of Personal Worth. To feel that he is well regarded by others, that others have faith in his future success, and believe he has average or better ability. He feels capable and reasonably attractive.

> Sample statement:
> *Do most of your friends have confidence in your ability?*
> (Sense of Personal Worth response: *Yes*)

Sense of Personal Freedom. One has a reasonable share in the determination of his conduct and in the governing of his own life. This includes selection of friends and some spending money.

Feeling of Belonging. To enjoy the love of family, well-wishes of friends, and a cordial relationship with people in general. To get along well with teachers or employers and feel proud of school or place of business.

Withdrawing Tendencies. A withdrawing person substitutes the joys of a fantasy world for actual successes in real life. He is characteristically sensitive, lonely, and given to self-concern. Normal adjustment is characterized by reasonable freedom from these tendencies.

Nervous Symptoms. One who suffers from a variety of physical symptoms which may be exhibiting physical expressions of emotional conflicts.

Social Adjustment Scales:

Social Standards. One who understands the rights of others and appreciates the necessity of subordinating certain desires to the needs of the group. To understand what is regarded as being right or wrong.

Social Skills. One who is diplomatic in his dealings with both friends and strangers and subordinates egoistic tendencies in favor of interest in the problems and activities of his associates.

Anti-Social Tendencies. One who endeavors to get his satisfactions in ways that are damaging and unfair to others. Normal adjustment is characterized by reasonable freedom from these tendencies.

Family Relations. To feel loved and well-treated at home and a sense of security and self-respect. Parental control that is neither too strict nor too lenient.

Occupation Relations. To feel happy in his job because he is assigned to work which fits his capacities and interests or when he has developed interest, sense of worth, and efficiency in a job previously deemed uncongenial.

Community Relations. One mingles happily with neighbors, takes pride in community improvements, and is tolerant in dealing with both strangers and foreigners.

Totals. Personal Adjustment Total, Social Adjustment Total, and Overall Adjustment Total.

ORDERING

Where To Order: CTB/McGraw-Hill
Del Monte Research Park
Monterey, California 93940
Phone: (408) 373-2932

Cost: *Specimen Set* (at any level: adult,
secondary, intermediate, elementary,
or primary.) Includes manual $ .75
35 Tests $3.85
50 separate answer sheets
(Can respond on test or on
answer sheet) $2.50
Hand Scoring Stencils $ .75

CALIFORNIA PSYCHOLOGICAL INVENTORY

Harrison G. Gough

DESCRIPTION

Length: 480 statements

Time: *Administering* forty-five to sixty minutes
Scoring fifteen to twenty minutes

Scales:

Dominance	*Tolerance*
Capacity for Status	*Good Impression*
Sociability	*Communality*
Social Presence	*Achievement via Conformance*
Self-acceptance	*Achievement via Independence*
Sense of Well-being	*Intellectual Efficiency*
Responsibility	*Psychological-mindedness*
Socialization	*Flexibility*
Self-control	*Femininity*

Poise, Ascendency, and Self-assurance

Dominance. Leadership ability, persistence, social intitiative, aggression confidence, planfullness.

Sample of Scored Statements:
+ *I think I would enjoy having authority over other people.*
- *I doubt whether I would make a good leader.*

Capacity for Status. Active, ambitious, forceful, insightful, resourceful, and ascendent.

Sociability. Confident, enterprising, competitive, original, and fluent in thought.

Social Presence. Clever, enthusiastic, imaginative, spontaneous, vigorous, and quick.

Self-acceptance. Intelligent, outspoken, versatile, witty, aggressive, and self-centered.

Sense of Well-being. Ambitious, alert, versatile, productive, and active.

Socialization, Maturity, and Responsibility

Responsibility. Responsible, thorough, progressive, capable, and conscientious.

Sample of Scored Statements:
+ *A person who doesn't vote is not a good citizen.*
- *There's no use in doing things for people; you only find that you get it in the neck in the long run.*

Socialization. Honest, industrious, obliging, self-denying, and conforming.

Self-Control. Calm, patient, practical, strict, thorough, and conscientious.

Tolerance. Enterprising, informal, quick, clear-thinking, and having broad and varied interests.

Good Impression. Cooperative, enterprising, outgoing, warm, and diligent.

Communality. Moderate, tactful, reliable, sincere, honest, and having common sense.

Achievement Potential and Intellectual Efficiency

Achievement via Conformance. Capable, cooperative, organized, responsible, and valuing intellectual activity and achievement.

Achievement via Independence. Mature, forceful, dominant, demanding, and independent and self-reliant.

Intellectual Efficiency. Efficient, clear-thinking, intelligent, progressive, and alert and well-informed.

Intellectual and Interest Modes

Psychological-Mindedness. Outgoing, spontaneous, quick, verbally fluent, and rebellious toward rules and restrictions.

Flexibility. Insightful, informal, adventurous, humorous, rebellious, and idealistic.

Femininity. Appreciative, patient, helpful, gentle, persevering, and sincere.

Uses: The *CPI* can be used to give people some insight into their personal make-up. It fosters self-examination and consideration of whether they are living their life in such a way that they make the most of their strengths and preferences and may help them to avoid spending time in areas they find distasteful or in which they are inept.

Positive Features: The *CPI* has been widely used: it has been given to over a million persons and is well-validated. It emphasizes the positive and normal aspects of personality rather than the pathological. It was developed using a technique that differentiates real groups of people who differ on some characteristics, rather than yielding mathematically pure scales that measure a characteristic that is of little practical importance. Norms are incorporated into the profile sheets provided. Finally, the scales are more relevant to interpersonal relations than are those of most of the large personality inventories.

Concerns: Although it is not as long as the *MMPI*, the *CPI* does have 480 statements and takes almost an hour to complete. There seems to be a fairly high overlap in the meaning of the scales measured, although there are very few statements that are scored in more than one scale.

ORDERING

Where To Order: Consulting Psychologists Press, Inc.
577 College Avenue,
Palo Alto, Calif. 94306
Phone: (415) 326-4448

Costs: *Specimen set*	$ 1.00
Hand scoring stencils	$ 5.00
25 booklets (reusable)	$ 6.25
100 booklets	$22.50
50 answer sheets	
(includes profile sheets)	$ 3.75
Manual	$ 3.00

OMNIBUS PERSONALITY INVENTORY

Paul Heist
George Yonge

DESCRIPTION

Length: 385 items

Time: *Administering* forty-five minutes to one hour
Scoring fifteen to twenty minutes

Scales:

Thinking Introversion	*Impulse Expression*
Theoretical Orientation	*Personal Integration*
Estheticism	*Anxiety Level*
Complexity	*Altruism*
Autonomy	*Practical Outlook*
Religious Orientation	*Masculinity-Femininity*
Social Extraversion	*Response Bias*

Thinking Introversion. Persons scoring high on this measure are characterized by a liking for reflective thought and academic activities. Persons scoring low show a preference for overt action and tend to evaluate ideas on the basis of their practical, immediate application or to entirely reject or avoid dealing with ideas and abstractions.

Theoretical Orientation. This scale measures an interest in or orientation toward a more restricted range of ideas. High scorers indicate a preference for dealing with theoretical concerns and problems and for using the scientific method in thinking. High scorers are generally logical, analytical, and critical in their approach to problems and situations.

Estheticism. High scorers endorse statements indicating diverse interest in artistic matters and activities and a high level of sensitivity and response to esthetic stimulation.

Complexity. This measure reflects an experimental and flexible orientation rather than a fixed way of viewing and organizing phenomena.

Autonomy. The characteristic measured by this scale is liberal, non-authoritarian thinking and a need for independence.

Religious Orientation. High scorers are skeptical of conventional religious beliefs and practices and tend to reject most of them, especially those that are orthodox or fundamentalistic in nature.

129

Social Extraversion. This measure reflects a preferred style of relating to people in a social context. High scorers display a strong interest in being with people, and they seek social activities and gain satisfaction from them.

Impulse Expression. This scale assesses a general readiness to express impulses and to seek gratification either in conscious thought or in overt action.

Personal Integration. The high scorer admits to few attitudes and behaviors that characterize socially alienated or emotionally disturbed persons. Low scorers often intentionally avoid others and experience feelings of hostility and aggression along with feelings of isolation, loneliness, and rejection.

Anxiety Level. High scorers deny that they have feelings or symptoms of anxiety and do not admit to being nervous or worried. Low scorers describe themselves as tense and high-strung.

Altruism. The high scorer is an affiliative person and trusting and ethical in his relations with others. Low scorers tend not to consider the feelings and welfare of others and often view people from an impersonal, distant perspective.

Practical Outlook. The high scorer on this measure is interested in practical, applied activities and tends to value material possessions and concrete accomplishments.

Masculinity-Femininity. This scale assesses some of the differences in attitudes and interests between college men and women. High scorers (masculine) deny interests in esthetic matters, and they admit to few adjustment problems, feelings of anxiety, or personal inadequacies. They tend to be somewhat less socially inclined than low scorers and more interested in scientific matters. Low scorers (feminine), besides having stronger esthetic and social inclinations, also admit to greater sensitivity and emotionality.

Response Bias. This measure represents an approach to assessing the student's test-taking attitude.

ORDERING

Where To Order: The Psychological Corporation
304 East Forty-Fifth Street
New York, N.Y. 10017
Phone: (212) 679-7070

Costs: *Specimen set* $3.00
25 Booklets $4.75
14 Hand-scoring Keys
with Manual $8.00
Manual $2.50

PERSONALITY RESEARCH FORM

Douglas N. Jackson

DESCRIPTION

Length: Standard Forms (A and B) 300 items
Long Forms (AA and BB) 440 items

Time: *Administering* forty-five to sixty minutes
Scoring fifteen to twenty minutes

Scales:

STANDARD FORM

Achievement	*Endurance*	*Order*
Affiliation	*Exhibition*	*Play*
Aggression	*Harm Avoidance*	*Social Recognition*
Autonomy	*Impulsivity*	*Understanding*
Dominance	*Nurturance*	*Infrequency*

LONG FORM: above scales plus:

Abasement	*Sentience*
Change	*Succorance*
Cognitive Structure	*Desirability*
Defendence	

Abasement. Shows a high degree of humility; accepts blame and criticism even when not deserved; exposes himself to situations where he is in an inferior position; tends to be self-effacing.

Achievement. Aspires to accomplish difficult tasks; maintains high standards and is willing to work toward distant goals; responds positively to competition; willing to put forth effort to attain excellence.

Sample statement:
+ *I get disgusted with myself when I have not learned something properly.*

Affiliation. Enjoys being with friends and people in general; accepts people readily; makes efforts to win friendships and maintain associations with people.

Sample statement:
- *Trying to please people is a waste of time. I have relatively few friends.*

Aggression. Enjoys combat and argument; easily annoyed; sometimes willing to

131

hurt people to get his way; may seek to "get even" with people whom he perceives as having harmed him.

Autonomy. Tries to break away from restraints, confinement, or restrictions of any kind; enjoys being unattached, free, not tied to people, places, or obligations; may be rebellious when faced with restraints.

Change. Likes new and different experiences; dislikes routine and avoids it; may readily change opinions or values in different circumstances; adapts readily to changes in environment.

Cognitive Structure. Does not like ambiguity or uncertainty in information; wants all questions answered completely; desires to make decisions based upon definite knowledge, rather than upon guesses or probabilities.

Defendence. Readily suspects that people mean him harm or are against him; ready to defend himself at all times; takes offense easily; does not accept criticism readily.

Dominance. Attempts to control his environment, and to influence or direct other people; expresses opinions forcefully; enjoys the role of leader and may assume it spontaneously.

Endurance. Willing to work long hours; doesn't give up quickly on a problem; persevering, even in the face of great difficulty; patient and unrelenting in his work habits.

Exhibition. Wants to be the center of attention; enjoys having an audience; engages in behavior which wins the notice of others; may enjoy being dramatic or witty.

Harmavoidance. Does not enjoy exciting activities, especially if danger is involved; avoids risk of bodily harm; seeks to maximize personal safety.

Impulsivity. Tends to act on the "spur of the moment" and without deliberation; gives vent readily to feelings and wishes; speaks freely; may be volatile in emotional expression.

Nurturance. Gives sympathy and comfort; assists others whenever possible, interested in caring for children, the disabled, or the infirm; offers a "helping hand" to those in need; readily performs favors for others.

Order. Concerned with keeping personal effects and surroundings neat and organized; dislikes clutter, confusion, lack of organization; interested in developing methods for keeping materials methodically organized.

Play. Does many things "just for fun;" spends a good deal of time participating in games, sports, social activities, and other amusements; enjoys jokes and funny stories; maintains a light-hearted, easy-going attitude toward life.

Sentience. Notices smells, sounds, sights, tastes, and the way things feel; remembers these sensations and believes that they are an important part of life; is sensitive to many forms of experience; may maintain an essentially hedonistic or aesthetic view of life.

Social Recognition. Desires to be held in high esteem by acquaintances; concerned about reputation and what other people think of him; works for the approval and recognition of others.

Succorance. Frequently seeks the sympathy, protection, love, advice, and reassurance of other people; may feel insecure or helpless without such support; confides difficulties readily to a receptive person.

Understanding. Wants to understand many areas of knowledge; values synthesis of ideas, verifiable generalization, logical thought, particularly when directed at satisfying intellectual curiosity.

Desirability. Describes self in terms judged as desirable; consciously or unconsciously, accurately or inaccurately, presents favorable picture of self in responses to personality statements.

Infrequency. Responds in implausible or pseudo-random manner, possibly due to carelessness, poor comprehension, passive non-compliance, confusion, or gross deviation.

ORDERING

Where To Order: Research Psychologists Press, Inc.
36 St. John's Street
Goshen, N.Y. 10924
Phone: (914) 294-6383

Cost:		
Specimen Set	$ 1.50
Examiner's Kit	12.00
Manual	4.00
Scoring Stencils	2.25

MINNESOTA MULTIPHASIC PERSONALITY INVENTORY

S. R. Hathaway
J. C. McKinley

DESCRIPTION

Length: 566 statements (Answered True, False, Cannot Say)

Time: *Administering* sixty to ninety minutes
       Scoring fifteen to twenty minutes

Scales:

Hypochondriasis	*Paranoia*
Depression	*Psychasthenia*
Hysteria	*Schizophrenia*
Psychopathic Deviate	*Hypomania*
Masculinity-Femininity	

Nine scales were originally developed for clinical use and were named for the abnormal conditions on which their construction was based. The scales were not expected to measure pure traits nor to represent discrete etiological or prognostic entities. Many other scales have subsequently been developed.

Hypochondriasis. Multiple complaints of somatic symptoms without organic basis

Depression. A sad, self-disparaging, apathetic, even suicidal, state.

Hysteria. A neurosis characterized by anxiety or blandness, naivete, ready displays of emotion, and certain bodily symptoms.

Psychopathic Deviate. A character disorder with impulsive, antisocial acting out.

Masculinity-Femininity. (based on responses of male overt homosexuals).

Paranoia. A rigid, suspicious, vengeful condition, which at its psychotic extreme includes delusions of persecution or of grandeur.

Psychasthenia. Obsessive-compulsive neurosis, with vacillation, indecisiveness, overconscientiousness, and overintellectuality.

Schizophrenia. The most common psychosis, marked by withdrawal, inappropriateness, peculiar thinking, delusions, and hallucinations.

Hypomania. An overactive, excited, elated, driven condition; at its psychotic extreme, often alternating with depression.

Non-trait oriented scales
"L (Lie)" Denial of trivial faults and symptoms,
"F (False validity)" Admission of rare, serious symptoms,
"K" Gives a score to apply to certain of the scales to correct for defensive understatement.

ORDERING

Where To Order: The Psychological Corporation
304 East Forty-Fifth Street
New York, New York 10017
Phone: (212) 679-7070

Costs:		
Specimen Set	$3.00	
Reusable booklet	$2.00	
50 answer sheets	$4.80	
Manual and Hand-scoring		
Keys (set of 14)	$4.50	

REFERENCES

Dahlstrom, W.G. and Welsh, G.S., *An MMPI Handbook: A Guide to Use in Clinical Practice and Research.* Minneapolis: University of Minnesota Press, 1960.
Hathaway, S.R. and Meehl, P.E., *An Atlas for the Clinical Use of the MMPI.* Minneapolis: University of Minnesota Press, 1951.

SECTION B
Instruments with an Interpersonal Focus

General

FUNDAMENTAL INTERPERSONAL RELATIONS ORIENTATION-BEHAVIOR

William C. Schutz

DESCRIPTION

Length: fifty-four statements, nine in each of six scales

Time: *Administering* five to twelve minutes
 Scoring five to ten minutes

Scales:

Inclusion (expressed)
Inclusion (wanted)
Control (expressed)
Control (wanted)
Affection (expressed)
Affection (wanted)

FIRO-B produces six scores: three on behavior expressed towards others and three on the behavior wanted from others in the areas of inclusion, control, and affection. It measures the *expression* of orientations by the degree to which one joins and includes others, controls and leads others, and is friendly and personal with others. It also measures the *desire* for such behavior from others by an indication of the extent to which one wants others to include him and invite him to join them, influence and lead him, and express friendly and affectionate feelings toward him. The six FIRO-B scores can be summarized in the following table:

Table 1. Description of the FIRO-B Scales

	I INCLUSION	C CONTROL	A AFFECTION
Expressed e (Toward Others)	I join other people, and I include others.	I take charge; I influence people.	I get close to people.
Wanted w (From Others)	I want people to include me.	I want people to lead me.	I want people to get close and personal with me.

139

Note that the *e* (expressed) row reflects an active-passive tendency in the person; a low score on an *e* subscale (e.g., expressed inclusion) indicates that the person is passive, whereas a high score on expressed indicates he is active. Note also that "want" does *not* mean "want to control" or "want to include others" but rather "want *others* to control me" and "want *others* to include me."

Table 2. Sample FIRO-B statements
(with responses that are counted in parentheses).

	I Inclusion	C Control	A Affection
Expressed e (Toward Others)	I try to be with people. (Usually, often, or sometimes.)	I try to take charge of things with people. (Most people, many people, or some people.)	I try to have close relationships with people. (Usually or often.)
Wanted w (From Others)	I like people to invite me to things. (Most people or many people.)	I let other people decide what to do. (Usually, often sometimes, or occasionally.)	I like people to act close and personal with me. (Most people or many people.)

Uses:

Generating a Personal Agenda: Giving the *FIRO-B* scale early in a training session can provide participants with insights into their inclusion, control, and affection desires and behavior which they may wish to modify or change by trying out new behaviors within the group setting.

Sensitization to Interpersonal Dimensions: Scoring and discussing the *FIRO-B* can make participants aware of dimensions of interpersonal relations with which they will be dealing during a training session. It introduces terminology for understanding inclusion, control, and affection problems.

Checking Self Understanding. Administering the *FIRO-B* can be preceded by asking members to estimate how they expect to score (high, medium, or low) on each scale. If the group has been in existence long enough, members can also predict how they expect the other members to score on the instrument. *FIRO-B* is not a deceptively-worded instrument, so pre-awareness should have little effect on the respondents' scores.

Individual Interpretation: FIRO-B can be given in a group followed by a general discussion of the subscales. Later the facilitator can meet with members individually to interpret each person's pattern of scores in detail and discuss how this feedback effects the individual's understanding of his or her past and future group behavior.

Positive Features: The primary appeal of *FIRO-B* is that it measures three characteristics of interpersonal relations—inclusion, control, and affection—that should be of concern to a person if his goal during his group experience is to come to increased self-understanding. A second positive aspect of the instrument is that it makes a meaningful distinction between what people want from others and what they express toward others. The relative scores in the six combinations of inclusion-control-affection and want-from, express-toward are extremely useful for gaining this self-understanding. A third positive feature is that the dimensions are also relevant for understanding some aspects of group process and are related to Schutz's (1966) theory of group development.

Other positive features include the following characteristics: 1) The items and scales have no assumed social desirability. Both extremes of the scales represent styles of living that people use with relative comfort. 2) The instrument is fairly brief. 3) The scales are reliable (average reproducibility index is .94). 4) It is non-threatening (i.e., does not suggest possible interpretations of psychological abnormality). 5) Scores are easy to interpret because all scales have the same number of items. 6) It is possible to look at score combinations for insight into both individual behavior and the relationship between two people.

Concerns: There is some feeling by respondents that the statements are repetitious. This feature is more a slight annoyance than a major problem.

FIRO-B is a self-report instrument; consequently, it is open to lying and self-deception biases. However, since the statements and the subscales are relatively free from overtones of psychological abnormality, the person should feel less need to be defensive.

Response style, *i.e.*, the tendency to be cautious and use only moderate response choices on any questionnaire, or the tendency to see all relationships in a basically negative (or positive) light, will affect a person's scores on all scales. Therefore, an inflation or depression of *all* scores could be interpreted as a possible response bias. Of course, the discovery of a response bias gives insight into the personality of the person and should be material for discussion and interpretation in its own right.

ORDERING

Where To Order: Consulting Psychologists Press, Inc.
577 College Avenue
Palo Alto, California 94306
Phone: (415) 326-4448

Cost: *Specimen Set* $ 3.50
  Set of Keys $ .50
  25 tests $ 3.00

ADMINISTERING, SCORING, AND INTERPRETING*

Administering:

1) Distribute *FIRO-B* booklets
2) Read the instructions on the front of the booklet aloud while the participants read along silently.
3) Re-emphasize the importance of honesty.
4) Let the participants begin to complete the instrument.
5) When they are finished, briefly discuss the scales using the six-cell box on the front of the instrument to explain the meaning of each scale.

*See "Chapter Two Instrumentation" for more details on Administering, Scoring, and Interpreting *FIRO-B*.

6) Participants may be asked to predict how they think they scored (High Medium, or Low) on each of the six scales.

7) Distribute the scoring keys and explain how to use them.

Scoring:

Templates are provided for individual scoring. A person can obtain a score ranging from zero to nine on each of the six subscales.

Scoring can be done in a group by reading the scored responses for each item aloud to the participants. Individual scoring can be accomplished in the group by having the participants use the templates. If enough scoring templates are not available, the scored responses for each subscale might be reproduced on mimeographed handouts, a chalkboard, or on newsprint. A third method of scoring is to use clerical assistance.

The oral group scoring technique can be satisfactory, but the leader must proceed slowly because the scoring procedure is somewhat complex.

Some Score Patterns. Ryan (1970) describes and interprets some "frequent and unique combinations of expressed and wanted scores" that might be obtained from *FIRO-B*. The discussion that follows borrows freely from his analysis. For simplicity of exposition, an "L" will represent a low score (0-2) and an "H" will represent a high score (7-9).

	I	C	A
e	–	–	–
w	L	–	–

"The Exclusive Club"

In focusing on the inclusion area, if a person has a low score (0-2) in the wanted category, he does not need to be with people and/or needs only a select circle of associates, regardless of what his expressed score indicates. A more specific pattern within the general category of low level of desire for others to include them is:

	I	C	A
e	L	–	–
w	L	–	–

"The Loner"

This person does not need people to include him in their activities, and he makes little attempt to be with people. Both low scores in the inclusion area reflect that the person may fear that people will think that he is not important or interesting. It could also mean that he is sure of himself and does not need to socialize widely to convince himself that he is a worthwhile person. Regardless, he does not involve himself with a lot of people.

	I	C	A
e	H	–	–
w	L	–	–

"Now you see him, now you don't"

Although this person does not have a need for people to include him, he can and does socialize. He has many acquaintances, but he desires to retain control over the socializing. His motto is "Don't call me, I'll call you!"

	I	C	A	
e	L	L	L	"Passive"
w	H	H	H	

A person with extremely low express scores and extremely high want scores may be a very frustrated individual. He wants people to seek him out, wants to be led, and wants affection, but he is too fearful or passive to initiate interpersonal relations. He may remain a frustrated person unless he shifts his interests to non-personal areas (stamp collecting, gardening, etc.) or begins to initiate behavior that will allow him to get what he wants from people. There is also the possibility that his passive orientation is working for him, that is, others are motivated to include, lead, and be close to him without his having to exert himself to initiate interpersonal relations.

	I	C	A	
e	H	H	H	"The Controller"
w	L	L	L	

This pattern reflects a person who is able to fool people; he appears to have motivations that he does not possess. He is socially almost too confident, and he is more friendly-appearing than he really wants or needs to be. He takes charge by initiating social contact, by influencing others, and by establishing a "warm rapport" with them. His behavior pattern makes it possible for him to control other people because, while he can "play off" others' needs in order to make them responsive to him, he has no needs for others to manipulate in order to make him responsive to them.

Congruence Between Persons

It is useful in a number of situations to look at the score patterns of two individuals for insight into their relationship (marriage, supervisor-subordinate, collegial). In marriage counseling, family therapy, couples groups, organization development, etc., it may help to compare basic interpersonal relations orientations of two parties.

Let us look at some interpersonal patterns as a demonstration of some kinds of information that can be obtained.

Wife

	I	C	A
e	H	-	-
w	H	-	-

Husband

	I	C	A
e	L	-	-
w	L	-	-

"John, why don't we give a party?"

144 Instrumentation in Human Relations Training

Depicted here is a low congruence pattern between a husband and wife. The husband has low needs for being with people and prefers to avoid them. His wife has a high need to be included in others' activities, and she joins others and includes them in her activities. She is a people person, and he is a loner. Both parties in this marriage are probably frustrated. He is irritated because his wife is continually bringing people into the house and planning activities with people; she is irritated because he is such a reluctant participant or because he refuses to engage in activities in which she wants to participate. If such a marriage lasts, it will probably settle into the pattern wherein the wife is active in women's activities or a high interaction job, and the husband is free to stay away from people and do other things (read books, watch television, work in the garden, sleep).

Wife				Husband		
	I	**C**	**A**	**I**	**C**	**A**
e	-	-	H	-	-	L
w	-	-	H	-	-	H

"John, do you still love me?"

We have above a potential problem in the affection area. The husband may be quite content, his affection needs being met by his wife. She, however, may be frustrated and feeling unloved. One of the problems that can develop after marriage is that the wife or husband with high needs to be close and personal with people is expected to limit such intimacy to his or her spouse. If the spouse is not demonstrative, he or she will likely be frustrated.

Husband				Wife		
	I	**C**	**A**	**I**	**C**	**A**
e	-	L	-	-	H	-
w	-	H	-	-	L	-

"Marsha, what do you think I ought to do?"

Here we have a case of complementary or balancing needs. The husband wants others to tell him what to do, and his wife is glad to oblige him. The husband does not lead and the wife does not want to be led.

The control area is often the seat of difficulties in the work situation.

Subordinates				Supervisor		
	I	**C**	**A**	**I**	**C**	**A**
e	-	L	-	-	L	-
w	-	H	-	-	L	-

"Boss, we're ready to go, tell us what you want us to do?
"Boys, look over the situation and do whatever you think is best."

The physical education department of a College had this type of pattern, *i.e.*, the subordinates wanted strong leadership. They would say, "Fred, what do you think we should do with the intramural program this year?" Fred would answer,

"I don't care fellows. Do whatever you want to do." Frustration!
The opposite case also occurs.

	Supervisor		
	I	**C**	**A**
e	-	H	-
w	-	L	-

	Subordinate		
	I	**C**	**A**
e	-	H	-
w	-	L	-

"Boss, let us do it our way and we'll give you the best sales
department in the country."
"You'll do things the way *I* say to do them."

Here we have a group of "young Turks" who do not want directive leadership but who are under a directive supervisor who does not want to be told what to do. The result is usually a loss of the energy and spirit that the subordinates could provide.

Summary Scores. In general, it helps to be able to look for a pattern among the six scores so that a person can get an indication of where his problem areas lie, and the relative size of the problems as compared to those of other people. There are a number of indices that may be useful to someone who is interpreting a set of scores.

Table 3. Average and Middle Ranges of FIRO-B Scores.
(Data abstracted based on plus and minus 1.5 added to the average scores
for adults and then rounded to the nearest whole number.)

	I Inclusion	**C** Control	**A** Affection	**Row Totals**
e Expressed (toward)	4 to 7 5.4	2 to 5 3.9	3 to 6 4.1	9 to 18 13.4
w Wanted (from)	5 to 8 6.5	3 to 6 4.6	3 to 6 4.8	11 to 20 15.9
Column Totals	9 to 15 11.9	5 to 11 8.5	6 to 12 8.9	20 to 38 29.3

The assumption that a score of 4.5 is average for a 0-9 point scale can lead to misinterpretations of results. For example, a 7 in "wanted inclusion" is about average, but the same score on expressed control would be significantly above average.

Therefore, the interpretation should take into account the normative or average scores on the scales.

The first and third quartiles (*i.e.*, the score that divides the bottom 25% of the scores from the rest, and the score that divides the top 25% of the scores from the rest) fall approximately 1.5 score points above and below the average on each of the scales. Thus, we shall consider a deviation of more than 1.5 score points from the normative average as large enough in magnitude to warrant special consideration. In order to interpret a score on one of the six *FIRO-B* Scales, it is useful to know whether it is typical, smaller, or larger than the score obtained by most people. This information is given by comparing the score with intervals that bracket the scores obtained by the middle 50% of the respondents in Schutz's normative sample:

Table 4. "Jack's" Sample Scores

	I Inclusion	C Control	A Affection
e Expressed (toward others)	4-7 2 (L)	2-5 2 (ML)	3-6 2 (L)
w Wanted (from others)	5-8 3 (L)	3-6 4 (M)	3-6 4 (M)

The average range is in the top half of each cell, and Jack's score is in the lower half of each cell, with an indication of whether it is high or low.

The scales on which Jack's score fell outside of the average range indicate that his style is to not seek out people (Low eI) and to prefer that they not seek him (Low wI). Furthermore, he does not attempt to control others (eC), nor does he become close and intimate with people (eA).

(*AL*) A persons *activity level* (level of expressed behavior) toward others is obtained by:

AL = e Row Total

Jack's score is 6, and the average interval is 9 to 18. Thus, Jack is low in his overall level of interpersonal activity or involvement. If he were high (higher than 18), we could assume that he is more outgoing and active than the average person. Since his score is lower than 9, we assume he is seldom an initiator, that he is more passive than the average person, or that he is getting all of the interpersonal contact he needs without seeking more.

(*NL.*) A person's overall *need level* for interpersonal contact is obtained by:

NL = w Row Total

Jack's need level score and the average range for NL are NL = 11 (11 to 20), which indicates that his general desire for contact of some sort from people is medium low. A high score (greater than 20) would have indicated a high desire for people to make contact with him. Since his score is low but still within average range, we can conclude that he has a below average desire for people to relate to him, possibly because of one of the following:

1) indifference to people,
2) distaste for the role of a relatively passive receiver of interpersonal approaches from others,
3) greater involvement in some other activity (such as work), or
4) getting all of the interpersonal contact he needs.

(IOP). The sum of the first column describes the *importance of people* to the respondent. This index is obtained bv: IOP = I column total

IOP = I column total

	I	C	A
e	×		
w	×		

(IOP)

which for Jack equals 5. The average range for *IOP* is 9 to 15. Jack is low in his valuing of interaction with people. A high score (greater than 15) would have indicated that being with people is very important to him and worth effort on his part; his low score indicates that being with people is not something he particularly wants or seeks.

(AR). The extent to which a person gets involved in task relations *assuming responsibility* is obtained by:

AR = C column total

	I	C	A
e		×	
w		×	

(AR)

which for Jack equals 6. The average range is 5 to 11. This indicates that he is average in his willingness to take responsibility and hold others responsible for things. A high score would have indicated more than average willingness to be held responsible and hold others responsible. A low score indicates a tendency to avoid task responsibility, to prefer to "live and let live," and to value freedom over responsibility.

(IOA). The *importance of affection* index measures the extent to which a person values intimate, close relations with people and is obtained by:

IOA = A column total

	I	C	A
e			×
w			×

(IOA)

which for Jack equals 6. The average range is 6 to 12. Jack's score is moderately low. Jack's score indicates that he is a person who tends either to avoid close relations in general or that he is quite selective about those with whom he becomes intimate. A high score would describe a person who regularly prefers and seeks interpersonal closeness.

(SII). The extent to which a person is a "people person" and who desires and is willing to get involved with others is indicated by the *Social Interaction Index:*

SII = grand total score

	I	C	A
e	×	×	×
w	×	×	×

(SII)

which for Jack yields 17. The average range is 20 to 38. Jack is low in his Social Interaction Index. A high score would describe a person for whom people are important, one who desires and seeks out relations with them. Jack's low score indicates that he has low people needs. This could be because he is interested in other things, people make him nervous, all the interpersonal contact he needs comes to him, or being with people is lower on his priorities than something else (e.g., being successful in work).

Interpretation of a Sample Pattern. Mary's scores will be listed for a demonstration of a score pattern analyzed with all indexes generated by the *FIRO-B*. Numbers at the top of the cells and margins are average scores for adults.

Table 5. Mary's FIRO-B Scores

	I Inclusion	C Control	A Affection		
e (toward others) expressed	4 to 7 1 [L]	2 to 5 1 [L]	3 to 6 7 [H]	9 to 18 9 [ML]	Activity Level (AL)
w (from others) wanted	5 to 8 1 [L]	3 to 6 1 [L]	3 to 6 8 [H]	11 to 20 10 [L]	Need Level (NL)
	9 to 15 2 [L] Importance of People (IOP)	5 to 11 2 [L] Assuming Respon- sibility (AR)	6 to 12 15 [H] Importance of Affection (IOA)	20 to 38 19 (L)	Social Interaction Index (SII)

It is useful to move from a discussion of the more general summary scores toward consideration of the specific scores that will explain them. We will therefore take the scores in approximately the reverse of the order in which they were calculated. Mary is low in her general behavior and need for interaction with people (SII). Her SII score could be even lower if it were not for the fact that affection is very important to her (IOA). Socializing with a lot of people is very unimportant to her (IOP), and she also prefers freedom from being held responsible and holding others responsible (AR). Both her overall need for people to approach her (NL) and her efforts to approach people (AL) are somewhat lower than average. As with SI I, these interaction and need levels would be lower if it were not for the high focus on affection and closeness (eA and wA) to counteract the low need and activity levels in the Inclusion and Control areas. Looking at her six basic scores we see that she describes herself as a person who does not join others and does not want them to invite her, does not influence others but is not comfortable being led, likes to get close and personal and likes people to approach her.

The facilitator may wish to reproduce the following score summary sheet (Table 6) for use in interpreting the *FIRO-B* in groups.

Table 6. FIRO-B Score Summary Sheet.
Place scores on lines and indicate low-high designations
(L, ML, MH, H) in brackets next to them.

	I Inclusion	C Control	A Affection	Row Totals	
express e (toward)	4 to 7 — [ ]	2 to 5 — [ ]	3 to 6 — [ ]	9 to 18 — [ ]	Activity Level (AL)
want w (from)	5 to 8 — [ ]	3 to 6 — [ ]	3 to 6 — [ ]	11 to 20 — [ ]	Need Level (NL)
Column Totals	9 to 15 — [ ]	5 to 11 — [ ]	6 to 12 — [ ]	20 to 38 — [ ]	Social Interaction Index (SII)
	Importance of People (IOP)	Assuming Respon- sibility (AR)	Importance of Affection (IOA)		

Interpersonal Compatibility Scores. The compatibility between two people is often separate from how personally well-integrated each of the two individuals are. Two happy people can come together with their needs clashing; it is possible for two unhappy people to find in each other the solution to their unhappiness. We will examine different bases for compatibility as described by Schutz (1958).

Reciprocal Compatibility (RC). This is an index of whether A's expressed behavior matches what B wants and whether B's expressed behavior matches what A wants. the formula is:

$$RC = |\text{Jack e} - \text{Mary w}| + |\text{Mary e} - \text{Jack w}|$$

for each of the inclusion, control, and affection areas. The vertical lines mean to drop the sign of the remainder from the subtraction within the lines.

	Jack				Mary		
	I	C	A		I	C	A
e	2	2	2	e	1	1	7
w	3	4	4	w	1	1	8

Looking at Jack's and Mary's scores, we have

Inclusion	$\lvert 2-1 \rvert + \lvert 1-3 \rvert$	=	3
Control	$\lvert 2-1 \rvert + \lvert 1-4 \rvert$	=	4
Affection	$\lvert 2-8 \rvert + \lvert 7-4 \rvert$	=	9

High scores (6 or above) indicate *incompatibility* in that area. Thus, Jack and Mary are most likely to have an incompatibility in the affection area. Specifically, Jack's low expressed affection will frustrate Mary's high need for affection. Incompatibility in the control area would indicate that one person wants more control than the other wants to give, or that one wants to control more than the other wants to be controlled. Incompatibility in the inclusion area indicates that one wants to include others more than the other wants to be included and/or that one wants to include others less than the other wants to be included.

Originator Compatibility (OC). The extent to which there may be conflict between two people because both want to initiate in an area, or because neither wants to initiate, is obtained by:

$$OC = (Jack\ e - Jack\ w) + (Mary\ e - Mary\ w)$$

for each of the three areas. For Jack and Mary we get:

Inclusion	(2-3)	+ (1-1) =	-1
Control	(2-4)	+ (1-1) =	-2
Affection	(2-4)	+ (7-8) =	-3

A zero means originator *compatibility*. A large negative score (-6 or below) indicates apathetic *incompatibility*, a large positive score (+6 or above) indicates competitive *incompatibility*. Jack and Mary's pattern indicates that they are basically compatible in the desire to initiate interpersonal activity.

Interchange Compatibility (IC). The extent to which a person is involved in an area (inclusion, control, affection) is given by the sum of his e and w scores in that area. This involvement can be shared with another person or not; the other person can have high or low behavior and feeling involvement in this area. Compatibility in interest and involvement is obtained by:

$$IC = \lvert (Jack\ e + Jack\ w) - (Mary\ e + Mary\ w) \rvert$$

which measures the difference in area involvement between the two people for each of the three areas. Jack and Mary's interchange compatibility is

Inclusion	$\lvert (2+3) - (1+1) \rvert$	=	3
Control	$\lvert (2+4) - (1+1) \rvert$	=	4
Affection	$\lvert (2+4) - (7+8) \rvert$	=	9

A high score (6 or above) indicates incompatibility in general concern for that kind of issue. Regarding affection issues, Mary has substantial concern over wanting to be close and intimate with many people. Jack probably considers such behavior promiscuous and indiscriminant. Regarding control issues, Jack is somewhat more willing to be held responsible and hold others responsible than is Mary. She prefers a "live and let live" approach to interpersonal control. Finally, Jack and Mary are compatible in the inclusion area. A high score would have meant that one of them had a much stronger "being with people" need than the other.

Reciprocal and interchange compatibility in this example yielded the same three scores. The two formulas are not equivalent, but they yield different scores ONLY UNDER two conditions: (1) when Jack's wanted is greater than Mary's expressed while *at the same time* Mary's wanted is greater than Jack's expressed, or (2) when Jack's wanted is less than Mary's expressed while *at the same time* Mary's wanted is also less than Jack's expressed score. If we count the times when wanted is equal to expressed score, there are 9 compatibility situations within an area (*e.g.*, one would be Jack's wanted = Mary's expressed while at the same time, Mary's wanted is less than Jack's expressed score). Since only two of these nine situations yield different scores for reciprocal and interchange compatibility, the two indices have high overlap.

	Need Areas		
	I	C	A
Reciprocal Compatibility	3	4	9
Originator Compatibility	-1	12	-3
Interchange Compatibility	3	4	9

In conclusion, two compatibility scores indicate compatibility problems in the affection area for Jack and Mary.

REFERENCES

Schutz, W.C. *FIRO: A Three-Dimensional Theory of Interpersonal Behavior.* (New York: Holt, Rinehart & Winston, Inc., 1958.) Reprinted in paperback as *The Interpersonal Underworld.* (Palo Alto, California: Consulting Psychologists Press, Inc., 1966.)

Ryan, Leo R. *Clinical Interpretation of the FIRO-B.* (Palo Alto, Consulting Psychologists Press, 1970.)

FUNDAMENTAL INTERPERSONAL RELATIONS ORIENTATION—FEELING

William C. Schutz

DESCRIPTION

Length: fifty-four statements (nine in each scale)

Time: *Administering* five to twelve minutes
Scoring five to ten minutes

Scales:°

Significance	*(perception of others)*
Significance	*(wanted to be perceived by others)*
Competence	*(perception of others)*
Competence	*(wanted to be perceived by others*
Lovability	*(perception of others)*
Lovability	*(wanted to be perceived by others)*

FIRO-F is meant to parallel *FIRO-B* but with a focus on feelings rather than on behavior. *FIRO-B* measures behavior in the areas of inclusion, control, and affection. *FIRO-F* measures feelings in the areas of *significance, competence,* and *lovability.* It is assumed that significance, competence, and lovability are the feelings that are behind inclusion, control, and affection behavior. As with the *FIRO-B* scale, a person obtains a score on both his expressed feelings toward others and how much he wants others to feel that way toward him. We can describe the six scales of the *FIRO-F* test by use of the following table:

Table 1. Description of FIRO-F Scales

		I Inclusion	C Control	A Affection
e	Expressed Feelings (toward others)	I think people are significant and I am interested in them.	I see others as competent and capable.	I feel people are likeable and loveable.
w	Wanted Feelings (from others)	I want others to consider me important and interesting.	I want others to feel that I am a competent person.	I want others to feel that I am a likeable and loveable person.

°Pragmatically restated.

152

The response categories are the same as those for *FIRO-B*. They range from "definitely not true" to "especially true" from "never" to "always" from "nobody" to "most people."

Table 2. Sample FIRO-F statements
(with responses that are counted in parentheses)

	I Inclusion	C Control	A Affection
e	Expressed Feelings (toward others)	I feel that each person is important (Especially true.)	I am skeptical of people's abilities (Definitely not true or not true.)	I feel cordial toward people (True or especially true.)
w	Wanted Feelings (from others)	It bothers me when people feel indifferent toward me (Sometimes, often, usually or always.)	I am very pleased when people show respect for my competence (Especially true.)	I want people to like me (True or especially true.)

Uses: Three major uses of *FIRO-F* are:

Self-insight. As with *FIRO-B*, *FIRO-F* can be used as a diagnostic instrument for interpersonal style. (See the **Uses** section under *FIRO-B*.)

Interpersonal Relations. Sharing (e.g., dyadic interpretation or posting) of *FIRO-F* scores can facilitate understanding of behavioral traits such as dominance, silence, defensiveness, avoidance of confrontation, hostility, and avoidance of intimacy.

Comparison. *FIRO-F* scores can be compared with *FIRO-B* scores to gain insight into feelings underlying preferred styles of behavior.

Positive Features: As with *FIRO-B*, a positive feature of *FIRO-F* is the highly meaningful nature of the six scales. Whether people view us as significant, competent, and lovable, and whether we are ready to see others in the same light is informative. *FIRO-F* has many of the positive features possessed by *FIRO-B*. *FIRO-F*:

a) is relatively short and non-threatening,

b) distinguishes between *expressed toward* and *wanted from* others,

c) has no assumed social desirability for a particular item or scale, and

d) lends to interpretation of *combinations* of scale scores.

In addition to these features, *FIRO-F*, (which was developed after *FIRO-B*), adds the possibility of detailed comparisons between a person's *feelings* about his relations with others and his *behavior* toward others.

Concerns: As with *FIRO-B*, *FIRO-F* falls victim to invalidities that attend self-report measures. It is possible that those who might benefit the most from an honest look at their feelings toward themselves and others may be the most likely to distort their self-report. In contrast to *FIRO-B*, *FIRO-F* has limited data on reliability and validity.

ORDERING

Where To Order: Consulting Psychologists Press, Inc.
577 College Avenue
Palo Alto, Ca. 94306
Phone: (415) 326-4448

Cost: *Specimen Set* $ 4.75
    Set of Keys   1.75
    25 Tests   3.00

ADMINISTERING, SCORING AND INTERPRETING

Scoring: Templates are available for rapid scoring. The scorer should be sure that he checks nine responses for each scale; items on the right hand margin of the template are easy to overlook. See the section on scoring under *FIRO-B* for some comments on group scoring or scoring through the use of clerical assistance.

Interpreting: The same summary scores described in the *FIRO-B* section can be applied to *FIRO-F* except that some changes in the score titles are necessary. The average interval is based on plus 1.5 and minus 1.5 from the norms for each scale.

Table 3. Normative scores and average range based on it
(plus and minus 1.5). Taken from "Supplementary Technical Data for FIRO Scales"

		I Inclusion	C Control	A Affection
e	Expressed feelings (toward others)	4.4 2.9 to 5.9	3.8 2.3 to 5.3	4.2 2.7 to 5.7
w	Wanted feelings (from others)	4.6 3.1 to 6.1	4.0 2.5 to 5.5	4.9 3.4 to 6.4

Since a person's scores may vary a point or two each time he completes the instrument, the decimal point implies an unrealistic level of accuracy for interpreting individual scores. Table 4 shows the average range to the nearest whole number.

Table 4. Average ranges to the nearest whole number.

		I Inclusion	C Control	A Affection	
e	Expressed feelings (toward others)	3 to 6	2 to 5	3 to 6	8 to 17
w	Wanted feelings (from others)	3 to 6	3 to 6	3 to 6	9 to 18
		6 to 12	5 to 11	6 to 12	17 to 35

Fred's scores can be compared to the average ranges, and a judgment can be made as to whether they are low (below the average range), medium low (at the bottom of the average range), average, medium high (at the top of the average range), or high (above the average range). See table 5.

Table 5. Fred's scores on scales and indices.

		I Inclusion	C Control	A Affection		
e	Expressed feelings (toward others)	3 to 6 0 [L]	2 to 5 5 [MH]	3 to 6 3 [ML]	8 to 17 8 [ML]	Appreciation Level (AL)
w	Wanted feelings (from others)	3 to 6 6 [MH]	3 to 6 6 [MH]	3 to 6 9 [H]	9 to 18 21 [H]	Need Level (NL)
		6 to 12 6 [ML]	5 to 11 11 [MH]	6 to 12 12 [MH]	17 to 35 29 [ ]	
		We're both Important (WBI)	We're both Competent (WBC)	We're both Lovable (WBL)		General Valuing (GV)

Table 6 provides a form for recording scores and indicating whether they deviate from the normative average.

Table 6. Form for recording scores and deviation indications.

	I Inclusion	C Control	A Affection		
e	Expressed feelings (toward others)	3 to 6 — [ ]	2 to 5 — [ ]	3 to 6 — [ ]	8 to 17 — [ ]	Appreciation Level (AL)
w	Wanted feelings (from others)	3 to 6 — [ ]	3 to 6 — [ ]	3 to 6 — [ ]	9 to 18 21 [ ]	Need Level (NL)
		6 to 12 — [ ]	5 to 11 — [ ]	6 to 12 — [ ]	17 to 35 — [ ]	
		We're both Important (WBI)	We're both Competent (WBC)	We're both Lovable (WBL)		General Valuing (GV)

Fred's *FIRO-F* scores indicate that he wants good feelings from others (regard, admiration, liking) but really does not appreciate others (AL and NL). When the desire for good feelings from others is greater than a willingness to appreciate them, it is marked in the areas of importance and lovability. Even though he wants more feelings of importance than he gives, his general feeling about the importance of people is low (WBI), whereas, even though his desire for love feelings is more than he gives, his involvement in love feelings is high (WBL). He feels that people (including himself) are competent (WBC). His very low estimation of the importance of people in general (eI) and his high need to be seen as lovable (wA) are the strongest deviations from average and should be viewed as important scores for Fred. The high need for respect (wC) and regard (wI) from others supports the image of a person who wants positive feelings from others.

Interpreting *FIRO-F* requires two cautions. First, it is possible for a person to have feelings for only a few people. Therefore, some low scores instead of indicating low feelings may indicate focused feelings, i.e., he may have strong feelings but concerning only a few people. Second, a low score may indicate a surfeit of stimulation in that area. If events change the amount of positive feelings from people or competence indications a person receives, then his score is expected to increase in those areas. Other information about him might indicate which of these alternatives generates the low score.

Comparison of FIRO-F Scores with FIRO-B Scores

Fred's FIRO-B

	I	C	A	Row Total
e	2 [L]	2 [ML]	2 [L]	6 [L]
w	3 [L]	4	4	11 [ML]
Col. Total	5 [L]	6	6 [ML]	17 [L]

Fred's FIRO-F

	I	C	A	Row Total
e	0 L	5 [MH]	3 [ML]	8 [ML]
w	6 [MH]	6 [MH]	9 [H]	21 [H]
	6 [ML]	11 [MH]	12 [MH]	29

Fred's *FIRO-B* scores indicate a generally low inclusion concern both in regard to joining people and wanting people to join him. His *FIRO-F* scores indicate, however, that his inclusion behavior may well be a compromise solution in that he sees little value in most people, but he has a big need to have other people see him as being interesting and important. Thus, his low inclusion behavior can be seen as something toward which he is driven by his need for admiration rather than by some strong level of interest he has in people.

Regarding control, it appears that Fred's attribution and wanting of competence feelings are greater than his desire to control or be controlled. Finally, his affection scores indicate greater desire for being liked than a desire for intimate relations with many people. Some of these differences between behavior (*B*) and feeling (*F*) scores may be due to Fred's desire to have relations with few people rather than many.

Another striking difference between his *FIRO-B* and *F* scores is the relatively smaller discrepancy between expressing and wanting *behavior* (5 points) compared to the larger discrepancy between expressed and wanted *feelings* (13 points). This discrepancy is caused by differences in wanted behavior versus wanted feelings. Fred needs people to feel he is interesting, competent, and especially to like him, much more than he wants them to approach him and involve him in their lives. Perhaps he fears that if they get to know him they will no longer feel that he is interesting and competent, and they will no longer like him.

In general, translation between *F* scores and *B* scores is relatively direct for the inclusion and affection areas, but the facilitator should be sure he understands the meaning of the scale scores in the case of the control area. That is, wC means "I want to be controlled" in *FIRO-B*, and "I want people to feel I am competent" in *FIRO-F*; eC means "I want to control" in *FIRO-B* and "I feel people are competent" in *FIRO-F*.

In the control area, *FIRO-B* and *FIRO-F* are not parallel; they imply the opposite of each other. In the inclusion and affection areas, an *expressed* feeling relates to an *expressed* behavior, in the control area an *expressed* feeling relates more to a *wanted* behavior.

SURVEY OF INTERPERSONAL VALUES

Leonard V. Gordon

DESCRIPTION

Length: thirty sets of three statements

Time: *Administering* fifteen minutes
Scoring five to ten minutes

Scales:

> *Support*
> *Conformity*
> *Recognition*
> *Independence*
> *Benevolence*
> *Leadership*

The *SIV* is designed to measure certain critical values involving the individual's relationships to other people or their relationships to him, which are important in the individual's personal, social, marital, and occupational adjustment. The scales are defined by what high-scoring individuals value. There are no separate descriptions for low-scoring individuals; they simply do not value what is defined by the particular scale.

For each set of three statements the individual is to choose the one statement he considers the *most* important to him and the one statement he considers the *least* important to him.

Support. Being treated with understanding, receiving encouragement from other people, being treated with kindness and consideration.

Sample statement:
To have people willing to offer me a helping hand.

Conformity. Doing what is socially correct, following regulations closely, doing what is accepted and proper, being a conformist.

Recognition. Being looked up to and admired, being considered important, attracting favorable notice, achieving recognition.

Sample statement:
To associate with people who are well known.

Independence. Having the right to do whatever one wants to do, being free to make one's own decisions, being able to do things in one's own way.

Sample statement:
To be allowed to do whatever I want to do.

Benevolence. Doing things for other people, sharing with others, helping the unfortunate, being generous.

Leadership. Being in charge of other people, having authority over others, being in a position of leadership or power.

Uses: Scores on various scales of the *SIV* can be used to point out the possibility that the disagreements among group members might derive from the differences in the interpersonal values they hold.

Positive Features: One of the positive features of the *SIV* is that it measures six values, chosen by factor analysis, critical to the individual's relationships to other people or their relationships to him in the individual's personal, social, marital, and occupational adjustment.

The *SIV* is brief, self-administering (all directions required are given on the title page of the booklet), easy to score, and fairly simple to interpret using the information provided in the test manual.

Concerns: Because the *SIV* is a self-description instrument, there is concern with lying and self-deception, but the forced-choice format and equating of triads in social desirability discourages these somewhat.

ORDERING

Where To Order: Science Research Associates, Inc.
259 East Erie Street
Chicago, Illinois 60611
Phone: (312) 944-7552

Cost:		
Specimen set	$2.10
Hand scoring stencil	.90
Manual	1.05
25 tests	4.75

ADMINISTERING, SCORING AND INTERPRETING

Scoring: Scoring is done through the use of a hand overlay stencil: count the number of responses showing through for each scale separately and record that number at the bottom of the page in the appropriate box. After each of the scales are scored in this way, the scores are totaled, and, if the *SIV* has been correctly marked, the number attained will be 90. If the scores fall between 85 and 95 and no more than two sets of statements have been mismarked or omitted, the obtained scores may be used.

Scoring could be done by one or more persons depending upon the number of hand overlay stencils available. It is, however, preferable to allow each person to score their own *SIV* for immediate feedback.

Interpreting: Interpretations of the score on the *SIV* is made by reference to norms prepared for each of the scales. The norms for men and women were obtained from colleges selected to represent regions of the country and are included in the test manual.

All norms are presented in percentiles, and the first step in the interpretation of scores is to convert the raw scores to percentiles by using the table given in the manual. The individual's percentile score provides an indication of his relative standing on a given value in comparison with other members of the same normative group.

INTERPERSONAL CHECK LIST

Rolfe LaForge

Robert Suczek

DESCRIPTION

Length: 128 adjectives

Time: *Administering* eight to twelve minutes
      Scoring sixteen segments—eight to twelve minutes

Scales:

> *Managerial-Autocratic*
> *Responsible-Hypernormal*
> *Cooperative-Over-conventional*
> *Docile-Dependent*
> *Self-effacing-Masochistic*
> *Rebellious-Distrustful*
> *Aggressive-Sadistic*
> *Competitive-Narcissistic*

The instrument is patterned after the interpersonal dimensions of personality described by Freedman, Leary, and their colleagues. There are sixteen sectors which are depicted in a wheel format. Figure 1 depicts the "wheel" which has as its two primary dimensions: Dominance-Submission, (vertical), and Love-Hate (horizontal). Radiating out from the center of the wheel is the third dimension—Intensity.

A number of indices are obtained from the *ICL*. First, there are the sixteen categories shown in Figure 1; second, there are the eight octants also shown in Figure 1; third, there are the indices for dominance, love, number of items checked, and average intensity of items checked (an index of attitude toward the person rated).

Uses: Since administration of the *ICL* takes only about ten minutes, a participant can complete it not only for himself, but also for his ideal self, or another members of the group or the organization. The *ICL* promotes discussion of the concept of weaknesses being strengths in excess and the gains and losses that acrue to both "top dogs" and "underdogs."

Positive Features: The most notable positive feature of the *ICL* is the dimensional view of interpersonal relations upon which it is built, in addition to the concept of strengths becoming weaknesses in excess. It is relatively brief and costs nothing.

Concerns: The *ICL* is not easily available which makes using it somewhat difficult. The user must make his own stencils or score answers without a stencil.

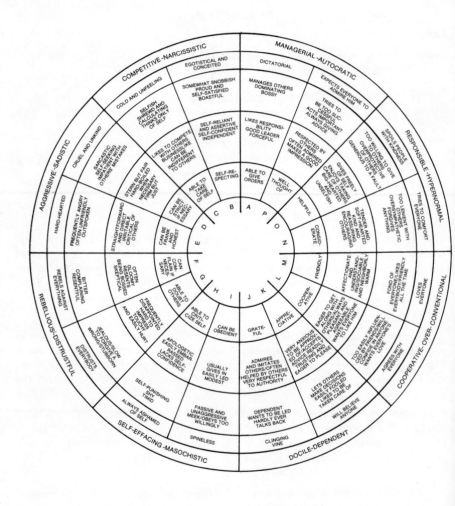

Figure 1. Classification of Interpersonal Behavior into sixteen Categories.

ORDERING

Where To Order: Copies of a technical report containing the instrument can be obtained from:

> Oregon Research Institute
> Eugene, Oregon 97401
> Phone: (503) 343-1674

Ask for "Research Use of the ICL" by Rolfe LaForge, ORI Technical Report Vol. 3, No. 4, October, 1963.

Costs: No Cost.

ADMINISTERING, SCORING AND INTERPRETING

Administering. Have the adjectives typed in alphabetical order. Responses could be made on the sheet with the adjectives or on a separate answer sheet or card. The response is usually a check (or blackened space on an IBM-type answer sheet) if the adjective applies and no response if it does not.

Scoring. Construct a template to show a score for each of the intensity levels within each of the sixteen sectors. See Figure 2 for a recording form for these scores.

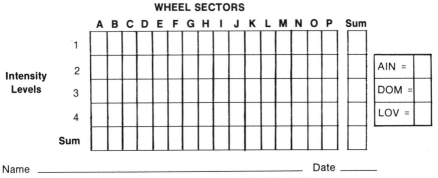

Figure 2. Recording Form For The ICL.

Interpreting. LaForge (1963) describes four indices that can be calculated from the scores in addition to the total number checked in each of the sixteen sectors and the eight octants. *Number of items checked* is the simple sum of the number of items that were checked. It is a measure of openness, a willingness to talk about that object or person. The *average intensity* is obtained by summing all of the level one adjectives checked, and adding to that sum double the sum of level two adjectives checked; to that new total, add triple the sum of level-three adjectives checked, and to that total add quadruple the sum of level four adjectives checked. Divide the overall total by the total number of adjectives checked.

$$\text{Average Intensity} = \frac{n_1 + 2n_2 + 3n_3 + 4n_4}{n \text{ checked}}$$

Average intensity is a measure of dislike or low evaluation. The higher the score, the more negatively you view the person you are rating.

The two dimensions of the wheel are obtained by taking the total number of adjectives for each sector and put them in the following formula:

Dominance = A-I + .9 (B+P-H-J) + .7 (C+O-G-K) + .4 (D+N-F-L)

Love = M-E + .9 (N+L-D-F) + .7 (O+K-C-G) + .4 (P+J-B-H)

INTERPERSONAL RATING FORM

Robert Freed Bales

DESCRIPTION

Length: twenty-six questions answered "yes," "no," or "?."

Time: *Administering* two to four minutes
Scoring   five to ten minutes

Scales: °

> *Material Success and Power*
> *Devaluation of Self*
> *Conservative Group Beliefs*
> *Rejection of Conservative Group Beliefs*
> *Equalitarianism*
> *Individualistic Isolationism*

There are 3 dimensions that are being assessed by the Interpersonal Rating Form. Bales refers to them as U-D (for Upward and Downward), F-B (for Forward-Backward) and P-N for (Positive-Negative). Thus he allows the reader to perceive of score patterns in terms of a three-dimensional space (positive is to the right and negative to the left). See Figure 1 for a depiction of the space.

The three-dimensional space is the result of a factor analysis (by A.S. Couch) of data from a variety of sources: 1) self report in a number of personality scales (e.g. *Minnesota Multiphase Personality Inventory (MMPI), Sixteen Personality Factor Scales, California Psychological Inventory* and the *Thurstone Temperament Schedule*), 2) interpersonal perceptions, 3) measure of talking in a group (*e.g.* to whom, how much, how often addressed, etc., using Bales' Interaction Process Analysis coding system), and 4) indices derived from content of value statements participants made during group meetings.

One must have Bales' book in order to interpret the meaning of a location because a location represents a large number of variables. Furthermore, the region surrounding a location gives much information about the location. Even the opposite location is informative as an example of what kinds of beliefs, attitudes, and values are counter to a position.

The kinds of statements that reflect the various locations are depicted in Figure 2.

°Pragmatically restated

164

(1) Slice where U is positive and other tendencies are neutral.

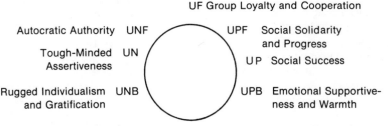

(U) (Upward) Material Success and Power

(2) Slice where U is positive but other tendencies are present also.

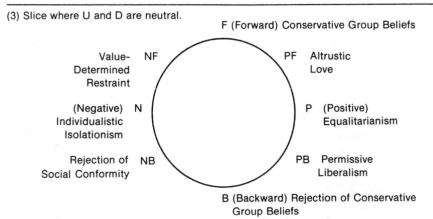

UF Group Loyalty and Cooperation

Autocratic Authority UNF   UPF Social Solidarity
                                      and Progress

Tough-Minded UN   U P Social Success
Assertiveness

Rugged Individualism UNB   UPB Emotional Supportive-
and Gratification   ness and Warmth

UB Value Relativism and Expression

(3) Slice where U and D are neutral.

F (Forward) Conservative Group Beliefs

Value-   NF   PF   Altrustic
Determined   Love
Restraint

(Negative) N   P   (Positive)
Individualistic   Equalitarianism
Isolationism

Rejection of NB   PB   Permissive
Social Conformity   Liberalism

B (Backward) Rejection of Conservative
Group Beliefs

(4) Slice where D is positive.

DF Self-knowledge and Subjectivity

Self-sacrifice for DNF   DPF Salvation through
Values   Love

Rejection of DN   DP   Trust in the
Social Success   Goodness of Others

Failure and DNB   DPB Identification with
Withdrawal   the Underprivileged

DB Withholding of Cooperation

(5) Slice where D is positive and other tendencies are neutral.

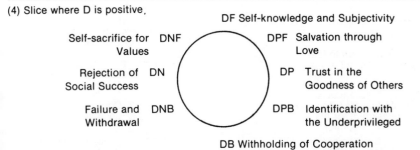

(D) (Downward) Devaluation of Self

Figure 1. Two-dimensional slices (of the sphere) through various levels of the U-D dimension. All locations should be read as "Toward...," indicating a tendency rather than an "everpresent" response style.

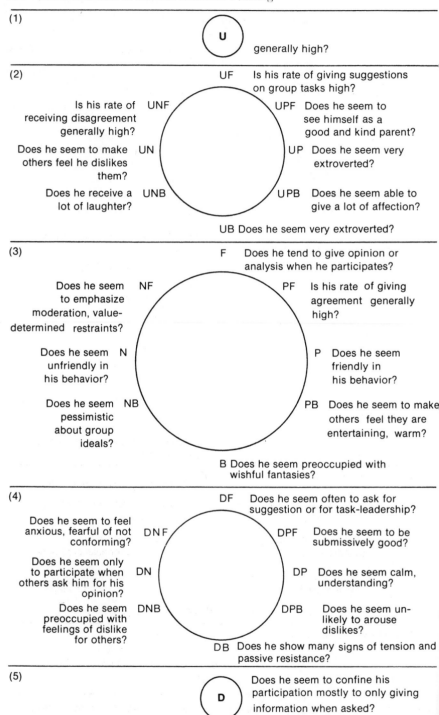

Figure 2. Sample statements.

Uses: *Group Mapping. Interpersonal Rating Form* can be used to give participants a view of the structure of the group regarding the distribution of the members. For example, some may have a high need for power and achievement while others may be passive and non-assertive (D), some may want to help others and be friendly (P), while others may be unfriendly, negative, and detached (N), and some may have a strong task and problem solving orientation (F), while these are antagonistic toward a down-to-earth practical orientation (B). By observing the locations of the other members, a participant can anticipate where he is likely to receive: general opposition, opposition on certain kinds of issues or procedures, support on certain issues or procedures, and general support.

Teaching a theory of interpersonal space: An important use of the instrument is as a springboard for learning a perception of three-dimensional space that is filled with personal traits, interpersonal predispositions, background experiences, goals, values, and people. A knowledge of such a space gives the participant useful concepts for understanding himself, others, and occurrences within the group. The idea of a three-dimensional space, even though a simplification of the complexity of interpersonal dimensions, is an improvement over the two-category approach people often use to look at themselves and others (with me versus against me; good people versus bad people; my kind of people versus different people).

Positive Features: Because Bales' *Interpersonal Rating Form* has only twenty-six short statements in it, and because there are three parallel forms, there are a great many alternatives possible in its effective use. For instance, we have asked a person to take one form to describe himself, a second form to describe the person on his left, and the third form to describe the person on his right. Each person describes two other people and is described by two other people. What he learns is whether he sees himself the way others see him, whether other people agree about how they see him, how he perceives himself, how others perceive him, in addition to the whole spatial configuration associated with the instrument.

A second positive feature is that it integrates characteristics, values, behavior in a group, childhood experiences, and self concept and shows how these personal elements cluster at various locations in the space. The person is given a unifying, integrating view of his social world.

Concerns: One problem with the instrument is the complexity of the spatial system. That is, it is easiest to describe a person's location and the locations of others on a one-dimensional scale like dominance, more difficult to communicate the various locations in a two-dimensional space such as love-hate and dominate-submit, and quite difficult to locate all of the members in a three dimensional space such as those described by Bales as: powerful—weak, interrelating—withdrawing, and task accomplishment—flight.

Furthermore, understanding the meaning of a location requires as an *absolute minimum* reading a paragraph of description of the characteristic associated with that location, and *ideally* reading the descriptions of the locations that touch on the designated one plus the one opposite to it. That is a great deal of information to absorb and is available only through copies of Bales' book. The facilitator may have to provide a number of copies of the book for the participants or insure that the participants have provided themselves with them.

It is also possible that the people in the group (all salesmen, all human relations trainers, all psychiatrists) may be so homogeneous that they cluster in the same sector of the sphere, thereby reducing some opportunity for the participants to compare themselves with people who are in distant locations.

ORDERING

Where To Order: The instrument, scoring key, and manual are all in: R.F. Bales, *Personality and Interpersonal Analysis*, 1970.

> Holt, Rinehart, and Winston
> 383 Madison Avenue
> New York, N.Y. 10017
> Phone: (212) 688-9100

Cost: $ 13.00

ADMINISTERING, SCORING AND INTERPRETING

Administering: Ask the respondents to try to envision a group situation wherein the group is held responsible for its performance by some higher authority; the group has a task focus and is rewarded for doing something well. "As you respond to the *Interpersonal Rating Form*, your frame of reference should be the kind of setting wherein you are held responsible for your behavior and performance. We recognize that you may not always be able to use such a setting as a frame of reference, but the more you can respond within that kind of setting the closer you will come toward the setting that was used to develop the scale locations."

Distribute the Interpersonal Rating Forms and ask people to rate the person on their left, themselves, and if time permits, the person on their right.

Scoring: The scoring key is on page 7 of the book. It assigns location designations to each response. For example, if the respondent answered question 1 "no" he receives a D, if "yes" a U. If he answers question 2 "no" he receives DN, if "yes" UP; question 3 "no" = DNB, "yes" = UPF; 4 "no" = DB, "yes" = UF, and so on. The key can be read aloud, reproduced and distributed, posted, or clerical assistance can be used.

After each of the twenty-six responses are classified, the respondent counts the number of U's, D's, P's, N's, F's and B's. He subtracts the U's from the D's, the P's from the N's, and the F's from the B's (placing the larger number in the position of menuend. The remainder is assigned the designation of the larger number, e.g. 4U, 1P, 13B. Any amount less than three is dropped, leaving 4U and 13B = UB.

The person can average his self rating with the rating made of him by the people on both sides of him. Figure 3 depicts an example of how this is done:

Ratings for Tony

Using letters only

Location	John's rating UPB	Helen's rating UPF	Tony's rating P
		U P B	
		U P F	
		P	

Total   2U3P O = UP (Summary Location)

You may wish require a minimum of "2" in front of a letter before it is carried to the summary location.

Using Numbers

	John's rating of Tony 5U 5P 12B	Helen's rating of Tony 9U 7P 8F	Tony's rating of Tony 1 U 12P 3B
	5U 5P 12B		
	9U 7P 8F *Reverse		
	1U 12P 3B		
Total	15U 24P 7B		
3 +	5U 8P 2.3B = UP		

Interpretation: Between pages 200 and 207 of Bales' book, the description of Tony's location—"Type UP: Toward Social Success"—is found. "The member located in the upward–positive part of the group space by his fellow members seems to be socially and sexually extroverted, ascendant but at the same time open and friendly."

How He Sees Himself and How Others See Him: "The UP member, in spite of deserved popularity, seems to have an over-expanded image of himself..."

His Place in the Interaction Network. "...higher than expected on the total interaction received (people addressing their ideas and comments to him...)"

What Ideas and Values will He Express?

...After respondents have had time to read about their location, ask them to locate themselves in the room, with the front of the room being forward, the rear of the room—backward, the right side—positive, the left side—negative, standing on chairs—upward, and lying on the floor—downward. Point out that those who are clustered together in their location (in our example UP) have a similar world view and approach to life: those who are in the 8 locations nearby (in our example, U, UF, UPF, PF, P, PB, UPB, and UB) are similar and compatible to an individual in the UP position, those at the 8 locations further removed (UN, UNF, F, DPF, DP, DPB, B and UNB) are different but will probably be neither unduly antagonistic nor supportive of him. The next level removed (N, NF, DF, DNB, D, DNF, DB, and NB) contains people who see the world quite differently from him and will probably oppose his ideas (either actively or passively) or dislike his style. Finally, the most removed location from him (in our example, DN) represents the persons whose values and style should be opposite to his.

After people have identified aloud those who are potential supporters, similar, indifferent, different, and potential opposition, ask them to form into groups that are as homogeneous as possible. Have each group discuss a group view on 1) the ideal interaction pattern, 2) the good life, and 3) what the group should be doing next. Discuss the difference in the group products. Ask each group to choose a group name to reflect its composition. If time permits, ask individuals to meet with the person as close to the opposite of their position as possible to draw up a list of similarities and differences between them.

PSYCHOLOGICAL AUDIT FOR INTERPERSONAL RELATIONS

Richard R. Stephenson

DESCRIPTION

Length: 500 true or false statements

Time: *Administering* about one hour
       Scoring   eight to ten minutes

Scales:

> *Social Status*
> *Intellectual Rigidity*
> *Family Cohesiveness*
> *Social Extraversion*
> *Political Conservatism*
> *Self-Rejection*
> *Aggressive Hostility*
> *Physical Affection*
> *Monetary Concern*
> *Change and Variety*
> *Dominant Leadership*
> *Nurturant Helpfulness*
> *Order and Routine*
> *Esthetic Pleasures*
> *Submissive Passivity*
> *Psychological Support*
> *Emotional Control*
> *Dependent Suggestibility*
> *Health Concern*
> *Outdoor Interests*
> *Self-Acceptance*

Social Status. Persons who score high on this scale are constantly striving, and not infrequently scheming, to accelerate their upward mobility. High scorers are status conscious and may be social snobs. Whatever their present status level, they are dissatisfied with it. There is no indication as to whether low scorers are *indifferent* to social status or are anti-class and anti-status.

    Sample of scored statement:
       "Living in a good neighborhood is very important to me."

Intellectual Rigidity. Persons who score high on this scale are opinionated and set in their ways. They are frequently prejudiced and intolerant regarding social, religious, or personal preference issues. However, they are not necessarily aggressive, malicious, or hostile. Low scorers tend to be intellectually flexible. In the usual case they are simply open-minded enough to admit the possibility that there is another side to most issues.

Sample of scored statement:
   "When I really believe something I almost never change my mind."

Family Cohesiveness. Persons who score high on this scale have traditional nineteenth-century, upper-middle-class attitudes toward marriage and family matters. Divorce is rare in such families with marriage seen primarily as a religious institution. Low scorers on this scale are representative of "modern," "liberal," or "progressive" family attitudes, using these terms descriptively rather than judgmentally.

Social Extraversion. High scorers on this scale are highly oriented to social interactions. Such persons may be loud, uninhibited, gregarious, and socially unconventional. Low scorers on this scale are probably seen as Self-Rejective, Passive, Dependent, Intellectually Rigid, and highly-controlled emotionally since they receive high ratings on criteria for those traits and behaviors.

Political Conservatism. High scorers are fiercely individualistic in the political laissez-faire sense (rather than in the rugged pioneer sense). Persons who score low on this scale are as politically liberal as high scorers are conservative. Thus, low scorers favor greater governmental intervention in such areas as regulation of profits, welfare programs, civil rights, control of education, and similar issues.

Self-Rejection. High scorers on this scale can generally be described in one word: unhappy. High scorers not only do not accept their good points but they may actually deny that they really have any. They tend to be listless, passive, dependent, and pessimistic about the future. The high *negative* correlations with Self-Rejection are, in descending order, with the criteria for Self-Acceptance, Dominant Leadership, Change and Variety, Emotional Control, and Social Extraversion.

Aggressive Hostility. High scorers are constantly and openly argumentative. They tend to be opinionated, frequently offering their opinions as fact; they tend to have few friends, tend to pout, and are usually seen as immature. Any hostility shown by a low scorer is probably indirect and the low scorer is probably seen as quite docile.

Physical Affection. High scorers express their affection in caressing, holding hands, or kissing. They have a need for little displays of romantic love, such as gifts, cards, or flowers. When considering the male-male relationship, a high-scoring male is usually a back-slapper, a frequent hand-shaker, and "arm-around-the-shoulder" type. Low scorers tend to be rated high on the criteria for those scales that measure conservatism, including especially Political Conservatism and Monetary Concern.

Monetary Concern. For persons who score high on this scale it is a rare penny that is ever spent foolishly. Thus, close and rigid control is maintained over all expenditures. To low scorers money is simply not important; it is something to be spent when one has it and not worried about when one does not have it. Low scorers generally have large monthly installment payments since they will buy on credit rather than save regularly for later purchases.

Change and Variety. High scorers are adventurous, enthusiastic, and energetic. They are always on the go, trying out new ideas or experiences. They may have difficulty in staying with a long-range goal. Low scores on this scale are correlated with: Self-Rejection; Submissive Passivity; and Dependent Suggestibility.

Dominant Leadership. Persons who score high on this scale are natural leaders. They are responsive to the desires of those they lead and subordinates are loyal to them, while they in turn, are loyal to their subordinates. Low scorers tend to be rated as high on the criterion for Submissive Passivity.

Nurturant Helpfulness. High scorers are seen by their associates as friendly, helpful, and considerate. They are quick to forgive and are sympathetic in listening to the troubles of others and seem always to have a kind word for others. Persons scoring low on this scale are most likely to have high ratings on Aggressive Hostility and Intellectual Rigidity.

Order and Routine. High scorers are conscientious, neat and orderly, frequently to an almost compulsive degree. The general rule is: a place for everything and everything *always* in its exact place. Low scorers probably tend to be careless and disorganized and in some respects may not seem conscientious.

Esthetic Pleasures. Persons who score high on this scale evidence a great deal of interest in cultural matters. They are seen as interested in art, classical music, drama, and literature. The low scorer is seen as one whose musical tastes are centered in popular songs rather than classical music and who would, seemingly, prefer television and popular movies to stage plays, and popular magazines to better literature.

Submissive Passivity. High scorers are characteristically seen as quiet, submissive, and non-threatening. They are frequently taken advantage of, a treatment to which they submit quite passively. Low scorers are generally rated high on Dominant Leadership and Aggressive Hostility.

Psychological Support. High scorers are psychologically quite dependent upon others since they are seen as having a great need for frequent personal encouragement. They frequently tend to view themselves as somewhat unworthy. Persons low on this need tend to be more emotionally controlled.

Emotional Control. Persons who score high constantly strive to give the impression of complete rationality. They avoid public display of personal emotion, and try to create the impression that they are intellectual machines. Low scorers are usually rated significantly high on: Social Extraversion; Physical Affection; and Change and Variety.

Dependent Suggestibility. High scorers are extremely indecisive and are reluctant to take independent action even in ordinary, every-day situations. They will attach themselves to a stronger person as the source of decision-making. Low scorers tend to be high on: Change and Variety; Self-Acceptance; and Emotional Control.

Health Concern. Persons with high scores have an inordinate concern with problems of their own health and with the state of their physical well-being.

High scorers tend to be passive, dependent, and self-rejective. Low scores are high on Dominant Leadership and Self-Acceptance.

Outdoor Interests. High scorers enjoy many active sports. While they would rather be sport participants, all enjoy being spectators. Low scorers eschew all interest in sports including, for very low scorers, even those occasional sports events of national interest.

Self-Acceptance. Persons with high scores are satisfied with their physical appearance, personalities, personal habits and traits, possessions, jobs, and accomplishments. In many respects, this scale is a measure of general adjustment and positive self-regard.

ORDERING

Where to Order: Richard R. Stephenson
3912 Third Avenue
San Diego, California 92103
Phone: (714) 298-1477

Costs: $25.00 (two answer sheets, profile sheet, manual, and test booklet)
Discounts for non-profit organizations, activities, and for research.

ASCENDANCE-SUBMISSION
REACTION STUDY

G. W. Allport

F. H. Allport

DESCRIPTION

Length: Women's form, thirty-four questions

Men's form, thirty-three questions

Time: *Administering* twelve minutes

Scoring eight minutes

Scale:

Ascendance-Submission

The *A-S Reaction Study* aims to discover the disposition of an individual to dominate his fellows (or to be dominated by them) in various face-to-face relationships of everyday life. A fairly large number of situations are verbally presented, and the respondent is required to select one of a group of standardized responses which most nearly characterizes his usual behavior in each situation.

Sample statements (with weight given to each response in parentheses):

(Form for Women)

1. *If the majority of your friends are having new costumes for a dance, are you disturbed by having to wear an old frock; one that you know will be recognized?*

   very much _____ *(-2)*

   somewhat _____ *(0)*

   not at all _____ *(+1)*

(Form for Men)

1. a) *At a reception or tea do you seek to meet the important person present?*

   usually _____ *(+1)*

   occasionally _____ *(-1)*

   never _____ *(-1)*

   b) *Do you feel reluctant to meet him?*

   Yes, usually _____ *(-1)*

   Sometimes _____ *(-1)*

   No _____ *(+2)*

Uses: This scale may be used for self-knowledge and for understanding interpersonal relations in the group. Members' scores may be posted to facilitate understanding each other. The participants should be encouraged to discuss any of the specific situations described that made them re-examine themselves or provided insight into their interpersonal style.

Positive Features: Ascendance-submission is an important interpersonal dimension in human relations and therapy groups. Because it is the sole score obtained from this instrument, it receives high focus and does not lose its impact among a group of scales as can happen with multiscale instruments.

The *A-S Reaction Study* is interesting, easy to take and score, and is reliable. Participants generally find their score quite meaningful to them.

Concerns: Although it is brief and easy to take and score, it still yields only one score for the time spent. Furthermore, the scale lumps a number of aspects of ascendance that the respondents might rather examine separately, (e.g., resistance to influence, social visibility, tolerance for ascendance from others).

The description of a few of the situations are somewhat dated ("streetcar," "frock," etc.) and are focussed at a college student population. Finally, the term "submission" is value-laden and carries the possibility of threat to someone who scores low. Effort should be made to emphasize some of the positive traits associated with a submissive style (e.g., easy to get along with, cooperative, flexible).

ORDERING

Where To Order: Houghton Mifflin Company
110 Tremont Street
Boston, Massachusetts 02107
Phone: (617) 423-5725

Cost: *Specimen Set* $ .75
       35 Tests $3.90

ADMINISTERING, SCORING, INTERPRETING

Administering. Refer to the instrument only as the *A-S Reaction Study* not as *The Ascendance Submission Scale.* Instruct all participants to respond as they *have done* under similar circumstances, *not* what they *would do* in that situation.

Scoring. The scoring key is in the manual. It will tell what numerical weight is given to each response to each situation. A large plus weight indicates a very ascendant response, large negative weight indicates a very submissive response, a zero weight indicates a response that is neither submissive nor ascendant. There are separate tables of score-values for men and for women.

Each item should be separately scored in the margin of the page. Omissions or items in which more than one choice is marked count as zero. The final score is the algebraic sum of the scores. This score may be obtained by first adding all the plus scores, then adding the minus scores, and finally subtracting the smaller sum from the larger, retaining the sign of the larger.

It is frequently convenient and entirely permissible to dictate the score-values, allowing the subjects to score their own papers.

Interpreting. Final scores are referred to the table of norms in the manual which are based on 2,578 cases for the Form for Men and six hundred cases for the Form for Women. These norms are derived from the three upper college classes in widely distributed institutions.

SECTION B
Instruments with an Interpersonal Focus

Pre-Marriage, Marriage, and Family

MARITAL ATTITUDES EVALUATION

William C. Schutz

DESCRIPTION

Length: Husband's Form, ninety statements (nine in each scale)
Wife's Form, ninety statements (nine in each scale)

Time: *Administering* seven to fourteen minutes
Scoring about twenty-five minutes

Scales:

Inclusion (behavior) wanted from wife/husband
Inclusion (feelings) wanted from wife/husband
Control (behavior) wanted from wife/husband
Control (feelings) wanted from wife/husband
Affection (behavior/feelings) wanted from wife/husband
Inclusion (behavior) wife/husband wants
Inclusion (feelings) wife/husband wants
Control (behavior) wife/husband wants
Control (feelings) wife/husband wants
Affection (behavior/feelings) wife/husband wants

MATE is highly similar to *LIPHE* except that it measures relations not between child and parent, but between husband and wife. There are two forms of *MATE*: one for the husband and one for the wife. The husband indicates what he wants from his wife and what he thinks his wife wants from him in the areas of inclusion, control, and affection. The wife indicates what she wants from her husband and what she thinks he wants from her. All statements are of the "want from others" type. Within that general class of statements, however, the person indicates what he wants from his spouse in terms of both feelings and behavior. Each person generates ten scores: five scores that indicate what he wants from his spouse and five that indicate what he thinks his spouse wants from him. Each couple thus gets twenty scores. See Table 1 for the categories.

Table 1. Description of Twenty MATE Scales

Husband's Form

I want my wife to:

	I Inclusion	C Control	ABF Affection
B Behavior	spend more time with me and give me more attention.	allow me more freedom and allow me to think more for myself.	show and feel more love and affection for me.
F Feelings	be more interested in me and feel more strongly that I am a significant person.	have more respect for my ability to think and do things well.	

My wife wants me to:

	I Inclusion	C Control	ABF Affection
B Behavior	spend more time with her and give her more attention.	allow her more freedom and allow her to think more for herself.	show and feel more love and affection for her.
F Feelings	be more interested in her and feel more strongly that she is a significant person.	have more respect for her ability to think and do things well.	

Uses: *MATE* lends itself to couples workshops, marriage counseling, family therapy, family labs, and pre-marital counseling. It is useful for getting participants to begin early to approach their relationship in a problem-oriented, low-defensive manner, focusing on specific aspects while at the same time seeing how the specifics fit together. It is sometimes useful to follow-up preliminary discussion of *MATE* scores with an administration of *FIRO-B* and perhaps *FIRO-F* since partners need to know, for example, whether the husband's low need to be with his wife is specific to her or is characteristic of his orientation toward people in general.

Positive Features: *MATE* has one feature that is especially useful: a wife's "I want my husband to" can be compared to the husband's "my wife wants me to." Similarly, the husbands expectations (and the wife's view of those expectations) of *her* behavior and feelings are highly useful. Discrepancies between what the wife wants and what the husband thinks she wants, for example, may indicate problems based on a failure to communicate.

A second positive feature of *MATE* is the use of wording that shows dissatisfaction (*e.g.*, "I want my husband to take me more on trips") rather than merely stating (*e.g.*, "My husband does not take me on trips"). A high score on an "I want my husband to" or an "I want my wife to" item clearly indicates dissatisfaction since the respondent wants more than is being given.

Concerns: The principle problem with *MATE* is that the Guttman scale key was lost and there are no large sample norms for each of the scales. It is hoped that the normative data provided in this discussion of the instrument is accurate enough to help generate insight into a marital relationship.

ORDERING

Where To Order: Consulting Psychologists Press, Inc.
577 College Avenue
Palo Alto, Ca. 94306
Phone: (415) 326-4448

Cost: No Keys available from publishers at this time
25 Tests $4.25

ADMINISTERING, SCORING AND INTERPRETING

Scoring: The original key to *MATE* was lost a number of years ago; however, the statements that are included in each scale are known. What is not available are the cutoff points on the response categories that make a Guttman Scale. However, we are able to use the nine statements in each scale. We can take the number that represents the response (Definitely not true -1, not true -2,... Especially true -6) to the first statement in a scale and add to that the number that represents the response to the second statement, and so on through the responses to the nine statements in the scale. Thus, scores for each scale may range from 9 (definitely not true responses) to 54 (especially true responses). Divide the total score for each scale by six and round off any decimal points (if the decimal is .5, round to the odd number). See Figure 1 for an indication of the statements that go in each scale and for a form for computing each scale score. To use Figure 1, merely transfer to the table the number the person wrote on the *MATE* form containing the statements. Next add the numbers in the score columns and write the sums in the Total row. Next, divide each total score by six and write the result in the Scale Score row.

After the scale scores have been calculated, transfer them to Figure 2 on the line next to the brackets. The numbers at the top of the cells (e.g., 2 to 5) describe the range for average scores on that scale.

In the brackets write "L" if the number is below the average range, "H" if it is above the range, "ML" if it is the same as the number defining the bottom of the range, and "MH" if it is the same as the number defining the top of the range. The "B" row total includes the ABF cell. The "F" row total also includes the ABF cell. However, the overall total is based on only five cells.

FIGURE 1. Form for calculating MATE scores
Wife's Form

I want my husband to—

Ib		Cb		Abf		If		Cf	
Item number	score	Item number	score	Item number	score	Item number	score	Item number	score
7	___	1	___	2	___	4	___	3	___
8	___	9	___	5	___	6	___	12	___
13	___	14	___	10	___	11	___	18	___
19	___	20	___	16	___	15	___	25	___
22	___	23	___	24	___	17	___	29	___
26	___	30	___	27	___	21	___	33	___
34	___	35	___	31	___	28	___	37	___
38	___	39	___	40	___	32	___	41	___
42	___	43	___	44	___	36	___	45	___
Total Ib = ___		Cb = ___		Abf = ___		If = ___		Cf = ___	
Scale Score ÷ 6* = ___		÷ 6 = ___		÷ 6 = ___		÷ 6 = ___		÷ 6 = ___	

My husband wants me to—

Ib		Cb		Abf		If		Cf	
Item number	score	Item number	score	Item number	score	Item number	score	Item number	score
4	___	1	___	2	___	3	___	7	___
8	___	5	___	12	___	6	___	14	___
11	___	9	___	21	___	10	___	18	___
15	___	16	___	24	___	13	___	22	___
19	___	20	___	30	___	17	___	27	___
28	___	23	___	33	___	25	___	35	___
32	___	29	___	37	___	26	___	38	___
39	___	36	___	41	___	31	___	42	___
43	___	40	___	44	___	34	___	45	___
Total Ib = ___		Cb = ___		Abf = ___		If = ___		Cf = ___	
Scale Score ÷ 6 = ___		÷ 6 = ___		÷ 6 = ___		÷ 6 = ___		÷ 6 = ___	

*Footnote, Round to nearest whole number. If quotient ends in .5 round to nearest odd number.

FIGURE 1 (continued)

Husband's Form

I want my wife to —

Ib		Cb		Abf		If		Cf	
Item number	score	Item number	score	Item number	score	Item number	score	Item number	score
4	_____	1	_____	2	_____	3	_____	7	_____
8	_____	5	_____	12	_____	6	_____	14	_____
11	_____	9	_____	21	_____	10	_____	18	_____
15	_____	16	_____	24	_____	13	_____	22	_____
19	_____	20	_____	30	_____	17	_____	27	_____
28	_____	23	_____	33	_____	25	_____	35	_____
32	_____	29	_____	37	_____	26	_____	38	_____
39	_____	36	_____	41	_____	31	_____	42	_____
43	_____	40	_____	44	_____	34	_____	45	_____
Total Ib = _____		Cb = _____		Abf = _____		If = _____		Cf = _____	
Scale Total ÷ 6 = _____		÷ 6 = _____		÷ 6 = _____		÷ 6 = _____		÷ 6 = _____	

My wife wants me to —

Ib		Cb		Abf		If		Cf	
Item number	score	Item number	score	Item number	score	Item number	score	Item number	score
7	_____	1	_____	2	_____	4	_____	3	_____
8	_____	9	_____	5	_____	6	_____	12	_____
13	_____	14	_____	10	_____	11	_____	18	_____
19	_____	20	_____	16	_____	15	_____	25	_____
22	_____	23	_____	24	_____	17	_____	29	_____
26	_____	30	_____	27	_____	21	_____	33	_____
34	_____	35	_____	31	_____	28	_____	37	_____
38	_____	39	_____	40	_____	32	_____	41	_____
42	_____	43	_____	44	_____	36	_____	45	_____
Total Ib = _____		Cb = _____		Abf = _____		If = _____		Cf = _____	
Scale Score ÷ 6 = _____		÷ 6 = _____		÷ 6 = _____		÷ 6 = _____		÷ 6 = _____	

FIGURE 2. Form for Interpreting MATE scores.

Wife's Form

I want my husband to:

	I Inclusion	C Control	Abf Affection		Ib + Cb + Abf
B Behavior	3 to 6 — [ ]	2 to 5 — [ ]	3 to 6 — [ ]	8 to 17 — [ ]	How he relates to me (R)
F Feelings	3 to 6 — [ ]	2 to 5 — [ ]		8 to 17 — [ ]	If + Cf + Abf How he feels about me (F)
	6 to 12 — [ ] More Interest (MI)	4 to 10 — [ ] More Confidence (MC)		13 to 28 — [ ]	Ib + Cb + Abf + If + Cf Dissatisfaction (D)

My husband wants me to:

	I Inclusion	C Control	Abf Affection		Ib + Cb + Abf
B Behavior	2 to 5 — [ ]	2 to 5 — [ ]	3 to 6 — [ ]	7 to 16 — [ ]	How I relate to him. (R)
F Feelings	2 to 5 — [ ]	2 to 5 — [ ]		7 to 16 — [ ]	If + Cf + Abf How I feel about him. (F)
	4 to 16 — [ ] More Interest (MI)	4 to 10 — [ ] More Confidence (MC)		11 to 26 — [ ]	Ib + Cb + Abf + If + Cf Dissatisfaction (D)

FIGURE 2. (continued)

Husband's Form

I want my wife to:

	I	C	Abf	Ib + Cb + Abf	
B Behavior	2 to 5 — [ ]	2 to 5 — [ ]	2 to 5 — [ ]	6 to 15 — [ ]	How she relates to me. (R)
F Feelings	2 to 5 — [ ]	2 to 5 — [ ]		6 to 15 — [ ]	How she feels about me. (F)
	4 to 10 — [ ] More Interest (MI)	4 to 10 — [ ] More Confidence (MC)		10 to 25 — [ ]	Ib + Cb + Abf + If + Cf Dissatisfaction (D)

My wife wants me to:

	I Inclusion	C Control	Abf Affection	If + Cf + Abf	
B Behavior	3 to 6 — [ ]	2 to 5 — [ ]	3 to 6 — [ ]	8 to 17 — [ ]	How I relate to her. (R)
F Feelings	3 to 6 — [ ]	2 to 5 — [ ]		8 to 17 — [ ]	How I feel toward her. (F)
	6 to 12 — [ ] More Interest (MI)	4 to 10 — [ ] More Confidence (MC)		13 to 28 — [ ]	Ib + Cb + Abf + If + Cf Dissatisfaction (D)

Interpreting: In addition to the five cell scores that represent what the respondent wants and the five scores that represent what the respondent thinks his or her spouse wants, there are some summary scores that may give an overview of some patterns in the relationship. To illustrate the calculation of the indices, Glen and Shirley's scores are shown in Table 3 and 4.

Five summary scores obtainable from one person's sheet are:

Dissatisfaction (D) Dissatisfaction over *not enough* attention, freedom, and love, from one's spouse reflected by high scores (above 25 for husbands) on the Dissatisfaction index. Low scores (below 10) are ambiguous. They may mean he is happy or he is getting too much attention, freedom, and love. This index is calculated by summing the five cells:

$$D = \text{Sum of five cell scores}$$
which for Glen yields
$$D = 3+8+3+3+4 = 21 \ (10 \ to \ 25) \ average$$

How she relates to me (R). A high score (above 15 for men) on this index means the husband wants more attention, freedom, and affectionate behavior from his wife; a low score (below 6) means either he is getting too much of these things from her or he is satisfied with her behavior. "R" is calculated by summing the three behavior cells (Ib, Cb, Abf) across the B row:

$$R = Ib + Cb + Abf$$
which for Glen yields
$$R = 3+8+3 = 14 \ (6 \ to \ 15)$$
which is average

How she feels about me (F). A high score (above 15 for men) means the husband wants his wife to feel more interest, respect, and love toward him; a low score (less than 6) indicates he certainly does not need more positive feelings from his wife. "How she feels about me" is calculated by adding the two cells in the "F" row (If and Cf) with Abf.

$$F = If + Cf + Abf$$
which for Glen yields
$$F = 3+4+3 = 10$$
which is average (i.e., within 6 to 15)

Table 3. **Glen's Scores**

I want Shirley to:

	I Inclusion	C Control	Abf Affection		
B Behavior	2 to 5 3 [ ]	2 to 5 8 [H]	2 to 5 3 [ ]	6 to 15 14 [ ]	How she relates to me (R)
F Feelings	2 to 5 3 [ ]	2 to 5 4 [ ]		6 to 15 10 [ ]	How she feels about me. (F)
	4 to 10 6 [ ] More Interest (MI)	4 to 10 12 [H] More Confidence (MC)		10 to 25 21 [ ]	Dissatisfaction (D)

Shirley wants me to:

	I Inclusion	C Control	Abf Affection		
B Behavior	3 to 6 7 [H]	2 to 5 3 [ ]	3 to 6 7 [H]	8 to 17 17 [MH]	How I relate to her (R)
F Feelings	3 to 6 6 [MH]	2 to 5 3 [ ]		8 to 17 16 [ ]	How I feel about her. (F)
	6 to 12 13 [H] More Interest (MI)	4 to 10 6 [ ] More Confidence (MC)		13 to 28 26 [ ]	Dissatisfaction (D)

Table 4. Shirley's Scores

I want Glen to:

	I Inclusion	C Control	Abf Affection		
B Behavior	3 to 6 2 [L]	2 to 5 3 [ ]	2 to 6 2 [ML]	8 to 17 7 [L]	How he relates to me. (R)
F Feelings	3 to 6 2 [L]	2 to 5 2 [ML]		8 to 17 6 [L]	How he feels about me. (F)
	6 to 12 4 [L] More Interest (MI)	4 to 10 5 [ ] More Confidence (MC)		13 to 28 11 [L]	Dissatisfaction (D)

Glen wants me to:

	I Inclusion	C Control	Abf Affection		
B Behavior	2 to 5 4 [ ]	2 to 5 2 [ML]	3 to 6 5 [ ]	7 to 16 11 [ ]	How I relate to him. (R)
F Feelings	2 to 5 3 [ ]	2 to 5 2 [ML]		7 to 11 10 [ ]	How I feel about him (F)
	4 to 10 7 [ ] More Interest (MI)	4 to 10 4 [ML] More Confidence (MC)		11 to 26 16 [ ]	Dissatisfaction (D)

More Interest (MI). A high score (above 10 for men) indicates that he feels he is not getting sufficient interest from his wife; a low score (below 4) indicates strong denial that he is not getting enough attention (he may be getting too much attention from her, or just enough). "More Interest" is calculated by adding the "I" column.

$$MI = Ib + If$$
which for Glen yields
$$MI = 3+3 = 6$$
which is average (between 4 and 10)

More Confidence (MC). A high score (above 10 for men) indicates that his wife does not have enough confidence in him and does not give him enough freedom to think for himself. A low score (below 4) means his wife gives him all the freedom and confidence he wants (and perhaps more than he wants). "More Confidence" is calculated by adding up the numbers in the "C" column.

$$MC = Cb + Cf$$
which for Glen yields
$$MC = 8+4 = 12$$
which is high (i.e., above 10)

The above five indices can be calculated for each of the four clusters, yielding twenty summary scores. Figure 2 which contains the form for organizing scores makes it easy to calculate the summary indices.

Summary Scores — Interpersonal

Comparisons between clusters may be informative. Perhaps the most informative comparisons are between the man's "my wife wants" and his wife's "I want" and between the woman's "my husband wants" and her husband's "I want." Looking at Glen's "My wife wants" and Shirley's "I want" score we see an extreme example of failure to communicate. Glen is convinced that Shirley wants his attention, interest, and love. Shirley is quite content with the attention and interest he shows her; she may even be getting more than she wants.

Similarly looking at Shirley's "My husband wants" and Glen's "I want" scores regarding control issues, Shirley thinks that Glen has no need for more freedom, but rather is unusually happy with the freedom and respect he is getting from her. In fact, Glen seems to want Shirley to give him more freedom than she is giving.

The difference between Glen and Shirley's scores are more marked than usual and reflect a serious communication gap; even less extreme differences may prove to be informative when discussed by a husband and wife.

SCALE OF FEELINGS AND BEHAVIOR OF LOVE

Clifford H. Swenson
Frank Gilner

DESCRIPTION

Length: 120 items

Time: *Administering* about twenty minutes
      Scoring   five to ten minutes

Scales:

Verbal Expression
Self-Disclosure
Tolerance
Support (Non-Material Evidence)
Support (Material Evidence)
Feelings (Not Expressed Verbally)

The *Love Scale* is a measure of the patterns of behavior and feelings people exhibit and experience in their relationships (relationships between two people) as an indirect measure of "love."

The 120 test items are divided into six subscales developed through repeated factor analysis. The subscales are:

Verbal expression of affection.

    Sample statement:
      You tell the loved one that you have a warm, happy feeling when you are with him (her).
        a) You never tell him (her) this.
        b) You occasionally tell him (her) this.
        c) You frequently tell him (her) this.

Self-disclosure.

    Sample statement:
      The loved one tells you what his (her) chief health concern, worry, or problem is at the present time.
        a) He (she) never tells you this.
        b) He (she) occasionally tells you this.
        c) He (she) frequently tells you this.

Toleration of the less pleasant aspects (of the loved person).

    Sample statement:
> *You tell the loved one whether or not you have sex problems and the nature of these problems.*
>> *a) You* never *tell him (her) this.*
>> *b) You* occasionally *tell him (her) this.*
>> *c) You* frequently *tell him (her) this.*

Non-material evidence — support, encouragement.

Feelings not expressed verbally (to the loved person).

Material evidence — gifts, financial support, chores performed.

Uses: Given within a group, the *Love Scale* can give insight into individual differences of group members in each of the six aspects (subscales) of the scale as concerns their relationships with other group members.

Positive Features: One of the positive features of the *Love Scale* is that it measures individual differences in six aspects of love relationships. It would be a good instrument to use within groups because it would make the group members aware of these individual differences as they affect relationships between group members.

    The Love Scale is self-administering, easy to score, and simple to interpret.

ORDERING

Where To Order: For the instrument:
University Associates
Box 615
Iowa City, Iowa
Phone: (319) 351-7322

For the Manual:
Prof. C. H. Swenson
Dept. of Psychological Sciences
Purdue University
Lafayette, IN. 47907
Phone: (317) 749-8111

Cost: 25 tests $12.55 $2.00

ADMINISTERING, SCORING, AND INTERPRETING

Administering: The respondant should be instructed to fill out the scale for a specific relationship as it exists at the present time.

Scoring: The scale is scored by adding the numbers of the choices made by the respondents to each item in a subscale. The lowest score possible for each item is "1" and the highest score possible for an item is "3."

THE MARRIAGE-PREDICTION SCHEDULE

E. W. Burgess
Leonard S. Cottrell

DESCRIPTION

Length: Part I   seventeen multiple choice questions.

Part II   twenty-one traits on which the subject rates himself, his (her) fiance (e), father and mother.

Part III   twelve multiple choice questions

Part IV   fifteen multiple choice and one rating with eleven sub-divisions for which the subject rates the fiance (e).

Part V   nine multiple choice items.

Time: *Administering:*   thirty minutes
       Scoring: five minutes

Scale:

Marriage Prediction

Selected background items significantly associated with marital adjustment were combined into an expectancy table for premarital prediction of success in marriage.

Sample statements: (weighting in parenthesis)
Part I:
(1) *What is your present state of health?*
     chronic ill-health _____ (4)
     temporary ill-health _____ (5)
     average health _____ (6)
     healthy _____ (7)
     very healthy _____ (8)

Part II: *Trait:*	*very much* *so*	*consid-* *erably*	*some-* *what*	*a* *little*	*not* *at all*
Angers easily	(4)	(5)	(6)	(7)	(8)

Part III:
(9) *Give the attitude of your father and mother toward your marriage*
     both approve _____ (8)
     both disapprove _____ (4)
     one disapproves:
         your father _____ (4)
         your mother _____ (4)

Part IV:
(6) Who generally takes the initiative in the demonstration of affection:
     mutual   _____ *(8)*
     you   _____ *(5)*
     your fiance(e)   _____ *(5)*

Part V:
(8) How many children would you like to have?
     four or more   _____ *(8)*
     three   _____ *(7)*
     two   _____ *(6)*
     one   _____ *(5)*
     none   _____ *(4)*

Uses: The marriage prediction schedule is used in assessing the probabilities of engaged couples being able to establish happy marital adjustment.

The instrument can be used as diagnostic tool in assessing social areas where difficulties exist in close interpersonal relationships, such as engagement and marriage, and in studying adjustment within interpersonal relationships to new situations. Responses to individual questions may indicate disagreement about how the marriage may be or a partner is. Even when there is agreement about questions, both may be agreeing that their marriage situation may be bad.

Concerns: There are no reliability or validity measures given for *The Marriage Prediction Schedule.* Also, as stated before, the prediction does not apply directly to the individual, but gives the statistical probabilities of marital success for a group of which the individual is a member.

ORDERING

Where To Order: The instrument is located in Burgess, E.W. and Locke, H.J. *The Family* New York: Van Nostrand Reinhold, 1971.
     Van Nostrand Reinhold Company
     450 W. 33rd Street
     New York, New York 10001
     Phone: (212) 594-8660

Cost: $10.50

ADMINISTERING, SCORING AND INTERPRETING

Scoring: The two-digit numbers after each subdivision provide the code for scoring. The score value of each response is obtained by adding the two digits in the number that is a subscript of the response that has been checked.

For each item, enter the two-digit number that appears as a subscript of the answer to each question in column 1 at the right-hand side of each page. In Part Two place only the score for the Fiance (e) in the blank on the right-hand margin.

Enter the sum of the two digits appearing in column one for each item in column two. For each part of the questionnaire, compute the total of the values appearing in column two and enter that figure in the spaces provided at the end of the section.

Enter the total score for each part in the spaces provided at the end of the questionnaire.

Interpreting: High scores on *The Marriage Prediction Schedule,* (those above 630) are favorable for marital adjustment, as indicated by research findings.

Low scores (those below 567) are much less favorable for happiness in marriage.

The prediction does not apply directly to the individual; it states the statistical probabilities of marital success for the group of persons of which that individual is a part. In the majority of cases, the specific matrimonial risk of a couple may be roughly estimated from the two general matrimonial-risk groups to which the two persons are assigned. One average of the two scores will generally be close to what may be expected from a specific matrimonial-risk group assignment.

REFERENCES

Burgess, E.W. and Cottrell, L.S.: *Predicting Success or Failure in Marriage,* Prentice-Hall, 1939, cf.

Huruitz, Nathan; The measurement of marital strain, *American Journal of Sociology,* May 1960, 65; 610-15.

Burgess, E.W. and Wallin, P: *Engagement and Marriage,* J.B. Lippincott, 1953.

THE MARRIAGE-ADJUSTMENT SCHEDULE

E. W. Burgess
Leonard S. Cottrell

DESCRIPTION

Length: Part I consists of thirty-six questions of which thirty-four are multiple choice and two are ratings.

Part II consists of fifty-seven items for which there are four ratings.

Time: *Administering* thirty minutes

Scoring five minutes

Scale:

Marriage Adjustment

Marital adjustment was defined as agreement between husband and wife upon matters that might be made critical issues; common interests and joint activites; frequent overt demonstrations of affection and mutual confidence; few complaints; and few reports of feeling lonely, miserable, and irritable.

Sample statements: (weighting in parenthesis)
Part I:
To what extent were you in love with your spouse before marriage?

"head over heels" _____ (8)

very much _____ (7)

somewhat _____ (5)

a little _____ (4)

not at all _____ (4)

Uses: The marriage-adjustment schedule is for married couples. It can be used as a diagnostic instrument to help the marriage counselor detect the social areas where difficulties exist. The researcher may use it to assess new relationships such as the role of parent-child relations and marital adjustment.

There are a number of questions on which a couple may disagree. There are many others that indicate problems whether they agree or not.

Positive Features: Each form may be completed in approximately thirty minutes. The measures may be used for both research and counseling purposes.

ORDERING

Where To Order: The scale is located in Burgess, E.W. and Locke, H.J. *The Family* New York: Van Nostrand Reinhold, 1971.

> Van Nostrand Reinhold Company
> 450 W. 33rd Street
> New York, New York 10001
> Phone: (212) 594-8660

Cost: $10.50

ADMINISTERING, SCORING AND INTERPRETING

Interpreting: In evaluating the total score, see the following table:

Marital Adjustment Scores	Adjustment in Marriage
720 and over	extremely well-adjusted
700 to 719	decidedly well-adjusted
680 to 699	fairly adjusted
660 to 679	somewhat adjusted
640 to 659	indifferently adjusted
620 to 639	somewhat unadjusted
600 to 619	unadjusted
580 to 599	decidedly unadjusted
579 and under	extremely unadjusted

REFERENCES

See the section in *The Marriage Prediction Schedule* description.

LIFE INTERPERSONAL
HISTORY ENQUIRY

William C. Schutz

Length: 108 statements (nine each of twelve scales)

Time: *Administering* twelve to twenty minutes
      Scoring   six to fifteen minutes

Scales:

Inclusion (Behavior) (Father)	*Affection (Behavior/Feelings)*
Inclusion (Behavior) (Mother)	*(Father)*
Control (Behavior) (Father)	*Affection (Behavior/Feelings)*
Control (Behavior) (Mother)	*(Mother)*
Inclusion (Feelings) (Father)	*Parental Approval (Perceived)*
Inclusion (Feelings) (Mother)	*(Father)*
Control (Feelings) (Father)	*Parental Approval (Perceived)*
Control (Feelings) (Mother)	*(Mother)*

LIPHE (pronounced "Life") asks the respondent to react to statements that might describe his relations with his father and mother when he was about six years old. As with other *FIRO* instruments, the three main areas of inquiry are *inclusion, control,* and *affection* relations, examining both feelings and behavior. Note that this instrument measures only behavior and feelings *wanted from* parents. It does not measure behavior and feelings *expressed toward* parents. The *LIPHE* focus is on the child's needs that were not met by his parents (ten scales), for example, "I wanted my father to feel more affection for me," and perceived parental expectations (two scales), for example, "My mother wanted me to be more sociable."

The twelve *LIPHE* scales can be seen in the table below.

Table 1. Description of twelve scales

Father	I **Inclusion**	C **Control**	Abf **Affection**
B Behavior	I wanted my father to spend more time with me.	I wanted my father to allow me more freedom.	I wanted my father to share and feel more love for me.
F Feelings	I wanted my father to be more interested in me.	I wanted my father to have more respect for me.	My father wanted me to be a better person.

ICA
Parental Approval

Mother	I Inclusion	C Control	Abf Affection
B Behavior	I wanted my mother to spend more time with me.	I wanted my mother to allow me more freedom.	I wanted my mother to feel more love for me.
F Feelings	I wanted my mother to be more interested in me.	I wanted my mother to have more respect for me.	My mother wanted me to be a better person.

ICA
Parental Approval

Table 2. (with responses that are counted in parentheses):

Father — I wanted my father to...

	I Inclusion	C Control	Abf Affection
B Behavior	Play with me more (tends to be true, true, especially true).	Allow me to think more for myself (tends to be true, true, especially true).	Treat me in a warmer and friendlier manner (true, especially true).
F Feelings	Feel more attached to me (true, especially true).	Have more confidence in my ability to take care of myself (tends to be true, true, especially true).	My father wanted me to get better grades in school (true, especially true).

ICA
Parental Approval

The statements for mother are essentially the same as those described for father.

Uses: In group therapy or where it seems appropriate in a human relations group, the instrument may facilitate member's focussing on early childhood sources of current, interpersonal difficulties. Transference behavior could be more easily and more confidently identified if the member's scores indicate that he had similar behavior patterns with his parents.

Even if a group is committed to a here-and-now focus, occasions arise when group behavior of a member indicates that he is reacting to someone in the group as a parental figure. He could be given *LIPHE* to complete during a break, and his scores could be used to help him understand his current behavior and feelings.

A third use of *LIPHE* is with family laboratory or therapy groups. Both parents could complete the *LIPHE* as they think one of their children (specifying which one) would complete it. They could also complete it as their estimate of the average of their children's responses.

Positive Features: It is possible that one of the drawbacks of retrospective tests can be an advantage: the possibility of distortion in trying to remember events when the respondent was six years old. Distortions that people impose on their recollection may represent wishes or justifications for current conditions; whatever they represent, they may be a vehicle for the person to indicate concerns about himself. It may well be that a person's memory of his childhood is really a more meaningful insight-producer than the actual childhood events.

Secondly, the *LIPHE* scales have the advantage of giving twelve scales for within-instrument comparison. Various discrepancies among the twelve scales—between father and mother, between their behavior and their feelings, between the respondent's perception of what he wanted from his parents and his perception of what they expected of him—may be useful in understanding the respondent's behavior and feelings in the present.

Concerns: One problem with *LIPHE* not encountered in *FIRO-B* or *FIRO-F* is its length. The fact that *LIPHE* has 108 statements places it in the moderately-long instrument category. Although it is not as long as the *MMPI* or some other instruments (500 statements or more), it is long enough to begin creating some hardship in completing it. However, as indicated in the "Time" section, fifteen minutes is usually sufficient for completing *LIPHE*.

There is some information in the *LIPHE* section of the manual that might be confusing to a user. Never developed are six scales that were to deal with behavior and feelings of the father toward the mother in the three areas of inclusion, control, and affection, plus six scales that were to deal with the behavior and feelings of the mother toward the father. Furthermore, there is mention of four other scales that do not seem to exist or have other names. Other than the slight confusion created by the description of scales that do not exist, there is no substantial problem regarding the administration or interpretation of *LIPHE*.

Perhaps the major drawback with LIPHE is that it seems less relevant to the kind of issues dealt with in human relation groups than FIRO-B or FIRO-F. Its focus on early childhood runs counter to the human relations norm of dealing with here-and-now behavior, feelings, and issues. Of course, adherence to this particular human relations norm varies with the setting and facilitator.

ORDERING

Where To Order: Consulting Psychologists Press
577 College Avenue
Palo Alto, California 94306
Phone: (415) 326-4448

Cost:		
Specimen Set		$ 4.75
Manual		$ 3.00
Set of Keys		$ 1.50
Packages of Tests	25 tests	$ 3.25

ADMINISTERING, SCORING, AND INTERPRETING

Administering: Use the design for administering *FIRO-B* or *F*.

Scoring: Templates are available for the twelve *LIPHE* scales. See the section for scoring the *FIRO-B* scale for detailed comments on group and individual scoring.

Interpreting: Some summary scores from the LIPHE instrument are as follows. The average adult score range is given at the top of the cells and summary scores in the margins. For illustrative purposes, Dave's scores have been placed in the cells below the average range, with an indication of whether his score is higher or lower than average. Both the "Wanted Fellowship" and "Wanted Liking" summary scores include the ABF cell (upper right hand corner of the box).

Table 3. Dave's Scores

Father

	I Inclusion	C Control	Abf Affection		
B Behavior	2 to 6 7 [H]	2 to 6 6 [MH]	2 to 6 7 [H]	6 to 18 20 [H]	Wanted fellowship from father.
F Feelings	2 to 6 7 [H]	2 to 6 5 [M]	2 to 6 8 [H]	6 to 18 19 [H]	Wanted liking from father.
	4 to 12 14 [H] Be more interested in me.	4 to 12 11 [MH] Have more confidence in me.	ICA		

Mother

	I Inclusion	C Control	Abf Affection		
B Behavior	2 to 6 8 [H]	2 to 6 7 [H]	2 to 6 2 [ML]	6 to 18 17 [MH]	Wanted fellowship from mother.
F Feelings	2 to 6 5 [M]	2 to 6 5 [M]	2 to 6 3 [ML]	6 to 18	Wanted liking from mother.
	4 to 12 13 [H] Be more interested in me.	4 to 12 12 [MH] Have more confidence in me.	ICA		

Since the variability of *LIPHE* scales was greater than for the *FIRO-B* and *FIRO-F* scales, an interval of 2.0 above and below average was selected to bracket the normative average score.

Indices similar to those developed for *FIRO-B* and *FIRO-F* can be developed for LIPHE. A few will be described for illustrative purposes.

Wanted Fellowships from Father (WFFF) =
WFFF = IB + CB + ABF
which for Dave equals
WFFF = 7 + 6 + 7 = 20   (6 to 18) H

Wanted Liking from Father (WLFF) =
WLFF = IF + CF + ABF
which for Dave equals
WLFF = 7 + 5 + 7 = 19   (6 to 18) H

Parental Pressure (PP) =
    Father Mother
    PP = ICA + ICA
    which for Dave equals
    PP = 8 + 3 = 11   (4 to 12)

The general conclusion one can draw from Dave's scores on *LIPHE* is that, in general, he was more dissatisfied with his childhood than the average person (assuming, of course, that everyone (average person and Dave) is being honest). His parents tended to spend less time with him and seemed to be less interested in him than he would have liked.

THE FAMILY SCALE

E. A. Rundquist
R. F. Sletto

DESCRIPTION

Length: twenty-one statements, one response to each statement

Time: *Administering* five minutes
      Scoring   four minutes

Scale:

Attitude Toward Family

One scale is being measured: favorability of attitude toward the family. It is designed to reflect family tensions.

Sample statements:
> *One ought to discuss important plans with the members of his family.*
> *(Favorable Attitude)*
> *Parents too often expect their grown-up children to obey them.*
> *(Unfavorable Attitude)*

To each statement the respondent chooses from the usual five Likert-type responses ranging from "Strongly Agree" to "Strongly Disagree."

ORDERING

Where To Order: The scale is located in Shaw, M.E., and Wright, J.M. *Scales for the Measurement of Attitudes.* New York: McGraw-Hill, 1967.
> McGraw-Hill Book Company
> 1121 Avenue of the Americas
> New York, N.Y. 10020
> Phone: (212) 997-1221

Cost: $17.80

REFERENCES

Rundquist, E.A., and Sletto, R.F. *Personality in the Depression.* Minneapolis: University of Minnesota Press, 1936.

FAMILY ADJUSTMENT TEST

Gabriel Elias

DIRECTIONS

Length: 114 statements

Time: *Administering* thirty to thirty-five minutes
    Scoring   fifteen to twenty minutes

Scale:

Intra-Family Homeyness-Homelessness

Intra-Family Homeyness-Homelessness

Feelings of homeyness are considered central to interpersonal and personal adjustment. Homey feelings are positive, they are full of warmth, love, and harmony. Homeless feelings are negative, cold, hateful, loveless, and full of friction.

There are ten sub-tests in the *FAT* but the author recommends that it is usually unprofitable to obtain separate scores for them because they correlate so highly with each other.

The subtests are: Attitude toward Mother
                   Attitude toward Father
                   Father-Mother Attitude Quotient
                   Oedipal
                   Struggle for Independence
                   Parent Child Friction-Harmony
                   Interparental Friction-Harmony
                   Family Inferiority-Superiority
                   Rejection of Child, Parental Qualities

Concerns: It is a long instrument for obtaining a single score.

ORDERING

Where To Order: Psychometric Affiliates
                      Box 3167
                      Munster, Indiana 46321
                      Phone: (219) 836-1661

Cost: *Specimen Set* $1.00
       25 Tests $5.00

SECTION B
Instruments with an Interpersonal Focus

Group Dynamics

HILL INTERACTION MATRIX-B

Wm. Fawcett Hill

DESCRIPTION

Length: sixty-four statements (four in each subscale)

Time: *Administering* fifteen to twenty minutes
Scoring fifteen to twenty minutes

Scales:

> *Personal Interaction Content (Topic, Group, Personal, or Relationship)*
> *Personal Interaction Style (Conventional, Assertive, Speculative, or Confrontive)*
> *Total Acceptance Score*
> *Risk Ratio*

HIM-B gives a person sixteen scores, one for each of the cells in the interaction matrix. The matrix results from the intersection of two dimensions (see Table 1). The first dimension, *CONTENT*, contains four categories of increasing growth potential: I. Topic, II. Group, III. Personal, and IV. Relationship. *Topic* refers to the focus on general interest topics, things other than the group, the people in it, or the relationships among them. *Group* refers to focus on group processes and dynamics. *Personal* concerns focusing on one's own or another's personal problems and growth concerns. *Relationship* focuses on events and feelings that have occurred or exist between people in the group.

The second dimension of the matrix is *STYLE*. It contains four categories in ascending order of willingness to take a facilitative. or therapist role and risk interpersonal threat. They are: Category A, *Responsive*, indicates a style wherein members initiate no interaction but wait for the leader or therapist to ask questions and then give minimal answers. It is not scored in *HIM-B* and is usually found only in groups of persons who are retarded, severely disturbed, or antisocial.

Category B, *Conventional*, marked by "chit-chat," gossip, planning functions, and in general "Putting one's best foot forward." Category C, *Assertive*, discussion that is of a dominating or challenging nature. Help is neither sought nor accepted. Category D, *Speculative*, members ask questions or "speculate" about what is causing problems in life, the group, some member, or a relationship, and what might be done about them. Category E, *Confrontive*, a person gives his personal reaction regarding some topic: the group, someone else, himself, or a relationship. The intent is to make someone (himself included) pause and reconsider his behavior.

Table 1. Hill Interaction Matrix.

Statements in the cells are from the content analysis scoring manual.

Content Categories

		Non-member Centered		Member Centered	
		Topics I	**Group** II	**Personal** III	**Relationship** IV
Pre-Work	Conventional (B)	1* Where did you buy that tie pin?	2 Let's bring our coffee to the meetings from now on.	9 What are your plans for next year?	10 You look pretty in that dress.
Pre-Work	Assertive (C)	3 The girls on this campus act as if they are Cleopatras. I'm sick of it!	4 This group is getting no-where!	11 What did you expect her to do...thank you!	12 If you hate me, come out and say so!
Work	Speculative (D)	5 Do you think that religion helps more people than it hurts?	6 Why do you think this is a good group?	13 Were you a good student in school?	14 I think you are reserved, very hard to know.
Work	Confrontive (E)	7 It sounds as though in de-manding love from others we become unlov-able.	8 We are avoid-ing talking about Helen's death, Frank's homosexuality and Joe's rejection of Tom.	15 I give people the impression I am hiding something. What do I do?	16 Ben, I'd like to know what I do that makes you fear or hate me.

STYLE CATEGORIES

*Numbers in the cells indicate the potential of that behavior for personal growth.

Behavior that is considered growth-inducing is found toward the lower right hand corner of the matrix (Cells III-D, IV-D, III-E, and IV-E).

The order of increasing growthful orientation begins with the first two columns (Topic and Group content) and proceeds down the columns going from Conventional interaction through Confrontation. The cells in the next two columns (Personal and Relationship) are taken and, again, statements move from Conventional down to Confrontation. Thus, Hill assumes that confrontation about what the group issues is less therapeutic or growth-inducing than even conventional conversation about personal matters or relationships in the group.

The instructions ask the person to consider his behavior in a group he is in already or might enter (therapy group, group course, human relations group). After each statement he responds by marking a number on an answer sheet that corresponds to:

1	2	3	4	5	6
Usually	Often	Sometimes	Occasionally	Rarely	Never
1	2	3	4	5	6
Most People	Many People	Some People	Few People	One or Two People	Nobody

Sample statements are shown in Table 2.

Uses: *HIM-B* has been used as a screening device to exclude people whose Total Acceptance Score (overall total) is below 50 or 40 as being likely to hurt group process much more than they would help it. Discussion of the *HIM-B* can make participants aware of different kinds of interaction in which they may engage. Hopefully, such awareness can help them move toward the more growth-inducing cells. Posting *HIM-B* scores may facilitate confrontation of persons who use an assertive style in an effort to appear open and confrontive.

Positive Features: The primary positive feature of the *HIM-B* is the matrix itself. The matrix has a number of features that participants in therapy and human relations groups should be aware of:

1. Total acceptance level indicates your willingness to relate to people in general.
2. There is a work and non-work way to talk about things.
3. There is a distinction between being assertive and being confrontive.
4. Playing the speculation game is a low-risk procedure.
5. One's own and other members' statements are legitimate material for analysis and categorization.
6. Finally, the matrix as a whole gives the members a structure to use in mapping what goes on in the group.

Concerns: *HIM-B* is cumbersome to score. High *HIM-B* scores could mean either high involvement with people, the tendency to agree with statements (acquiescent response), or position response set (always checking left-hand column). Completing the instrument and learning about the matrix could make participants too self-conscious about their interaction style.

Table 2. Sample Statements

Content Categories

		Non-member Centered		Member Centered	
		Topics I	Group II	Personal III	Relationship IV
Pre-Work	Conventional (B)	1* I like to chat with people. (Most people, Many people).	2 I help plan a group's activ- ities. (usually, often).	9 I'm interested in people. (Usually, Often).	10 I try to support and encourage other people. (Most people, Many people).
STYLE CATEGORIES	Assertive (C)	3 Even though my ideas are un- popular, I tend to uphold them (Usually, Often, Sometimes).	4 I disagree with the way groups tend to operate (Usually, Often).	11 I side in with people who say they are getting a raw deal. (Most people, Many people, Some people, Few people).	12 I make fun of people. (Usual- ly, Often, Some- times, Occa- sionally).
Work	Speculative (D)	5 I like to dis- cuss what causes various kinds of emotional up- sets and mental illnesses. (Usually).	6 I offer sugges- tions as to how a group might improve its functioning. (Usually, Often, Sometimes).	13 I like for others to help me understand my- self. (Usually, Often, Some- times, Occa- sionally).	14 When I tell people how I react to them I try to do so but in a way that doesn't hurt their feelings. (Usually, Often, Sometimes).
	Confrontive (E)	7 I try to get peo- ple to discuss the kinds of de- fenses and psy- chological principles that their behavior illustrates. (Usually, Often).	8 If conflicting goals are foul- ing up a group I will point this out. (Usually, Often, Sometimes).	15 I point out dis- crepancies or contradictions between peo- ples behavior and what they say they are like. (Usually, Often, Sometimes).	16 It is my respon- sibility to give group members an honest statement of how I react to them even if it may hurt their feelings. (Usually, Often, Sometimes).

HIM-A: As indicated earlier, *HIM-A* is the same as *HIM-B* except that the wording of *HIM-A* is easier than the wording of *HIM-B*. For example, the *HIM-B* statement, "I tell other people specifically what kinds of reactions I have toward them when they ask me." becomes in *HIM-A* "I tell other people exactly what kind of feelings I have to- ward them when they ask me." The scoring of *HIM-A* is identical to *HIM-B*.

ORDERING

Where To Order: Youth Studies Center
University of Southern California
Los Angeles, California 90007
Phone: (213) 746-6292

Cost: There are no separate test manuals or keys. They must be reproduced by you. The *HIM-A*, *HIM-B*, and *HIM-G* are described in:

Hill, W. F. *Hill Interaction Matrix (HIM) Supplement, HIM Test Manual*. Los Angeles: Youth Studies Center, University of Southern California, 1969. $1.50
Briefly summarizes the *HIM* content and style dimensions and then describes in detail *HIM-G*, *HIM-A*, and *HIM-B*. The statements in all three instruments, the scoring keys, and some interpretational indices are presented.

Hill, W. F. *Hill Interaction Matrix (HIM) Monograph. — revised*. Los Angeles: Youth Studies Center, University of Southern California, 1963. $2.50
Sets out rationale, development, reliability, validity of *HIM* categories with focus on use of the sixteen-cell matrix for statement coding of group interaction. It contains a chapter on *HIM-B*, the self-report instrument emphasized here, with a listing of the statements in it. (No scoring key.)

Hill, W. F. *Hill Interaction Matrix (HIM) Scoring Manual*. Los Angeles: Youth Studies Center, University of Southern California, 1963. $1.50
Contains coding categories for the content analysis category system; it is useful for understanding the theory and value assumptions underlying *HIM-B* and *HIM-G*.

HIM Training Film: Purchase Price $65.00
HIM Training Film: Rental Price   6.00
The film is a "low-budget" production that appears to use non-professional actors, but it is still a useful way to familiarize people with the matrix.

ADMINISTERING, SCORING, AND INTERPRETING

Administering:

1. Reproduce (Xerox, mimeograph, ditto) instruction page, statement pages and an answer sheet.

2. Distribute the *HIM-B* or *HIM-A* booklet of statements and answer sheets.

3. Read the instructions out loud. Emphasize that the questions are to be answered in terms of a counseling, interpersonal growth, encounter, sensitivity training, or therapy group, not in terms of every day life.

4. When they are finished, give a short lecture on the Hill interaction matrix. (Describe the eight categories and sixteen cells.)

5. Ask the participants to guess on which of the eight categories they scored high or low.

6. Distribute the scoring key (Table 3) and the scoring aid (Table 4).

Table 3 Scoring Key for HIM-B (or HIM-A)

INSTRUCTIONS: Column one indicates the statement number. Column two indicates the cut-off level. Count the response if it is equal to or less than the number in column two. Column three indicates the cell number to be scored.

Page 1			Page 4			Page 7		
1	2	IIIB	25	2	IIB	49	2	IVB
2	4	IVE	26	2	IB	50	2	IE
3	2	ID	27	2	IC	51	2	IC
4	2	IIIC	28	4	IE	52	2	IID
----			----			----		
5	2	IVD	29	1	ID	53	3	IVD
6	3	ID	30	4	IID	54	2	ID
7	4	IVC	31	2	IIID	55	3	IIIC
8	2	IIE	32	2	IIIC	56	2	IIIC

Page 2			Page 5			Page 8		
9	3	IIB	33	3	IE	57	3	IC
10	4	IVC	34	4	IIE	58	2	IVB
11	2	IVB	35	3	IIIE	59	3	IIIC
12	2	IIIE	36	4	IIID	60	2	IID
----			----			----		
13	3	IC	37	2	IIB	61	1	IVD
14	3	IIC	38	3	IVB	62	3	IIIE
15	2	IIIB	39	2	IIC	63	2	IB
16	4	IVC	40	3	IVC	64	2	IIIB

Page 3			Page 6		
17	3	IID	41	2	IIIB
18	2	IIID	42	3	IVE
19	3	IIB	43	4	IIID
20	4	IIC	44	3	IVD
----			----		
21	3	IIE	45	2	IE
22	3	IIC	46	4	IIE
23	4	IVE	47	1	IVE
24	3	IB	48	2	IB

Table 4. Hill Interaction Matrix (HIM-B) Scoring Aid.
It contains 1) a place to write in the weight if the response qualified to make that statement counted; 2) a place to total the scores for each cell and category; 3) a place to indicate that the score is high or low (H, MH, ML, L); and 4) the average range to be used for making the decision about high or low.

	I General Interest	II Group	III Personal	IV Relationship	Row Total
B Conventional	24. ___ (1) 26. ___ (3) 48. ___ (4) 63. ___ (2)	9. ___ (2) 19. ___ (1) 25. ___ (3) 37. ___ (4)	1. ___ (4) 15. ___ (3) 41. ___ (1) 64. ___ (2)	11. ___ (3) 38. ___ (1) 49. ___ (2) 58. ___ (4)	B
Total	___ [ ] 3 to 6	___ [ ] 3 to 6	___ [ ] 4 to 7	___ [ ] 4 to 7	Total ___ [ ] 14 to 26
C Assertive	13. ___ (1) 27. ___ (4) 51. ___ (3) 57. ___ (2)	14. ___ (3) 20. ___ (1) 22. ___ (2) 39. ___ (4)	4. ___ (1) 32. ___ (4) 55. ___ (3) 59. ___ (2)	7. ___ (3) 10. ___ (2) 16. ___ (1) 40. ___ (4)	
Total	___ [ ] 2 to 5	___ [ ] 2 to 5	___ [ ] 3 to 6	___ [ ] 3 to 6	Total ___ [ ] 10 to 22
D Speculative	3. ___ (3) 6. ___ (1) 29. ___ (4) 54. ___ (2)	17. ___ (2) 30. ___ (1) 52. ___ (4) 60. ___ (3)	18. ___ (4) 31. ___ (3) 36. ___ (1) 43. ___ (2)	5. ___ (4) 44. ___ (1) 53. ___ (2) 61. ___ (3)	D
Total	___ [ ] 2 to 5	___ [ ] 3 to 6	___ [ ] 3 to 6	___ [ ] 3 to 6	Total ___ [ ] 11 to 23
E Confrontive	28. ___ (1) 33. ___ (2) 45. ___ (3) 50. ___ (4)	8. ___ (4) 21. ___ (2) 34. ___ (1) 46. ___ (3)	12. ___ (2) 35. ___ (3) 56. ___ (4) 62. ___ (1)	2. ___ (1) 23. ___ (2) 42. ___ (3) 47. ___ (4)	E
Total	___ [ ] 2 to 5	___ [ ] 3 to 6	___ [ ] 3 to 6	___ [ ] 3 to 6	Total ___ [ ] 11 to 23
Column Total	I Tot. ___ [ ] 9 to 21	II Tot. ___ [ ] 11 to 23	III Tot. ___ [ ] 13 to 25	IV Tot. ___ [ ] 13 to 25	Overall Tot. ___ [ ] 46 to 26

Scoring: Table 3 and Table 4 are useful for scoring *HIM-B* or *A*. There is a cut-off for the responses to each statement: if the response is to the right of the cut-off (more than the number in column 2 of Table 3), it is not counted (or scored zero which amounts to the same thing); if it is to the left of the cutoff (equal to or less than the number in column 2 of Table 3), then it is counted. The number in column 3 indicates the cell being scored. In Table 4, next to each line in each cell, in parenthesis, is a weight. If the statement is to be counted, write the weight on the line next to it. The total scores in each cell can range from 0 (0+0+0+0) to 10 (1+2+3+4). The scores are not in any order because the statements were scrambled before they were placed in the questionnaire.

Interpreting: Some indices can be quickly made to help a participant understand his interpersonal style or to help decide whether a person would be a contributing member in a therapy or personal growth group. For illustrative purposes, we will look at Al's scores compared to average scores obtained by Hill. Average scores are shown in Table 5.

Table 5. Average Score for HIM-B and A based on normative sample.

	Topic I	Group II	Personal III	Relation IV	
Conventional B	4.3	4.9	5.4	5.4	20
Assertive C	3.2	3.6	4.1	4.1	15
Speculative D	3.6	4.1	4.6	4.6	17
Confrontive E	3.9	4.4	4.9	4.9	18
	15	17	19	19	70

Let us look at Al's scores for comparison and change the average score to an average range based upon plus and minus 1.5 of the average score rounded off. If Al's score is above the average, an H is placed next to it; if below, an L. MH and ML describe scores at the margins.

Table 6. Average range, Al's score, and High-Low Indication

	Topic I	Group II	Personal III	Relation IV	Row Total
Conventional B	3 to 6 / 0 L	3 to 6 / 3 ML	4 to 7 / 8 H	4 to 7 / 1 L	14 to 26 / 12 L
Assertive C	2 to 5 / 6 H	2 to 5 / 5 MH	3 to 6 / 4 H	3 to 6 / 4	10 to 22 / 19
Speculative D	2 to 5 / 6 H	3 to 6 / 6 MH	3 to 6 / 6 MH	3 to 6 / 10 H	11 to 23 / 28 H
Confrontive E	2 to 5 / 6 H	3 to 6 / 10 H	3 to 6 / 6 MH	3 to 6 / 6 H	11 to 23 / 28 H
Column Total	9 to 21 / 18	11 to 23 / 24 H	13 to 25 / 24	13 to 25 / 21	46 to 94 / 87

Summary Scores

Column and Row Totals. The sum of the total scores in a column or row show the person's preference for a given content across styles or a given style across contents. According to Al's description of his interactions, he uses conventional style less than most people but speculative and confrontive styles more than most people. He also talks about the group more than do most people.

Total Acceptance Score (TAS). This score is the person's total score (sum of row totals or sum of column totals). The average TAS is 70. Hill reports that one standard deviation for TAS scores is 20, therefore, scores below 50 or above 90 represent persons in the bottom 17% and top 17% of people who have taken the test. People who obtain a score below 50 (or particularly below 40) would probably not help themselves, nor the other members if they participated in a therapy or personal growth group. Hill suggests that their participation in a group is contraindicated, that they would find it difficult to give and accept help. Al's TAS of 87 indicates that he is a high-average participator.

Risk Ratio. The extent to which a person behaves in a way that may engender negative reactions from someone or from the group is given by:

$$\text{Risk Ratio} \quad \frac{\text{Assertive Row} + \text{Confrontive Row}}{\text{Conventional Row} + \text{Speculative Row}}$$

Which for normative scores is:

Low Average	**Average**	**High Average**
$\frac{10 + 11}{26 + 23} = \frac{21}{49} = .43$	$\frac{15 + 18}{20 + 17} = \frac{33}{37} = .89$	$\frac{22 + 23}{14 + 11} = \frac{45}{25} = 1.80$

For Al we have

$$\frac{19 + 28}{12 + 28} = \frac{47}{40} = 1.18$$

This indicates that he is about average in his willingness to risk the displeasure of the group members.

Growth-Work vs. Flight Ratio (GWVF). The extent to which a person is willing to get involved in working on problems and relations is given by the ratio of the four cells in the lower right corner of the matrix to the four cells in the upper left hand corner:

$$\text{Group Work vs. Flight (GWVF) Ratio} = \frac{\text{IIID} + \text{IVD} + \text{IIIE} + \text{IVE}}{\text{IB} + \text{IIB} + \text{IC} + \text{IIC}}$$

For the normative data (rounded) we have:

Low Average	**Average**	**High Average**
$\frac{3 + 3 + 3 + 3}{6 + 6 + 5 + 5} = \frac{12}{22} = .54$	$\frac{5 + 5 + 5 + 5}{4 + 5 + 3 + 4} = \frac{20}{16} = 1.25$	$\frac{6 + 6 + 6 + 6}{3 + 3 + 2 + 2} = \frac{24}{10} = 2.40$

For Al's scores we have:

$$\text{GWVF:} \quad \frac{6 + 10 + 6 + 6}{0 + 3 + 6 + 5} = \frac{28}{14} = 2.00$$

indicating that he is close to high average in his preference to relate to people at a more confrontive personal-interpersonal level.

REFERENCES

Hill, W.F. Hill Interaction Matrix (HIM) conceptual framework for understanding groups, J.W. Pfeiffer and J.E. Jones, Editors, *The 1973 Annual Handbook for Group Facilitators* 159-176: Iowa City: University Associates, 1973.

HILL INTERACTION MATRIX—
GROUP

Wm. Fawcett Hill

DESCRIPTION

Length: seventy-two statements (four in each of the sixteen subscales, plus eight others of interest)

Time: *Administering* Twenty minutes
Scoring Ten to fifteen minutes

Scale:

> *Group Interaction Content (Topic, Group, Personal, or Relationship)*
> *Group Interaction Style (Responsive, Conventional,*
> *Assertive, Speculative, or Confrontive)*
> *Therapist Activity*

See this section of the *HIM-B* presentation. *HIM-G* focuses on group and leader behavior rather than on individual member's preferred style and content of interacting. *HIM-G* is meant to be a way of obtaining measures of group behavior that is quicker then the content analysis method that was the original application of the interaction matrix. *HIM-G* consists of seventy-two descriptions of group behaviors to which an observer, leader, or member assigns a rating to describe the group.

For each cell of the matrix there are four statements that describe a given behavior with four emphases. These emphases are (1) trainer sponsored behavior (2) trainer encouraged or maintained behavior (3) member behavior (number of members) and (4) member behavior (proportion of time).

For statements that are counted therapist (leader) sponsoring (Ts), therapist going along with (Tm), or frequency of member participation (Mf) the response categories are:

0	1	2	3	4	5	6
Not at all	0-1% of time	1-5% of time	5-10% of time	10-20% of time	20-40% of time	40-100% of time

Statements coded as "member participating (Mp)" have the following response categories:

0	1	2	3	4	5	6
no members	one members	two members	three members	four/five members	five/six members	seven or more members

For the HIM-G, all twenty cells are used.

Table 1. Sample Statements, HIM-G

	I	II	III	IV
A	**#30** Ts Group leader attempts to stimulate interaction by probing and sponsoring members about discussing current events, gossip and other everyday subjects.	**#14** Ts Group leader attempts to stimulate interaction by probing and sponsoring members about the group with members responding perfunctorily or not at all.	**#19** Ts Group leader attempts to stimulate interaction by probing and sponsoring members about themselves; their family, educational background, military experience, etc.	**#3** Ts Group leader attempts to stimulate interaction by probing and sponsoring members about reacting to or showing awareness of each other with members responding perfunctorily or not at all.
B	**#17** Mf Members socialize informally by talking about current events, gossip and other everyday subjects.	**#27** Mp Members socialize informally by talking about the group and its activities.	**#45** Ts Group leader sponsors, probes, or otherwise encourages members to socialize informally by getting them to discuss themselves.	**#35** Tm Group leader socializes informally by good-natured give-and-take and joking, indulging in inside-jokes or offering pairing and support.
C	**#11** Mp Members express negative, or hostile feelings or delusional ideas about certain conditions, institutions or events.	**#2** Mf Members express negative, critical or hostile feelings toward the group and its activities.	**#57** Tm Group leader is critical of a member's formulation or report of his past, out-group behavior or way-of-life, or the group leader defends his past, out-group behavior or way-of-life.	**#23** Ts Group leader sponsors, probes or otherwise encourages members to indulge in ribbing, embarrassing, needling or verbally attacking others.
D	**#22** Ts Group leader sponsors, probes or otherwise encourages members for understanding their problems.	**#31** Tm Group leader discusses the manner in which the group operates or might function.	**#41** Tm Members explore aspects of a certain member's problem.	**#34** Mp Members give impressions or reactions they have to another member.
E	**#36** Tm Group leader points out in a topic discussion of non-personal matters, conclusions or insights derived from the discussion which have implications for the members' personal problems.	**#40** Ts Group leader sponsors, probes or otherwise encourages members to point out characteristic malfunctions or collaborative avoidances of certain topics of other inadequacies.	**#43** Mp Members reality test a certain member's formulation of his problem by pointing out distortions, omissions or contradictions in member's presentation of his problem.	**#51** Mf Members point out how certain members have characteristic patterns of interacting, members ask for or give reactions to specific behaviors of a member.

Uses: *HIM- G* could be used to sensitize members to their transactions by having the leader or some member give feedback to the group every five to ten minutes. Leaders and members can complete a scale after selected meetings or at the end of a laboratory.

Positive Features: This is one of the few instruments designed to obtain an explicit measure of group processes. The fact that the measure is based on the Hill Interaction Matrix—an excellent tool for examining group interaction—enhances it value.

Concerns: The manual (Supplement to *HIM Monograph*) is occasionally confusing. For example, page three of the supplement discusses a response of "5-10% of time" receiving a check in box three would be scored as a 2 when tallied or punched on an IBM card. A 3 should either remain as a 3 or become a 4 if the investigator wanted to avoid using zeroes, but it would not become a 2. Hill, in a personal communication, says he prefers it to remain a 3. Another problem is the absence of normative data for the *HIM-G*. Hill does acknowledge this problem but indicates that the norms in the monograph (1965) for the category-system use of the matrix on pages 62 and 63 which show percentile norms for percentage of time spent in each cell can easily be applied to the *HIM-G* results with some validity since *HIM-G* correlates over .90 with scores from the content analysis system.

ORDERING

See the section on *Hill Interaction Matrix—Behavior* (*HIM-B*) for information on addresses and costs.

ADMINISTERING, SCORING AND INTERPRETING

Scoring: The key for the *HIM-G* is in the *Supplement to the HIM Monograph*. Table 2 depicts a simplified scoring form for the *HIM-G*.

Interpreting: A number of indices can be derived from the matrix. A number of them are shown at the bottom of Table 2. In order to use the tables of percentiles in the monograph, it is necessary to convert cell, column, and row totals to percentages. You do this by dividing each total by the "Overall Total".

Table 2. HIM-G Scoring Form

	I	II	III	IV	
A	30 ____ Ts	14 ____ Ts	19 ____ Ts	3 ____ Ts	A (Ts) Total ____
B	66 ____ Ts	63 ____ Ts	45 ____ Ts	65 ____ Ts	B Ts Total ____
	12 ____ Tm	48 ____ Tm	21 ____ Tm	35 ____ Tm	B Tm Total ____
	61 ____ Mp	27 ____ Mp	28 ____ Mp	47 ____ Mp	B Mp Total ____
	17 ____ Mf	67 ____ Mf	60 ____ Mf	16 ____ Mf	B Mf Total ____
Total	_____	_____	_____	_____	B Total ____
C	69 ____ Ts	29 ____ Ts	39 ____ Ts	23 ____ Ts	C Ts Total ____
	62 ____ Tm	37 ____ Tm	57 ____ Tm	26 ____ Tm	C Tm Total ____
	11 ____ Mp	24 ____ Mp	7 ____ Mp	53 ____ Mp	C Mp Total ____
	32 ____ Mf	2 ____ Mf	15 ____ Mf	42 ____ Mf	C Mf Total ____
Total	_____	_____	_____	_____	C Total ____
D	22 ____ Ts	9 ____ Ts	49 ____ Ts	72 ____ Ts	D Ts Total ____
	52 ____ Tm	31 ____ Tm	59 ____ Tm	4 ____ Tm	D Tm Total ____
	6 ____ Mp	18 ____ Mp	68 ____ Mp	34 ____ Mp	D Mp Total ____
	71 ____ Mf	44 ____ Mf	41 ____ Mf	20 ____ Mf	D Mf Total ____
Total	_____	_____	_____	_____	D Total ____
E	55 ____ Ts	40 ____ Ts	8 ____ Ts	54 ____ Ts	E Ts Total ____
	36 ____ Tm	13 ____ Tm	70 ____ Tm	46 ____ Tm	E Tm Total ____
	38 ____ Mp	5 ____ Mp	43 ____ Mp	1 ____ Mp	E Mp Total ____
	25 ____ Mf	33 ____ Mf	58 ____ Mf	51 ____ Mf	E Mf Total ____
Total	_____	_____	_____	_____	E Total ____

Total	I ____ Ts	II ____ Ts	III ____ Ts	IV ____ Ts	Ts Total ____
	____ Tm	____ Tm	____ Tm	____ Tm	Tm Total ____
	____ Mp	____ Mp	____ Mp	____ Mp	Mp Total ____
	____ Mf	____ Mf	____ Mf	____ Mf	Mf Total ____
Total	I _____	II _____	III _____	IV _____	Overall Total ____

Member Silence: 10 ____   50 ____   56 ____   Total MS ____

Amount of Leader Participation: 64 ____

Risk Ratio = $\dfrac{C + E}{B + D}$

Therapist Activity = $\dfrac{Ts + Tm}{Mp + Mf}$

Abreviations: Ts = Therapist Sponsoring; Tm = Therapist Maintaining; Mp = Number of Members Participating; Mf = Frequency of Members Participating; MS = Member Silence

REACTIONS TO GROUP SITUATIONS

Herbert A. Thelen

DESCRIPTION

Length: fifty items

Time: *Administering* ten to fifteen minutes
Scoring twelve to eighteen minutes

Scales: These five scores indicate preferences for certain kinds of behavior in group settings.

> *Inquiry Mode*
> *Fight Mode*
> *Pairing Mode*
> *Dependency Mode*
> *Flight Mode*

Inquiry Mode. Indicated preferences are: task-oriented behavior; group-oriented responses aimed at helping accomplish group objectives; a problem-solving orientation; attempting to understand and deal with issues; and making suggestions for analyzing and for dealing with a problem.

Sample of scored statements:
When the group wanted his views about the task, Sam...
A. *wondered why they wanted his views.*
B. *thought of what he might tell them.*
Inquiry response: B

Fight Mode. Indicated preference is an angry response.

Pairing Mode. Indicated preferences are: supporting another person's idea; expressing intimacy, warmth, and supportiveness to another member; and expressions of warmth and commitment directed to whole group.

Sample of scored statements:
When the group wanted his views about the task, Sam...
A. *wondered why they wanted his views.*
B. *thought of what he might tell them.*
Fight response: A

Dependency Mode. Indicated preferences are appeals for support and direction; reliance on a definite structure, rules, and regulations; reliance on leader or on outside authority; and expressions of weakness or inadequacy.

Sample of scored statements:
When I wanted to work with Frank, I...
  A. *felt we could do well together.*
  B. *asked if it would be all right with him.*
Pairing response: A

Flight Mode. Indicated preferences are: tuning out (withdrawal or lessened involvement); joking, fantasy and daydreaming; inappropriate theorizing over-intellectualized, overgeneralized statements; total irrelevancy; changing the subject; leaving the group; and excess activity in busywork.

Positive Features: *Reactions to Group Situations* is a useful way to sensitize participants to important dimensions of group relations. It is a way of introducing them to Bion's influential theory of basic assumptions of people in therapy and similar groups. The instrument is also pleasant to take and, short and easy to score.

ORDERING

Where To Order: The instrument is located in Herbert Thelen's *Classroom Groupings for Teachability,* John Wiley, 1967.
  John Wiley & Sons, Inc.
  605 Third Avenue
  New York, New York 10016
  Phone: (212) 867-9800

Cost: $9.75

REFERENCES

Bion, W.R. *Experiences in Groups.* Basic Books, 1959.

GROUP LEADERSHIP QUESTIONNAIRE

Daniel B. Wile

DESCRIPTION

Length: twenty-one situations, nineteen alternative responses for each situation
Time: *Administering* about three minutes per situation or slightly over an hour
if all twenty-one situations are responded to.

    Scoring ten minutes

Scales:

Silence Intervention	Group Dynamics Question
Group Directed Intervention	Intervention
Reassurance-Approval	Group Atmosphere Interpretation
Intervention	Intervention
Subtle Guidance Intervention	Group Dynamics Interpretation
Structure Intervention	Intervention
Attack Intervention	Psychodynamic Interpretation
Member Feeling Intervention	Intervention
Leader Feeling Intervention	Personal Life Intervention
Leader Experience Intervention	Past and Parents Intervention
Clarification-Confrontation	Behavioral Change Intervention
Question Intervention	Non Verbal Intervention
Role-Playing Intervention	

The Group Leadership Questionnaire (GTQ-C; so abbreviated because it used to
be called the Group Therapy Questionnaire) describes twenty-one situations that
may occur in an encounter or therapy group and for each situation provides nineteen alternative ways in which the facilitator can respond to the occurrence. The
respondent deals with each of these twenty-one situations in two ways. First, he
lists any of the nineteen alternatives he might make. Second, he selects the one
responses he is most likely to make. Some of the situations are described below.

Sample Situations

Situation 1. Starting the Group

    You are the leader in a group which is meeting today for the first time. All
eight members, young adults, are present as you enter the room and sit down.
You introduce yourself and the members introduce themselves. Then everyone
turns and looks at you expectantly. There is silence. What do you do?

    Sample response statements:

        1. Silence

           Do nothing.

   2. *Group Directed*
      Say that the group is theirs to make use of as they wish.
   3. *Reassurance-Approval*
      Reassure them that a certain amount of tension is typical in the beginning of a group.
   4. *Subtle Guidance*
      Break the ice with casual conversation.
   5. *Structure*
      Describe the purposes and procedures of the group.
   6. *Attack*
      Say that everyone seems so uptight that you wonder if the group is going to get off the ground.
   7. *Member feeling*
      Ask how they feel in this first meeting (about being in the group or about each other).
   8. *Leader Feeling*
      Say how you are feeling (example: tense and expectant).
   9. *Leader Experience*
      Share an experience in your own life.
  10. *Clarification-Confrontation Question*
      Ask why everyone is silent.
  11. *Group Dynamics Question*
      Ask what they think might be going on in the group.
  12. *Group Atmosphere Interpretation*
      Describe how they seem to be expecting you to start things.
  13. *Group Dynamics Interpretation*
      Suggest that they are wanting you to be an inspirational and protective leader.
  14. *Psychodynamic Interpretation*
      Describe the silence as an expression of their anxieties about the group.
  15. *Personal Life*
      Ask everyone to say why he came to the group.
  16. *Past and Parents*
      Lead into a discussion of their family relationships and past experiences.
  17. *Behavioral Change*
      Encourage them to discuss their goals in behavioral terms.
  18. *Nonverbal*
      Use a nonverbal procedure (example: milling around, focusing on bodily tensions).
  19. *Role-Playing*
      Use a role-playing or psychodrama procedure (example: encourage a member to act out one of his problems).

Situation 2. Personal Questions

Near the beginning of the first meeting, the members ask you personal questions about your family and background. What do you do?

Situation 5. An Attack Upon the leader

After spending much of this second meeting talking about dieting and politics, the group suddenly turns on you, accusing you of being uninvolved, distant and uncaring. What do you do?

Situation 14. A Member Cries

It is the middle of the sixth meeting. A woman who had been unusually silent for the first half of this meeting, makes a brief attempt to fight back tears and then begins to cry. No one says anything about it. What do you do?

Situation 21. The Sexualized Meeting

The tenth meeting begins in a mood of seductiveness. At the center of the interaction is a girl who for several meetings now has repeated a pattern of flirting with a man until he begins to show interest in her. In the present meeting she has just stopped flirting with one man and has begun with another. Everyone seems to be taking part in the sexual mood, if not as an active participant, at least as a fascinated observer. What do you do?

A person's scores are the number of times he uses each response a) as a possible choice, and b) as a first choice.

Positive Features: The *GTQ-C* is one of the most stimulating instruments we have used in workshops. The situation and responses presented generate involving discussion among participants regarding basic assumptions about what helps other people. The individual situations are meaningful in their own right for discussing assumptions about what are growthful or therapeutic experiences.

Completing the total test (or even half of the situations) may tell the respondent if he favors a certain response pattern. He may wish to examine why he has the preferences he has.

Another positive feature of the *GTQ-C* is that it makes the respondent aware of alternatives available to a trainer, *i.e.*, it may expand his repertoire of possible responses to a situation.

Concerns: The instrument is long. However, it is not boring, and can be shortened easily.

ORDERING

Where To Order: University Associates
P. O. Box 615
Iowa City, Iowa 52240
Phone: (319) 351-7322

Cost: *Package of 25 tests* $12.50
Package of 25 answer sheets $12.50

ADMINISTERING, SCORING, AND INTERPRETING THE INSTRUMENT

Before you administer the *GTQ-C* you need to decide whether you want to use the complete instrument. The entire instrument takes over an hour to complete. We have used as few as five of the twenty-one situations with good results, *i.e.*, discussion of the situations was active, and the participants were highly involved and interested. If you decide to use only a part of the instrument we recommend selecting the following:

1. Starting the group
4. A filibuster
6. A group silence
7. A distressed woman
10. The quiet member

12. Marital problem
14. A member cries
16. The polite group
17. A group attack
20. The fight
21. The sexualized meeting

Scoring: Table 1 provides a sheet on which to record responses. Count the number of blackened circles in each column and place the total at the foot of each column. Similarily, count the number of X's in each column and write the totals below the column. You should also note the written in responses at the right of the answer sheet. If one kind of response is written in more than other responses, it should be indicated in the space to the right of the row where the X responses are totaled.

Interpreting: The labels given to the scales "subtle guidance" and "leader feeling" are the best first approximation to the meaning of the scales and the respondents preferred style. However, when a group of people are available, participants can use their responses to the *GTQ-C* as a springboard for a searching analysis of their own and other's styles of handling groups and individuals. The learning which comes from using the instrument generates from examining the assumptions about people, what is healthful for participants, what is healthful for the leader, and the short and long term effects of various behaviors by the leader. The process of arguing for the chosen leader responses lends itself to observing the process of resolving conflict in a positive manner.

In general both the overall scores and the situation-by-situation responses give a great deal of insight into a person's interpersonal assumptions and leadership style.

REFERENCES

Wile, D.B. Nonresearch Uses of the Group Leadership Questionnaire (GTQ-C). J.W. Pfeiffer and J. Jones (eds.) *The 1972 Annual Handbook for Group Facilitators.* Iowa City: University Associates, 1972.

Wile, D.B., Bron, G.D., and Pollack, H.B. The Group Therapy Questionnaire: An Instrument for the Study of Leadership in Small Groups. *Psychological Reports,* 1970, *27,* 263,273.

Wile, D.B., Bron, G.D. and Pollack, H.B. Preliminary Validational Evidence for the Group Therapy Questionnaire. *Journal of Consulting and Clinical Psychology,* 1970, *34,* 367-374.

Table 1 Answer Form

Darken the circle under all the responses that you might consider making if you were the leader faced with that situation. Place an X through the one response you have darkened which you feel is most important to make. To the right of the page write any responses that you might make which have not been included on the list.

Responses

Situation	1	2	3	4	5	6	7	8	9	10	11	12	13	14	15	16	17	18	19	Other Responses
1	0	0	0	0	0	0	0	0	0	0	0	0	0	0	0	0	0	0	0	_____
2	0	0	0	0	0	0	0	0	0	0	0	0	0	0	0	0	0	0	0	_____
3	0	0	0	0	0	0	0	0	0	0	0	0	0	0	0	0	0	0	0	_____
4	0	0	0	0	0	0	0	0	0	0	0	0	0	0	0	0	0	0	0	_____
5	0	0	0	0	0	0	0	0	0	0	0	0	0	0	0	0	0	0	0	_____
6	0	0	0	0	0	0	0	0	0	0	0	0	0	0	0	0	0	0	0	_____
7	0	0	0	0	0	0	0	0	0	0	0	0	0	0	0	0	0	0	0	_____
8	0	0	0	0	0	0	0	0	0	0	0	0	0	0	0	0	0	0	0	_____
9	0	0	0	0	0	0	0	0	0	0	0	0	0	0	0	0	0	0	0	_____
10	0	0	0	0	0	0	0	0	0	0	0	0	0	0	0	0	0	0	0	_____
11	0	0	0	0	0	0	0	0	0	0	0	0	0	0	0	0	0	0	0	_____
12	0	0	0	0	0	0	0	0	0	0	0	0	0	0	0	0	0	0	0	_____
13	0	0	0	0	0	0	0	0	0	0	0	0	0	0	0	0	0	0	0	_____
14	0	0	0	0	0	0	0	0	0	0	0	0	0	0	0	0	0	0	0	_____
15	0	0	0	0	0	0	0	0	0	0	0	0	0	0	0	0	0	0	0	_____
16	0	0	0	0	0	0	0	0	0	0	0	0	0	0	0	0	0	0	0	_____
17	0	0	0	0	0	0	0	0	0	0	0	0	0	0	0	0	0	0	0	_____
18	0	0	0	0	0	0	0	0	0	0	0	0	0	0	0	0	0	0	0	_____
19	0	0	0	0	0	0	0	0	0	0	0	0	0	0	0	0	0	0	0	_____
20	0	0	0	0	0	0	0	0	0	0	0	0	0	0	0	0	0	0	0	_____
21	0	0	0	0	0	0	0	0	0	0	0	0	0	0	0	0	0	0	0	_____

Total
number of
blackened
circles   _ _ _ _ _ _ _ _ _ _ _ _ _ _ _ _ _ _ _

Total
number
of X's   _ _ _ _ _ _ _ _ _ _ _ _ _ _ _ _ _ _ _   _____

Circle the two response totals receiving the highest number of blackenings and X's

HELPING RELATIONSHIP INVENTORY

E. H. Porter
Adapted by John E. Jones

DESCRIPTION

Length: twenty-five questions with five responses in each question.

Time: *Administering* thirty to forty-five minutes
Scoring ten to fifteen minutes

Scales: The respondent ranks alternatives in order of preferred responses from
one to five, "most apt" to "least apt."

> *Understanding*
> *Probing*
> *Interpretive*
> *Supportive*
> *Evaluative*

Understanding. A response tendency which indicates that the counselor's intent
is to respond in a manner which asks the client whether the counselor understands
what the client is "saying," how the client "feels" about it, how it "strikes" the
client, how the client "sees" it. This is the Rogerian reflection-of-feeling approach.

> Sample statement:
> *It's really a tough decision, isn't it? Whether to take the risks of starting out
> in a new field or to stick by the security of the irritating teaching job.*

Probing. A response tendency which indicates that the counselor's intent is to
gather further information, provoke further discussion along a certain line, to
query. He is some way implies that the client ought to or might profitably develop
or discuss a point further.

> Sample statement:
> *Could you tell me a little more about your new field of interest? It is quite
> important that we think about this clearly.*

Interpretive. A response tendency which indicates that the counselor's intent
is to teach, to impart meaning to the client, to show him. He in some way implies
what the client might or ought to think, however grossly or subtly.

> Sample statement:
> *This indecision of yours is an understandable thing and stems from the con-
> flict between your uncertainty over the new line of interest and your mixed*

228

feelings of dissatisfaction with the teaching job, yet hesitance to leave the security which it affords

Supportive. A response tendency which indicates that the counselor's intent is to reassure, to reduce the client's intensity of feeling, to pacify. He in some way implies that the client need not feel the way he does.

Evaluative. A response tendency which indicates that the counselor has made a judgment of relative goodness, appropriateness, effectiveness, rightness. He in some way implies what the client might or ought to do, however grossly or subtly.

ORDERING

Where To Order: University Associates
P. O. Box 615
Iowa City, Iowa 52240
Phone: (319) 351-7322

Cost: *25 tests* $10.50

GROUP ENCOUNTER SURVEY

Jay Hall
Martha S. Williams

DESCRIPTION

Length: eighty statements

Time: *Administering* fifteen to twenty minutes
      Scoring   ten to fifteen minutes

Scales:

> *Self-sufficient Decision Making*
> *Good Neighbor Decision Making*
> *Default Decision Making*
> *Traditional Decision Making*
> *Integrated Decision Making*

The *GES* measures the dimensional categories of individual attitudes, leadership preference, conflict resolution, and intergroup relations in terms of the five alternative patterns of individual behavior or attitude.

The grid model represents a two dimensional analysis of individual decision-making behaviors. The two most basic concerns an individual is thought to have when confronted with group situations serve as the two dimensions. These are a concern for decision quality, as he subjectively defines this and a concern for the commitment of other people to decisions reached. Individuals have personal "theories" about how these concerns should be related to one another, and, depending upon the particular "theory" they hold, people will adopt a particular set of behaviors in satisfying these concerns. These behaviors may be considered to constitute a style of group behavior. Three general theories of related concerns have been identified, and these give rise to five distinct or "pure" styles of group encounter behavior.

Responses are made on a line scale.

Sample statement:
> Each of us has been associated at one time or another with groups which fail to make truly adequate decisions. In your opinion, to what is such failure most often attributable?
> a. *Lack of sensitivity to the individual feelings and personal interests of one another among group members, as well as unreasonable demands on others for ideas, most often leads to group failure in decision making.*
> b. *The tendency of group members to view both complete agreement coupled with adequate decisions as unattainable, and the preoccupation or concern with time limits, status differences between group members, etc., rather than an integration of available resources most often leads to group failure in decision.*
> c. *Either the inability or the reluctance of group members to face up to the requirements of the task directly and not holding irrelevant discussion and personal feelings to a minimum, most often lead to group failure in decision making.*
> d. *The failure of the group leader—either formal or informal—to provide guidance, control and structure for other members of the group as well as a general lack of precedent for the decision most often leads to group failure in decision making.*
> e. *The tendency of group members to place total emphasis on either getting the job done or keeping harmony in the group rather than getting a little of both through compromise most often leads to group failure in decision making.*

Positive Features: The ten-point scale gives a weighting to each response preference. Attention is given to back up styles that indicate what kind of behaviors one is likely to adopt once stress forces the abandonment of the most prefered or dominant group encounter style.

The four graphs of component scores permits a focusing on the consistency between the weakest and strongest plots in each of the major categories.

Concerns: The graphs of component scores uses the concept of "stronger/weaker than desirable." This presupposes that there is a genuine ideal behavior towards which all individuals should strive. A more palatable pervasive assumption might give more credence to the strengths of individual differences and focus on knowing and accepting those differences rather than getting into a set where the goal is loaded with the shoulds and oughts of trying to become more "desirable".

ORDERING

Where To Order: Teleometrics, Int'l.
2210 North Frazier
Conroe, Texas 77301
Phone: (713) 756-1185

Cost: $3.00 (Includes "How to Interpret Your Scores on the Group Encounter Survey" booklet.)

TEAM EFFECTIVENESS SURVEY

Jay Hall

DESCRIPTION

Length: twenty descriptions of a "team member"
Time: *Administering* ten to twelve minutes
     Scoring   twelve to fifteen minutes

> *Exposure*
> *Feedback*

Scales: Scale values are from one (extremely uncharacteristic) to ten (extremely characteristic).

Exposure. Open about one's opinions and feelings about people and situations. Not guarded, defensive, or suspicious of others' motives. Willing to admit when he is wrong, confused, or ignorant.

    Sample statement:
> *He is open and candid in his dealings with the entire team.*
> As opposed to being closed, cautious, and under wraps in his relationships.

Feedback. Is open to other peoples' opinions, feelings and reactions. Solicits reservations and concerns; does not roll over opposition. He is not defensive or concerned only about himself.

    Sample statement:
> *He encourages collaboration on problems and solicits others' definitions and*
> *solutions on mutual problems.* As opposed to insisting on mechanical decision rules or trying to railroad his own judgments through.

Positive Features: A large amount of information is generated, and it has the advantage of not all being self-report information. Members rate each other on each of the twenty descriptions in addition to rating themselves. The participant is shown how he perceives members in comparison with how other members perceive them, discrepancies between his estimate of others and the other members' estimates of themselves, and discrepancies between his estimate of himself and how others estimate him.

ORDERING

Where To Order: Teleometrics, Int'l.
                 2210 North Frazier
                 Conroe, Texas 77301
                 Phone: (713) 756-1185

Cost: $3.00 (Includes "How to Interpret Your Scores on the Team Effectiveness Survey" booklet.)

GROUP DIMENSIONS
DESCRIPTIONS QUESTIONNAIRE

John K. Hemphill

DESCRIPTION

Length: one hundred fifty statements

Time: *Administering* fifteen to twenty minutes
        Scoring   ten minutes

Scales:

Control	*Hedonic Tone*	*Permeability*
Stability	*Autonomy*	*Participation*
Intimacy	*Potency*	*Polarization*
Stratification	*Viscidity*	*Flexibility*
		Homogeneity

The questionnaire differentiates characteristics of groups in certain dimensions as stated by individual group members. The respondent to the questionnaire expresses his answers for (attitudes toward, perceptions of, impressions or knowledge about) a specific group by indicating to what degree he regards each of the 150 statements as stating something that is true about the group.

The 150 statements are arranged to yield scores on thirteen group dimensions.

Control. The degree to which a group regulates the behavior of individuals while they are functioning as group members. It is reflected by the modifications which group membership imposes on complete freedom of individual behavior and by the intensity of group-derived government.

Sample of scored statement:
 - *A member may leave the group by resigning at any time he wishes.*

Stability. The degree to which a group persists over a period of time with essentially the same characteristics. It is reflected by the rate of membership turnover, by frequency of reorganization, and by constancy of group size.

Sample of scored statement:
 - *Members are constantly leaving the group.*

Intimacy. The degree to which members of a group are mutually acquainted with one another and are familiar with the most personal details of one another's lives. It is reflected by the nature of topics discussed by members, by modes of

233

greeting, forms of address, and by interactions which presuppose a knowledge of the probable reaction of others under widely differing circumstances, as well as by the extent and type of knowledge each member has about other members of the group.

Sample of scored statement:
+ *Members of the group know the family background of other members of the group.*

Stratification. The degree to which a group orders its members into status hierarchies. It is reflected by differential distribution of power, privileges, obligations and duties, and by asymmetrical patterns of differential behavior among members.

Sample of scored statement:
+ *Experienced members are in charge of the group.*

Hedonic Tone. The degree to which group membership is accompanied by a general feeling of pleasantness or agreeableness. It is reflected by the frequency of laughter, conviviality, pleasant anticipation of group meetings, and by the absence of griping and complaining.

Autonomy. The degree to which a group functions independently of other groups and occupies an independent position in society. It is reflected by the degree to which a group determines its own activities, by its absence of allegiance, deference, and dependence relative to other groups.

Potency. The degree to which a group has primary significance for its members. This is reflected by the kind of needs which a group is satisfying or has the potentiality of satisfying, by the extent of readjustment which would be required of members should the group fail, and by the degree to which a group has meaning to the members with reference to their central values.

Viscidity. The degree to which members of the group function as a unit. It is reflected by absence of dissention and personal conflict among members, by absence of dissention and personal conflict among members, by absency of activities serving to advance only the interests of individual group members, by the ability of the group to resist disrupting forces, and by the belief on the part of members that the group does function as a unit.

Permeability. The degree to which a group permits ready access to membership. It is reflected by absence of entrance requirements of various kinds and by the degree to which membership is solicited.

Participation. The degree to which members of a group apply time and effort to group activities. It is reflected by the number and kinds of duties members perform, by voluntary assumption of non-assigned duties, and by the amount of time spent in group activities.

Polarization. The degree to which a group is oriented and works toward a single goal which is clear and specific to all members.

Flexibility. The degree to which a group's activities are marked by informal procedures rather than by adherence to established procedures. It is reflected by the extent to which duties of members are free from specification through custom, tradition, written rules, regulations, codes of procedure, or even un-written but clearly-prescribed ways of behaving.

Homogeneity. The degree to which members of a group are similar with re-spect to socially-relevant characteristics. It is reflected by relative uniformity of members with respect to age, sex, race, socio-economic status, interests, attitudes, and habits.

Uses: The questionnaire would be a valuable instrument to use with organized or natural groups. After completing and scoring the questionnaire, the members would have an idea of their group's strength and weakness in each of the thirteen dimensions.

Positive Features: The scales have been shown to have adequate reliability for many useful purposes. There is evidence of relationships between dimension scores and degree of group satisfaction or productivity.

ORDERING

Where To Order: Bureau of Business Research,
College of Commerce & Administration
1775 South College Road
The Ohio State University
Columbus, Ohio 43210
Phone: (614) 422-6446

Cost: Hemphill, J.K. *Group Dimensions: A Manual For Their Measurement* Co-lumbus: The Ohio State University, Bureau of Business Research Mono-graph, No. 87, 1956. (contains the instrument and scoring key) $2.00

ADMINISTERING, SCORING, INTERPRETING

Scoring: A respondent's answer to each of the 150 statements may be one of five alternatives: (A) definitely true, (B) mostly true, (C) neither true nor false, (D) mostly false, (E) definitely false. Each of the responses has a weight in the determination of the raw score of the dimension which it describes. The weights are shown in the Scoring Key in Appendix B of the manual.

The responses of an individual are scored to yield a raw score for each of the thirteen dimensions. The raw score for a dimension is the sum of the item scores (weights) for that dimension. For example, the score for "Control" is the sum of the scoring weights of the responses marked by the subject for items one to twelve inclusive.

The raw scores on the thirteen dimensions may be converted into normalized scores, expressed in stanines. Conversion information for the translation of raw scores into stanine scores is in Table I of the manual.

The questionnaire could be scored by any number of people depending upon the number of keys available. It would be to the group's benefit to score the ques-tionnaire as soon as possible and discuss the results in terms of their relevance to the group.

Interpretation. Interpretation and understanding of stanine scores are dependent upon knowledge of the characteristics of the standard population. There are five sub-samples of respondents who compose the standard population. Sample A consists of one hundred respondents' descriptions of one hundred miscellaneous groups. Sample B is composed of the descriptions supplied by one hundred thirty members of the faculty of a liberal arts college. Each member provided a description of his department considered as a social group. Two or more descriptions were obtained for eighteen departments. Sample C is composed of one hundred eighty five women office workers. Sample D consists of 215 college students who were members of nine organizations affiliated with the religious council of a large university. Sample E consists of descriptions of school staffs supplied by 320 public school teachers.

SECTION C
Instruments with an Organizational Focus

Organizational Climate

ORGANIZATION HEALTH SURVEY

P. T. Kehoe
W. J. Reddin

DESCRIPTION

Length: eighty statements

Time: *Administering* ten minutes
  Scoring   eight to twelve minutes

Scales:

> *Productivity*
> *Leadership*
> *Organization Structure*
> *Communication*
> *Conflict Management*
> *Human Resource Management*
> *Participation*
> *Creativity*

Productivity. The degree to which the organization is seen as placing a high value on productivity.

Sample statements:
> *My superior often discusses my productivity with me.*
> *Very little time is wasted here.*

Leadership. The degree to which the organization is seen as having effective leadership.

Sample statements:
> *The recent decisions of management have clearly benefited the organization.*
> *Management is highly respected here.*

Organization Structure. The degree to which the organization structure is seen as appropriate.

Sample statements:
> *Managers know their jobs here.*
> *I know how this organization operates.*

Communication. The degree to which the organization is seen as having open communication.

239

Conflict Management. The degree to which disagreement is seen to occur when necessary and to be used productively.

Human Resource Management. The degree to which the organization's human resources are seen to be well utilized.

Participation. The degree to which participation is seen to be used.

Creativity. The degree to which the organization is seen as creative.

ORDERING

Where To Order: Organizational Tests, Ltd.
P. O. Box 324
Fredericton, N.B. Canada
Phone: (506) 455-8366

Cost: $20.00 per kit (10 tests in Kit)

ORGANIZATIONAL CLIMATE

Rensis Likert

DESCRIPTION

Length: twenty line scales

Time: *Administering* four to five minutes
Scoring   five minutes

Scales:

> *Authoritarian (System I)*
> *Paternalistic (System II)*
> *Consultative (System III)*
> *Participative (System IV)*

System I: Authoritarian. A very hierarchical system with virtually no participation by subordinates. Decisions are made by superiors, and subordinates are expected to comply.

Sample statement
How much confidence is shown in subordinates?
None
Condescending
Substantial
Complete
(*SYSTEM I RESPONSE: None*)

System II: Paternalistic. Some attempt is made to avoid being completely autocratic. Power remains at the top, but subordinates are given some few opportunities for limited participation in decision process.

Sample statement
Are subordinates' ideas sought and used if worthy?
Seldom
Sometimes
Usually
Always
(*SYSTEM II RESPONSE: Sometimes*)

System III: Consultative. Superiors are still superiors, but they show a lot of interest and confidence in subordinates. Power resides in superiors, but there is good communication and participation throughout the organization.

System IV: Participative. Energy and power reside in the logical focus of interest and concern for a problem. Subordinates have high latitude to initiate, coordinate, and execute plans to accomplish goals. Communication between subordinates and superiors is completely open, involving, unguarded.

ORDERING

Where To Order: The instrument is located in the book: Rensis Likert, *The Human Organization.* New York: McGraw-Hill, 1967.

McGraw-Hill Book Company
1121 Avenue of the Americas
New York, New York 10020
Phone: (212) 997-1221

Cost: $9.65

EDUCATIONAL VALUES

William C. Schutz

DESCRIPTION

Length: 126 statements (nine in each scale)

Time: *Administering* fifteen to twenty minutes
      Scoring   ten to fifteen minutes

Scales:

Importance (of Education)	*Control (School-Child)*	*Affection (Teacher-Child)*
Mind (Development of)	*Control (Teacher-Child)*	*Affection (Teacher-Community)*
Inclusion (Teacher-Community)	*Control (Teacher-Community)*	*Affection (Administrator-Teacher)*
Inclusion (Administrator-Teacher)	*Control (Administrator-Community)*	*Affection (Administrator-Community)*
Inclusion (Administrator-Community)	*Control (Administrator-Teacher)*	

This instrument measures the respondent's ideal of appropriate relations between teachers and pupils, between teachers and the community, between administrators and teachers, and between the administrators and the community. The dimensions of inclusion, control, and affection are the focus of these inquiries.

In addition to measuring the interpersonal relations between pairs of these sectors, *VAL-ED* measures attitude toward the importance of education (Imp), toward the need to focus on intellectual teaching (Mind), and toward the idea that the school should strive to allow the child to achieve his highest potential (SC:C). The fourteen *VAL-ED* scales are described in Table 1.

Uses: Since *VAL-ED* deals with a number of important interpersonal relations that bear on the administration of an educational system, it would be useful for examining attitudes toward educational relationships in seminars or workshops on community relations, higher education, and race relations. *VAL-ED* is readily modifiable for use with colleges rather than elementary and secondary schools; the facilitator instructs the respondents to substitute the word "student" for "children." The only statement that might present some difficulty concerns the PTA. Since this item bears on teachers-community relations the term PTA might be replaced by something like "the local town-gown organization" whether or not one exists in the particular community (It is the *attitude* that is important, not the accident of whether such an organization has been formed.) Uses in higher education include Faculty-Student Labs, Administration workshops, and any other combination of students (or student organizations) and faculty and administrators.

VAL-ED is useful in helping people to sort out their priorities: whose needs are paramount and who is answerable to whom? It is also useful to clarify any discrepancies that exist between ideals and actual practice so that people know at least what they would like to move toward.

Table 1. Description of Scales in the VAL-ED_

	I Inclusion	C Control	A Affection		
T-Cm (Teacher- Community)	The teacher should partici- pate in com- munity activities and be en- couraged to do so by com- munity mem- bers.	The teacher should conform to the domi- nant values of the comunity.	The teachers and people in the community should be personally friendly with each other.	The school should help the child to realize and use his own abilities and judgement most effectively.	Sc-C (School- Child— Potential Achieve- ment.)
A-T (Adminis- trator- Teacher)	The adminis- trator should take account of teachers' opin- ions when making policy decisions.	The adminis- trator should control the activities of the teachers, both in the class- room and the community.	The adminis- trator should be personally close with teachers and express his feelings openly.	Education has intrinisic value beyond its occupa- tional advan- tages.	IMP (Impor- tance of Education)
A-Cm (Adminis- trator- Com- munity)	The adminis- trator and the people in the community should be in- volved jointly in school and community affairs.	The desires of the community should deter- mine school policy.	The adminis- trator and the people in the community should be personally friendly with each other.	The school should concern itself primar- ily with de- veloping the mind of the student rather than with de- veloping his whole per- sonality.	Mind (Focus on Develop- ing *Mind* —Intel- lectual Teaching)
T-C (Teacher- Child)		The teacher should regu- late completely classroom les- sons and activities.	The teacher should be per- sonally friendly and warm toward the children.		

Table 2. Sample Statements and Responses that Reflect the Scales

	I Inclusion	C Control	A Affection		
T-Cm (Teacher-Community)	A teacher should stay out of community activities (strongly disagree).	A teacher should live his personal life as he chooses (strongly disagree, mildly disagree).	People in the community should not be too personal with teachers (strongly disagree, disagree).	The school should help the child to be original (strongly agree).	Sc-C (School-Child)
A-T (Administrator-Teacher)	A school administrator should have teacher representation on all administrative communities (strongly agree).	A school administrator should allow a teacher to teach anything the teacher believes to be true, no matter how unpopular (strongly disagree, disagree).	A school administrator should be personal friends with teachers (agree, strongly agree).	A college education makes a person more aware of important world issues (strongly agree).	IMP (Importance of Education)
A-Cm (Administrator-Community)	A school administrator should include the community in school activities (strongly agree).	A school administrator should be sure the school program is acceptable to the community (agree, strongly agree).	People in the community should invite administrators to their homes (agree, strongly agree).	Today's schools need to devote some time to subjects other than the basic subjects (English science, mathematics) (strongly disagree, disagree, mildly disagree, mildly agree).	Mind (Focus on developing Mind)
T-C (Teacher-Child)		A teacher should let the children decide many classroom matters by majority decision strongly disagree, disagree, mildly disagree, mildly agree).	A teacher should not express personal feelings to the children. (strongly disagree, disagree, mildly disagree).		

Positive Features: *VAL-ED* does a thorough job of accounting for any important interpersonal relations that exist in an educational enterprise. The fourteen scales provide a number of points of comparison both for different groups and people who take *VAL-ED* (teachers, parents, administrators) and within a person.

The focus on-ought ("A teacher should..."), rather than on behavior ("Teachers in our school system usually..."), helps to avoid ambiguities that occur with behavior involving an implied question, "Does the respondent approve of the reported behavior?" or, if it is his own behavior "Is he happy with the situation or is his behavior a reflection of pressure from others?"

Since the statements are not personal to the respondent and are non-threatening, there is a little motivation to lie on the instrument.

Concerns: As with *LIPHE*, *VAL-ED* has the problem of being larger (126 statements) than *FIRO-B* or *FIRO-F*. Whether this is a substantial problem may well depend on whether you have made a strong case for the value of instruments in helping people to understand things.

ORDERING

Where To Order Consulting Psychologists Press, Inc.
577 College Avenue
Palo Alto, California 94306
Phone: (415) 326-4448

Cost: *Specimen set* $ 5.00
  Manual $ 3.00
  Set of keys $ 1.75
  Packages of tests
   25 tests $ 4.00
   100 tests $11.50
   500 tests $52.50

ADMINISTERING, SCORING, AND INTERPRETING

Scoring: Templates are available for scoring. There are six of them so that six respondents can use one set to score their booklets, passing the six templates around as they go. The administrator may also transfer the key to a mimeograph format such as:

TCm:I	TCm:C
46) 1	47) 5-6
48) 6	49) 2-3-4-5-6
50) 4-5-6	51) 2-3-4-5-6
52) 1-2	53) 1-2-3
etc.	etc.

This key allows the participant to work at his own pace and to take the key away with him in case he wants to check on his responses to some of the scales. Table 3 is a form for recording scores and evaluating five summary scores.

Table 3. Form for Recording Scores on VAL-ED

	Inclusion	Control	Affection		
T-Cm	3 to 6 —( )	3 to 6 —( )	3 to 6 —( )	3 to 6 —( )	Sc-C
A-T	3 to 6 —( )	3 to 6 —( )	3 to 6 —( )	3 to 6 —( )	IMP
A-Cm	2 to 5 —( )	3 to 6 —( )	2 to 5 —( )	2 to 5 —( )	Mind
T-C		1 to 4 —( )	3 to 6 —( )		

	Inclusion	Control	Affection		
	8 to 17 —( ) Likes high participation	10 to 22 —( ) Authority should be exercised	11 to 23 —( ) People should be friendly	29 to 62 —( ) People should be active	
		6 to 12 —( ) Teacher should be controlled Add T-Cm + A-T			

Interpreting: The normative scores for *VAL-ED* are shown in table 4.

Table 4. Normative Averages for VAL-ED scales

	Inclusion	Control	Affection		
T-Cm	4.6	4.8	4.6	4.5	Sc-C
A-T	4.3	4.8	4.9	4.2	IMP
A-Cm	3.9	4.6	3.7	3.8	Mind
T-C		2.5	4.5		

For illustrative purposes we will examine Stan's scores compared to an average range based upon plus and minus 1.5 of the normative average score.

Table 5. Average range and Stan's scores on VAL-ED

	Inclusion	Control	Affection		
T-Cm	3.1 to 6.1 5	3.3 to 6.3 2	3.1 to 6.1 7	3.0 to 6.0 4	Sc-C
A-T	2.8 to 5.8 7	3.3 to 6.3 3	3.4 to 6.4 7	2.7 to 5.7 3	IMP
A-Cm	2.4 to 5.4 7	3.1 to 6.1 6	2.2 to 5.2 8	2.3 to 5.3 6	Mind
T-C		1.0 to 4.0 3	3.0 to 6.0 6		

Since scores fluctuate depending on the respondent's set, the use of decimal points to define the average range seems to be artificially precise. We will round off the decimal points and at the same time indicate if Stan's scores is high, medium, or low.

Table 6. Average Range (rounded).
Stan's scores, and Five Summary Scores

	Inclusion	Control	Affection		
T-Cm	3 to 6 5 (M)	3 to 6 2 (L)	3 to 6 7 (H)	3 to 6 4 (M)	Sc-C
A-T	3 to 6 7 (H)	3 to 6 3 (ML)	3 to 6 7 (H)	3 to 6 3 (ML)	IMP
A-Cm	2 to 5 7 (H)	3 to 6 6 (MH)	2 to 5 8 (H)	2 to 5 6 (H)	Mind
T-C		1 to 4 3 (M)	3 to 6 6 (H)		
	8 to 17 19 (H) Likes high participation	10 to 22 14 (M) Authority should be exercised	11 to 23 28 (H) People should be friendly		29 to 62 61 (MH) People should be active
		6 to 12 5 (L) Teacher should be controlled T-Cm plus A-t			

Stan's scores indicate that he values autonomy for teachers (low T-Cm:C and A-T:C), but not for administrators (high A-Cm:C). He thinks that teachers and administrators should get involved with each other and with the community (high A-T:I and A-Cm:I). Perhaps the most striking thing about Stan's scores is that he values close, open, warm relations between all sectors measured high in all four affection scales. Finally he feels that schools should concentrate on developing the student's mind rather than his whole personality (High Mind) and that education's value is primarily in its occupational preparation (Medium low IMP).

Stan's scores have been described in a way that implies some summary scores that could be derived from them. Table 6 shows five summary scores. Stan believes that the teacher should have personal and academic freedom, that joint decision-making and high participation is important, and most of all that people should be friendly and open with each other.

ORGANIZATIONAL CLIMATE INDEX

George G. Stern

DESCRIPTION

Length: three hundred statements

Time: *Administering* approximately fifteen minutes
      Scoring   hand scoring stencils in preparation. Sixty to seventy-five minutes from book.

Scales: The *OCI* parallels the *Activities Index*, by Stern.

Abasement-
  Assurance
	Dominance-
	  Tolerance
		Narcissism

Achievement	Ego Achievement	Nurturance
Adaptability- Defensiveness	Emotionality-Placidity	Objectivity-Projectivity
Affiliation	Energy-Passivity	Order-Disorder

Aggression-Blame
  Avoidance
	Exhibitionism-
	  Inferiority Avoidance
		Play-Work

Change-Sameness	Fantasied Achievement	Practicalness- Impracticalness

Conjunctivity-
  Disjunctivity
	Harm Avoidance-
	  Risktaking
		Reflectiveness

Counteraction	Humanities-Social Science	Science

Deference-
  Restiveness
	Impulsiveness-
	  Deliberation
		Sensuality-Puritanism
		Sexuality-Prudishness
		Supplication-Autonomy
		Understanding

Abasement-Assurance. Self-depreciation and self-devaluation as reflected in the ready acknowledgment of inadequacy, ineptitude, or inferiority; the acceptance of humiliation and other forms of self-degradation *versus* certainty, self-confidence, or self-glorification.

    Sample of scored statements:
        (True) People who work hard here do so in spite of the realization that some-
                one else will be getting the credit.
        (False) Criticism of administrative policies and practices is encouraged.

Achievement. Surmounting obstacles and attaining a successful conclusion in order to prove one's worth; striving for success through personal effort.

    Sample of scored statements:
        (True) The competition for recognition is intense.
        (False) People will have it in for you if you work too hard.

Adaptability-Defensiveness. Accepting criticism, advice, or humiliation publicly *versus* resistance to suggestion, guidance, direction, or advice, concealment or justification of failure.

> Sample of scored statement:
> *(True) Errors and failures are talked about freely so the others may learn from them.*

Affiliation. Gregariousness, group-centered, friendly, participatory associations with others *versus* social detachment, social independence, self-isolation, or unsociableness.

Aggression-Blame Avoidance. Indifference or disregard for the feelings of others as manifested in hostility either overt or covert, direct or indirect *versus* the denial or inhibition of such impulses.

Change-Sameness Variable or flexible behavior *versus* repetition and routine.

Conjunctivity-Disjunctivity. Organized, purposeful, or planned activity patterns *versus* uncoordinated, disorganized, diffuse, or self-indulgent behavior.

Counteraction. Persistent striving to overcome difficult, frustrating, humiliating, or embarrassing experiences and failures *versus* avoidance or hasty withdrawal from tasks or situations that might result in such outcomes.

Deference-Restiveness. Respect for authority, submission to the opinions and preferences of others perceived as superior *versus* noncompliance, insubordination, rebelliousness, resistance, or defiance.

Dominance-Tolerance. Ascendancy over others by means of assertive or manipulative control *versus* nonintervention, forbearance, acceptance, equalitarianism, permissiveness, humility, or meekness.

Ego-Achievement. Self-dramatizing, idealistic social action, active or fantasied realization of dominance, power, or influence achieved through socio-political activities in the name of social improvement or reform.

Emotionality-Placidity. Intense, open emotional expression *versus* stolidness, restraint, control, or constriction.

Energy-Passivity. High activity level, in tense, sustained, vigorous effort *versus* sluggishness or inertia.

Exhibitionism-Inferiority Avoidance. Self-display and attention-seeking *versus* shyness, embarrassment, self-consciousness, or withdrawal from situations in which the attention of others might be attracted.

Fantasied Achievement. Daydreams of success in achieving extraordinary public recognition, narcissistic aspirations for fame, personal distinction, or power.

Harm Avoidance-Risktaking. Fearfulness, avoidance, withdrawal, or excessive caution in situations that might result in physical pain, injury, illness, or death *versus* careless indifference to danger, challenging or provocative disregard for personal safety, thrill-seeking, boldness, venturesomeness, or temerity.

Humanities-Social Science. The symbolic manipulation of social objects or artifacts through empirical analysis, reflection, discussion, and criticism.

Impulsiveness-Deliberation. Rash, impulsive, spontaneous, or impetuous behavior *versus* care, caution or reflectiveness.

Narcissism. Self-centered, vain, egotistical, preoccupation with self, erotic feelings associated with one's own body or personality.

Nurturance. Supporting others by providing love, assistance, or protection *versus* disassociation from others, indifference, withholding support, friendship, or affection.

Objectivity-Projectivity. Detached, nonmagical, unprejudiced, impersonal thinking *versus* autistic, irrational, paranoid, or otherwise egocentric perceptions and beliefs-superstition, suspicion.

Order-Disorder. Compulsive organization of the immediate physical environment manifested in a preoccupation with neatness, orderliness, arrangement, and meticulous attention to detail *versus* habitual disorder, confusion, disarray, or carelessness.

Play-Work. Pleasure-seeking, sustained pursuit of amusement and entertainment *versus* persistently purposeful, serious, task-oriented behavior.

Practicalness-Impracticalness. Useful, tangibly productive, business-like applications of skill or experience in manual arts, social affairs, or commercial activities *versus* a speculative, theoretical, whimsical, or indifferent attitude toward practical affairs.

Reflectiveness. Contemplation, intraception, introspection, preoccupation with private psychological, spiritual, esthetic, or metaphysical experience.

Science. The symbolic manipulation of physical objects through empirical analysis, reflection, discussion, and criticism.

Sensuality-Puritanism. Sensory stimulation and gratification, voluptuousness, hedonism, preoccupation with esthetic experience *versus* austerity, self-denial, temperance or abstinence, frugality, self-abnegation.

Sexuality-Prudishness. Erotic heterosexual interest or activity *versus* the restraint, denial, or inhibition of such impulses, prudishness, priggishness, asceticism.

Supplication-Autonomy. Dependence on others for love, assistance, and protection *versus* detachment, independence, or self-reliance.

Understanding. Detached intellectualization, problem-solving, analysis, theorizing, or abstraction as ends in themselves.

ORDERING

Where To Order: Psychological Research Center
Syracuse University
Syracuse, New York 13210
Phone: (315) 476-5541, ext. 2295

Costs: *Specimen Set* $ .55
Answer Sheet $ .08
Test Booklet $ .30

REFERENCE

Stern, G.G. *People in Context.* Wiley and Sons, Inc., New York. 1970.

ORGANIZATIONAL CLIMATE QUESTIONNAIRE

George H. Litwin
Robert A. Stringer, Jr.

DESCRIPTION

Length: fifty items

Time: *Administering* five minutes
    Scoring . five minutes

Scale:

Structure	*Risk*	*Standards*
Responsibility	*Warmth*	*Conflict*
Reward	*Support*	*Identity*

Structure. The feeling that employees have about the constraints in the group: how many rules, regulations, procedures there are; is there an emphasis on "red tape" and going through channels or is there a loose and informal atmosphere.

Sample statement:
> *Excessive rules, administrative details, and red tape make it difficult for new and original ideas to receive consideration.*

Responsibility. The feeling of being your own boss; not having to double-check all your decisions; when you have a job to do, knowing that it is *your* job.

Sample statement:
> *Around here management resents your checking everything with them; if you think you've got the right approach you just go ahead.*

Reward. The feeling of being rewarded for a job well done; emphasizing positive rewards rather than punishments; the perceived fairness of the pay and promotion policies.

Sample statement:
> *We have a promotion system here that helps the best man to rise to the top.*

Risk. The sense of riskiness and challenge in the job and in the organization; is there an emphasis on taking calculated risks, or is playing it safe the best way to operate.

Warmth. The feeling of general good fellowship that prevails in the work group atmosphere; the emphasis on being well-liked; the prevalence of friendly and informal social groups.

253

Support. The preceived helpfulness of the managers and other employees in the group; emphasis on mutual support from above and below.

Standards. The perceived importance of implicit and explicit goals and performance standards; the emphasis on doing a good job; the challenge represented in personal and group goals.

Conflict. The feeling that managers and other workers *want* to hear different opinions; the emphasis placed on getting problems out in the open, rather than smoothing them over or ignoring them.

Identity. The feeling that you belong to a company and you are a valuable member of a working team; the importance placed on this kind of spirit.

ORDERING

Where To Order: The instrument is located in Litwin, George H. and Stringer, Robert A., Jr. *Motivation and Organizational Climate*. Cambridge, Massachusetts: Harvard University, 1968.

> Harvard Business School
> Division of Research
> Soldiers Field
> Boston, Massachusetts 02103
> Phone: (617) 495-6000

Cost: $6.00

SECTION C
Instruments with an Organizational Focus

Management/Leadership Style

THE ORIENTATION INVENTORY

Bernard M. Bass

DESCRIPTION

Length: twenty-seven statements, two responses to each statement

Time: *Administering* fifteen to twenty minutes
        Scoring   ten to fifteen minutes

Scales:

> Self-Orientation
> Interaction-Orientation
> Task-Orientation

Self-Orientation. This scale reflects the extent to which a person wants direct rewards to himself separate from his relations with others and the task he is doing. A high scorer enjoys the limelight and aspires to it in both positive and negative fashions.

Sample statement:
> *One of the greatest satisfactions in life is:*
> A. *Recognition for your efforts.*
> B. *The feeling of a job well done.*
> C. *The fun of being with friends.*

(Self-Orientation Response: A)

Interaction-Orientation. This scale reflects the extent to which a person is concerned with maintaining happy, harmonious relationships in a superficial sort of way, often making it difficult for him to contribute to the task at hand or to be of real help to others.

Sample statement:
> *The trouble with organizations like the Army or Navy is:*
> A. *The rank system is undemocratic.*
> B. *The individual gets lost in the organization.*
> C. *You can never get anything done with all the red tape.*

(Interaction-Orientation Response: A)

Task-Orientation. This scale reflects the extent to which a person is concerned about completing a job, solving problems, working persistently, and doing the best job possible. If he is involved in a task, he will fight hard for what he thinks is right.

257

Sample statement:
I am considerably disturbed by:
A. Hostile arguments.
B. Rigidity and refusal to see the value of new ways.
C. Persons who degrade themselves.
(Task-Orientation Response: B)

Uses: One way in which the *Ori* can work effectively is to use the data to form participants into homogeneous groups and give them a task to see the effect of the three orientations on task accomplishment and group process. It has been our experience that groups composed of self-oriented people frequently get into a somewhat frustrating sharing of insights with little effort to build on each other's ideas in working toward solutions to problems. This is punctuated with periodic struggles for dominance within the group. The groups composed of interaction-oriented people often fail to complete the task, but they seem to enjoy themselves. The groups composed of task-oriented people tend to get right to the task and finish it in a relatively short time.

Positive Features: The *Ori* is brief and easy to administer. The statements are intrinsically interesting and enjoyable to answer. The three orientations measured are important ones for interpersonal relations and organizational functioning. There are a number of validational findings reported in the manual.

Concerns: The description of the scales in the manual for the self- and inter-action-orientation scales is quite negative and seems likely to cause people with high scores on those scales to feel depressed or defensive. Read the descriptions of the scales in the manual to decide whether you want to use these verbatim with those to whom you have administered the instrument. Bass places a high value on task orientation. Sometimes participants express annoyance at the forced-choice nature of the response format. An additional disadvantage is that one cannot have all high scores or all low scores because the total of the three scores must be 81.

The *Ori* is somewhat difficult to score when using the scoring strips available from the publisher. Be sure that you are familiar with the scoring procedure before you administer the instrument. There are a number of checks in the scoring procedure that help in detecting errors.

ORDERING

Where to Order: Consulting Psychologists Press, Inc.
577 College Avenue
Palo Alto, California 94306
Phone (415) 326-4448

Cost:
Specimen Set	$ 1.25
Manual and Key	$ 1.00
Packages of Tests	
25 tests	$ 3.00
100 tests	$11.00
500 tests	$50.00

ADMINISTERING, SCORING, AND INTERPRETING

Interpreting: Below is a sample of scores on the *Ori* and an example of how to

understand and interpret some score combinations. The raw data and the percentiles for the example are as follows:

Scale	Raw Score	Percentile (Males)
S	35	94
I	15	7
T	31	44

The score profile indicates that the person is motivated to work at tasks when
he will get credit and recognition for his efforts and that he will be concerned for
his own needs and feelings. His low score on inter-action-orientation indicates
that he is not likely to help members of his group express their ideas. He is concerned with intra-group relationships in only a superficial way. His moderate
score on task-orientation indicates only an "average" concern about getting the
job done.

(These interrelationships among the scores were derived from tables showing
the relations between the scales and peer ratings of management personnel.)

A SURVEY OF LIFE ORIENTATIONS

Stuart Atkins
Allan Katcher

DESCRIPTION

Length: seventy statements organized in eighteen four-statement blocks to which the respondent allocates four scores: 4, 3, 2, and 1.

Time: *Administering* fifteen to twenty minutes
      Scoring   fifteen to twenty minutes

Scales:

> *Supporting/Giving*
> *Controlling/Taking*
> *Conserving/Holding*
> *Adapting/Dealing*

The philosophy behind the instrument is that your weaknesses are your strengths in excess. Within each of these four scales the respondent obtains an index of his use of a style in his *intentions*, his *behavior*, and his *impact* on others. Furthermore, each of the four *LIFO* style scores is divided into use of a style *productively* (+) and use of a style *excessively* (-). (See table 1 for a recording form.)

Supporting/Giving LIFO style Characterized as thoughtful, modest, loyal, receptive. People with these traits in excess are characterized as self-denying, gullible, obligated, and passive.

> Sample statement
> + *intention. I feel most pleased with myself when I act idealistically and with optimism.*
> - *behavior. In the face of failure, I feel it is best to turn to others and count on them to help me out.*

Controlling/Taking LIFO style Tends to be quick to act, seeks change, forceful, a risk taker. In excess he is impulsive, arrogant, coercive, and a gambler.

Table 1. My Scores Are:

	SP/GV	CT/TK	CS/HD	AD/DL
+ INT	A	B	C	D
+ BEH	E	F	G	H
+ IMP	I	J	K	L

	SP/GV	CT/TK	CS/HD	AD/DL	
TOTAL +					= 90
TOTAL −					= 90

	SP/GV	CT/TK	CS/HD	AD/DL
− INT	a	b	c	d
− BEH	e	f	g	h
− IMP	i	j	k	l

Sample statement

+ impact.   *I find it most satisfying when others see me as a person who can take ideas and make them work.*

− intention.   *If I don't get what I want from a person, I tend to claim my rights and try to talk him into doing it anyway.*

Conserving/Holding LIFO style Tends to be tenacious, economical, factual, and thorough. In excess he is uncreative, stingy, unfriendly, and stubborn.

Adapting/Dealing Lifo Style Characterized as flexible, experimenting, socially skilled and animated. In excess he is inconsistent, child-like, agitated, and without conviction.

Uses: *LIFO* can be used to make a person aware of his characteristic style of handling life problems. With awareness of his main style of approaching life plus knowledge of the style that he avoids, he can intelligently analyze where he should participate, where he may expect a conflict of styles, where he is most effective. Proper use of the instrument brings across the concept of compatibility of styles, that all styles may be useful for effective group activity, and that conflicts of styles are negotiable problems.

Positive Features: *LIFO* is interesting, and it is constructed so that it gives the various scale scores in a spatially understandable way. The concept of weaknesses being strengths in excess is simple, intuitively satisfying, and lends itself to correctional measures with confidence that modification is achievable. We are more willing to reduce an excess and gain a strength than we are to remove the offending behavior.

There are no "sick" or dysfunctional types. Each person can accept himself, realize what he can contribute, know where he needs help, and be aware of the dysfunctions his style is prone to.

Concerns: According to the authors, to be fully qualified to administer the instrument, a person must engage in a telephone conference with one of the authors in which he is given a two-hour tutorial on the instrument. This course qualifies the person to be what they refer to as a "Level I licensee." The cost of the telephonic training is $375 plus $30.50 for one practice kit per trainee, in addition to the cost of the telephone call. Up to three trainees can participate in a telephonic conference at once using extensions or a conference call arrangement.

There is a confound and confusion between whether a negative label refers to use of a style when under stress or use excessively, and between whether a positive label refers to use of a style when things are going well or use productively.

ORDERING

Where To Order: Atkins-Katcher Associates, Inc.
8383 Wilshire Boulevard
Beverly Hills, California 90211
Phone: (213) 653-0672

Cost: *LIFO Test* (non-reusable booklets)　　$2.50
　　Manual　　$5.50

ADMINISTERING, SCORING AND INTERPRETING

Administering: Distribute the *LIFO* booklet. Demonstrate how to tear the front sheet off of the booklet.

Scoring: If someone complains after he has scored his questionnaire that his most preferred style by the test is not at all like him, check to be sure he did not reverse-score the alternatives. A response of 4 means *most* like you.

Interpreting: Emphasize that there is really no dysfunctional score with *LIFO*, and each of us has a preferred style that is our strength and our weakness at the same time.

Ask the members to announce what their highest + (productive) style was. Make a tally on chalk board or newsprint.

Ask each one to announce what his next highest + style was. Describe the group as a person using the kinds of descriptions on pages 3-7 and section III of the manual. After you have characterized the group using the three highest raw scores in the positive part of the figure, obtain the same information for the minus scores and post them. Interpret this combination of scores using the description on pages 8-10 and section III of the manual.

To give them some insight into the four styles you may want to use such illustration as:

SP/GV "Ask not what your country will do for you, but rather ask what you can do for your country."

CT/TK "Damn the torpedoes. Full speed ahead!"

CS/HD "A penny saved is a penny earned."

AD/DL "Smile, and the world smiles with you."

Ask participants to write down examples of incidents in their lives when they have oriented in one of the four styles in intention, behavior, or impact both productively or in excess.

Have the participants for subgroups to discuss their examples and share their interpretation of their profile. Encourage them to consider how to best use their strengths and modify their excesses so that they become strengths.

MANAGEMENT STYLE DIAGNOSIS TEST

W. J. Reddin

DESCRIPTION

Length: sixty-four pairs of statements

Time: *Administering*   twenty to fifty minutes
  Scoring   twenty to thirty minutes

Scales:

> *Task Orientation*
> *Relationships Orientation*
> *Effectiveness*
> *Models of Management*

Task Orientation. The extent to which a manager directs his subordinates' efforts toward goal attainment; characterized by planning, organizing and controlling.

> Sample statement:
> *He usually reaches his decisions independently and then informs his subordinates of them.*

Relationships Orientation. The extent to which a manager has personal job relationships; characterized by mutual trust, respect for subordinates' ideas, and consideration of their feelings.

> Sample statement:
> *When possible he forms work teams out of people who are already good friends.*

Effectiveness . The extent to which a manager achieves the output requirements of his position.

Eight style models of management behavior. A person is classified as high or low on each of the three dimensions above; this classification yields eight combination scores.

Executive. A manager who is using a high Task Orientation and a high Relationships Orientation in a situation where such behavior is appropriate and who is therefore more effective. Seen as a good motivator who sets high standards, treats everyone somewhat differently, and prefers team management.

Compromiser. A manager who is using a high Task Orientation and a high Relationships Orientation in a situation that requires a high orientation to only one or neither and who is therefore less effective. Seen as being a poor decision-maker and as one who allows various pressures in the situation to influence him too much. Seen as minimizing immediate pressures and problems rather than maximizing long-term production.

Benevolent Autocrat. A manager who is using a high Task Orientation and a low Relationships Orientation in a situation where such behavior is appropriate and who is therefore more effective. Seen as knowing what he wants and knowing how to get it without creating resentment.

Autocrat. A manager who is using a high Task Orientation and a low Relationships Orientation in a situation where such behavior is inappropriate and who is therefore less effective. Seen as having no confidence in others, as unpleasant, and as being interested only in the immediate job.

Developer. A manager who is using a high Relationships Orientation and a low Task Orientation in a situation where such behavior is appropriate and who is therefore more effective. Seen as having implicit trust in people and as being primarily concerned with developing them as individuals.

Missionary. A manager who is using a high Relationships Orientation and a low Task Orientation in a situation where such behavior is inappropriate and who is therefore less effective. Seen as being primarily interested in harmony.

Bureaucrat. A manager who is using a low Task Orientation and a low Relationships Orientation in a situation where such behavior is appropriate and who is therefore more effective. Seen as being primarily interested in rules and procedures for their own sake and as wanting to maintain and control the situation by their use. Often seen as conscientious.

Deserter. A manager who is using a low Task Orientation and a low Relationships Orientation in a situation where such behavior is inappropriate and who is therefore less effective. Seen as uninvolved and passive.

ORDERING

Where To Order: Organizational Tests, Ltd.
Box 324
Fredericton, N.B., Canada
Phone: (506) 475-8366

Costs: Free sample (One test, manual and users guide)
1 kit of ten tests (includes Managerial Effectiveness)$30.00

REFERENCE

Reddin, W.J., *Managerial Effectiveness*, New York, McGraw-Hill, 1970.

XYZ TEST

W. J. Reddin
J. Brian Sullivan

DESCRIPTION

Length: eighty-four statements

Time: *Administering*   fifteen to twenty minutes
      Scoring   ten to fifteen minutes

Scales:

> Theory X
> Theory Y
> Theory Z

Theory "X" (Assumptions About the Nature of Man). Man is basically a beast who is best controlled by civilization. He is inherently evil and is driven by his biological impulses; his basic interactional mode is competition.

> Sample statement:
> *There is no real evidence that man can control his natural instincts.*

Theory "Y" (Assumptions About the Nature of Man). Man is basically a self-actualizing person who works best with few controls. He is inherently good and is driven by humanism; his basic interactional mode is cooperation.

> Sample statement:
> *Man does not need to be governed by laws.*

Theory "Z" (Assumptions about the Nature of Man). Man is basically a rational being open to and controlled by reason. He is inherently neither good nor evil but open to both and is driven by his intellect; his basic interactional mode is interdependence.

> Sample statement:
> *Lack of knowledge is the main thing holding mankind back.*

Positive Features: The XYZ instrument deals with a central and influential concept in management—the managers assumption about man. Furthermore, it extends McGregor's popular distinction between "theory X" and "theory Y" management thereby highlighting some disfunctions of both approaches.

265

Concerns: The *XYZ Test* uses rather general statements, e.g., "Man's future is promising," and "Man is essentially a naked ape." Because of this the leader may have some difficulty insuring that the participants make the transition to the organizational situation. They may wish to make a distinction between how they view man in general and how they relate to people in the organization.

ORDERING

Where To Order: Organizational Tests Ltd.
Box 324
Fredericton, N.B., Canada
Phone: (506) 475-8366

Cost: *Package of 10 tests* $30.00

LEADERSHIP APPRAISAL SURVEY

Jay Hall

DESCRIPTION

Length: twelve situations described.

Time: *Administering* fifteen to twenty minutes
       Scoring   eight to twelve minutes

Scales:

> *Concern For Purpose*
> *Concern For People*

This instrument is a parallel to the *Management Appraisal Survey*. See the description of the *MAS* for full details on the variables measured and the schema used to relate the two orientations (people and tasks). So that you may compare the difference between the two instruments, the same situation described in the *Management Appraisal Survey* is repeated below in the format for the *Leadership Appraisal Survey*.

Sample situation
> *While it is a rare occurrence for a member's mistakes to be serious enough to affect a total organization, the manner in which mistakes are treated can significantly influence organizational health. How does your leader react when those under his direction make mistakes on their assignments?*
>
>   *a. On the basis of a careful investigation of the facts surrounding the case, he decides what disciplinary action should be taken.*
>
>   *b. Because it is only natural for some mistakes to occur, he tries to avoid emphasizing those which do happen unless they call the attention of his superiors to his work group.*
>
>   *c. On the basis of his knowledge of the facts, he disciplines those who make mistakes, but, in addition, he tries to show them how they can learn from their mistakes.*
>
>   *d. In dealing with mistakes which occur, the thought he keeps uppermost in his mind is that the self-confidence and morale of the person involved must not be damaged.*
>
>   *e. When mistakes are made, my leader and those of us involved try to learn from them by analyzing their causes and by developing procedures which are designed to prevent similar mistakes in the future.*

| Completely
Characteristic | : : : : : : : : : :
10 9 8 7 6 5 4 3 2 1 | Completely
Uncharacteristic |

Positive Features: The *Leadership Appraisal Survey* is a companion for the *Styles of Leadership Survey* also published by Teleometrics. The *LAS* measures the impression the members have of the leader. The *SLS* measures the leader's impression of himself. Both instruments give indices on Blake and Mouton's two-dimensional grid thereby allowing meaningful and often confrontive comparisons between the two sets of scores. The leader's style in all four aspects of his work: philosophy, planning, implementation and evaluation are scored thereby indicating interesting shifts in style contingent on the task phase.

ORDERING

Where To Order: Teleometrics, Int'l.
2210 North Frazier
Conroe, Texas 77301
Phone: (713) 756-1185

Cost: $3.00 (Includes "How to Interpret the Leadership Appraisal Survey" booklet.)

MANAGEMENT APPRAISAL SURVEY

Jay Hall

DESCRIPTION

Length: eighty statements

Time: *Administering* fifteen to twenty minutes
        Scoring   ten to fifteen minutes

Scales:

> 9/9 *Participative Management*
> 9/1 *Task-Centered Management*
> 1/9 *People-Centered Management*
> 5/5 *Compromise Management*
> 1/1 *Custodial Management*

The Management Appraisal Survey Grid: The grid model represents a two-dimensional analysis of managerial behaviors. The two most basic concerns a manager is though to have serves as the two dimensions; these are a concern for production and a concern for people. Managers have personal "theories" about how these concerns should be related to one another and, depending upon the particular "theory" he holds, a manager will adopt a particular set of behaviors in satisfying his concerns; these behaviors may be considered to constitute a style of management. Three general "theories" of related concerns have been identified, and these give rise to five distinct or "pure" styles of management.

A special notation grid is used in identifying management styles. With the value 9 denoting a maximum concern and the value 1 denoting a minimal concern, styles can be interpreted in terms of the degree of concern for production *vis-a-vis* people which the manager experiences:

9/1 *Style* Maximal concern for production coupled with a minimal concern for people.

1/9 *Style* Maximal concern for people coupled with a minimal concern for production.

1/1 *Style* Minimal concern for both dimensions.

5/5 *Style* Moderate concern for each.

9/9 *Style* Maximal concern for production and people.

Obviously, different behaviors will be used by individuals adhering to the pressures of such different combinations of concerns; it is these behaviors—and the overall style which results—which the *Styles of Management Inventory* and *Management Appraisal Survey* have been designed to measure.

Each major category, *i.e.*, philosophy, planning, implementation and evaluation is presented under four different situations. Five alternative patterns of individual behavior or attitudes have been supplied as possible responses to each situation.

Sample statement

B. *While it is a rare occurrence for a subordinate's mistakes to be serious enough to affect organization, the manner in which mistakes are treated can significantly influence organizational health. How does your manager react when his subordinates make mistakes on the job?*

a. *On the basis of his knowledge of the facts he disciplines those subordinates who make mistakes; but, in addition, he tries to show them how they can learn from their mistakes.*

b. *When mistakes are made, he has those of us involved try to learn from them by analyzing the causes and by developing procedures which are designed to prevent similar mistakes in the future.*

c. *In dealing with mistakes which occur, the thought my manager keeps uppermost in his mind is that the self confidence and morale of the employee involved must not be damaged.*

d. *On the basis of a careful investigation of the facts surrounding the case he decides what disciplinary action should be taken.*

e. *Because it is only natural for some mistakes to occur, my manager tries to avoid emphasizing those which do happen unless they call the attention of his superiors to his department or agency.*

ORDERING

Where To Order: Teleometrics Int'l.
2210 North Frazier
Conroe, Texas 77301
Phone: (713) 756-1185

Cost: $3.00 (Includes "How to Interpret Your Scores from the *Management Appraisal Survey*" booklet.)

LEADERSHIP OPINION QUESTIONNAIRE

Edwin A. Fleishman

DESCRIPTION

Length: forty items

Time: *Administering* ten to fifteen minutes
Scoring six to eight minutes

Scales:

> *Consideration*
> *Structure*

Consideration. Reflects the extent to which an individual is likely to have job relationships with his subordinates characterized by mutual trust, respect for their ideas, consideration of their feelings, and a certain warmth between himself and them. A high score is indicative of a climate of good rapport and two-way communication. A low score indicates the individual is likely to be more impersonal in his relations with group members.

Structure. Reflects the extent to which an individual is likely to define and structure his own role and those of his subordinates toward goal attainment. A high score on this dimension characterizes individuals who play a very active role in directing group activities through planning, communicating information, scheduling, criticizing, and trying out new ideas. A low score characterizes individuals who are likely to be relatively inactive in giving direction in these ways.

ORDERING

Where To Order: Science Research Associates, Inc.
259 East Erie Street
Chicago, Illinois 60611
Phone: (312) 944-7552

Costs: *Specimen Set* $1.30
25 Test booklets $7.65
Manual $ .43

THE LEADERSHIP ABILITY EVALUATION

Russell N. Cassel
Edward J. Stancik

DESCRIPTION

Length: fifty problem situations, one response to each

Time: *Administering* fifteen minutes
      Scoring   three minutes

Scales:

> *Laissez-Faire*
> *Democratic-Cooperative*
> *Autocratic-Submissive*
> *Autocratic-Aggressive*

Laissez-Faire. Decision in which there is complete non-direction by the leader. Low scores represent too little dependency upon group members for arriving at decisions.

> Sample situation:
> *You receive a failing grade in a class in which you think you did as well as the students who passed. What do you do?*
> (Laissez-Faire Response: *Do nothing and repeat the course.*)

Democratic-Cooperative. A "parliamentary procedure-centered" decision process. Individual plays roles of both leader and member. Very high scores suggest excessive cooperation by the leader; very low scores suggest too little cooperation.

> Sample situation:
> *Several of your close friends decide to attend a symphony concert. You do not care for classical music. What do you do?*
> (Democratic-Cooperative Response: *Ask them to choose between a movie and a symphony; then abide by their decision*).

Autocratic-Submissive. A "resource person or committee-centered" decision process; resource persons are outside the group. Very high scores represent excessive use of resource persons; very low scores represent too little use of resource persons.

Autocratic-Aggressive. An "ego-centered" decision process. Complete development and implementation of the group activity is retained by the leader. High scorers (above 8) use leader-dominated thinking excessively; low scorers (below 2) use too little leader-dominated thinking.

Total Score. The weighted sum of the scores is the total. A heavy weight is given to laissez-faire and a moderate weight to autocratic-submissive. Weights are those that discern best between outstanding leaders and typical individuals. The lower the total score (10 and below) the more effective the leader.

Positive Features: The *LAE* is an interesting instrument to take. It presents provocative situations from five areas:

Home and family life
Work and Vocational Pursuits
Play and Avocational Pursuits
School and Educational Pursuits
Community Life

Concerns: No consideration seems to have been given to the possibility that a leadership style that is functional in one setting may be dysfunctional in another setting. The definition of outstanding leaders solely in terms of Air Force colonels seems unnecessarily narrow. Different occupations require different leadership styles, and norms of five or six groups of successful leaders (e.g., football coaches, camp directors, presidents of universities, leaders of construction groups, noncommissioned officers) would be helpful.

ORDERING

Where to Order: Western Psychological Services
12031 Wilshire Boulevard
Los Angeles, California 90025
Phone (213) 478-6730

Costs: *Specimen Set* $8.00 (Includes manual plus 25 tests)
      25 Tests $7.50
      Manual $2.00

SECTION C
Instruments with an Organizational Focus

Supervisor-Subordinate Relations

LEADERSHIP: EMPLOYEE-ORIENTATION AND DIFFERENTIATION

Russell Doré

DESCRIPTION

Length: sixty pairs of statements, respondent chooses one

Time: *Administering* fifteen to twenty minutes
Scoring ten to fifteen minutes

Scales:

> *Employee-Orientation*
> *Differentiation*

Employee-orientation. A high score tends to agree with the following leadership techniques: being oriented toward employees as people rather than as a means of production, delegating authority and responsibility for decisions to the employees where possible, and creating an atmosphere of teamwork and cooperation. A low scorer agrees with these methods: assigning all tasks to employees rather than letting them help decide assignments, making most decisions yourself, supervising closely, stressing rules and work standards, and focusing on individual performance and competition rather than cooperation.

Differentiation. A high scorer tends to agree that a leader's activities are different from those of his employees and include: explaining and discussing changes in the work, planning and scheduling the overall group's activity, training employees, explaining their job responsibilities, giving them feedback on good and poor performance, and trying out new ideas. A low scorer tends to feel that a leader should stress: doing the same kind of activities as the employees, being a high individual performer himself, being an outstanding technical expert in his field, and working hard personally to get a big share of the work done.

Positive Features: Employee orientation and differentiation are two aspects of management style that have been emphasized elsewhere and are clearly distinct dimension of it. They have been called "consideration" and "initiating structure" by Fleishman. The instrument orients participants to two of the four successful leadership methods identified by the Michigan Survey Research Center: employee orientation, differentiation, delegation of authority, and creation of teamwork.

Concerns: The instrument provides a method of estimating a total score using a nomograph but provides little indication of the meaning of such a score.

ORDERING

Where to Order: University Associates
P.O. Box 615
Iowa City, Iowa 52240
Phone (319) 351-7322

Costs: *25 tests* $3.50
25 answer sheets and profile sheets $2.75

REFERENCES

Jones, J.E. and Pfeiffer, J.W. *The 1973 Annual Handbook for Group Facilitators.* Iowa City: University Associates, 1973.

RATE YOUR BOSS AS A LEADER

Robert Townsend

DESCRIPTION

Length: ten items, each scored from zero to ten

Time: *Administering* five minutes
     Scoring   two minutes

Scale:

Leadership

Rating Your Boss. This is his or her rating as a leader on a scale of 0 to 100. If the obtained rating is below fifty, he or she is low in leadership qualities and probably unsatisfactory as a superior.

   Sample statement:
   He is fair. And concerned about me and how I'm doing. Gives credit where credit is due, but holds me to my promise.
   (Assign a value of 0 to 10 points.)

Positive Features: The scale points up ten dimensions of leadership and causes respondents to attend to them. All of this is done in a very short period of time.

Concerns: The scale is unvalidated, contains no reliability data, and looks like what it is: a "quick and dirty" way of generating some data that should be useful for people looking at the needs of those in subordinate roles.

ORDERING

Where To Order: The scale is located in Robert Townsend, *Up the Organization.*

> Fawcett World Library
> Fawcett Place
> Greenwich, Connecticut 06380
> (203) 661-6700

Cost: $1.25

PERSONNEL RELATIONS SURVEY

Jay Hall
Martha S. Williams

DESCRIPTION

Length: sixty items (three sections, twenty items in each section)

Time: *Administering*   thirty to forty minutes
        Scoring   twelve to fifteen minutes

Scales:

> *Exposure*
> *Feedback*

There are two dimensions measured by the *PRS—Exposure* and *Feedback*. You obtain these two scores for three target persons: your *employees or subordinates, colleagues,* and *supervisors.*

Exposure. Let the other person know how you feel about his behavior or about some situation. High scorers disclose their reactions and inner feelings.

Feedback. High scorers solicit feedback from other people about their behavior or about the relationship between them.

Positive Features: The *Personnel Relations Survey* is an excellent tool for making people both aware of their Johari Window.

Figure 1. Johari Window

	Known to self	Not known to self
Know to others	I. Area of free activity (public self)	II. Blind area ("bad breath" area)
Not known to others	III. Avoided or hidden area (private self)	IV. Area of unknown activity

Participants often find that they are, say, very open to their subordinates and superiors but very closed with their colleagues. Whatever the pattern that emerges, the participant is given some indication of where he feels trust and lack of trust in his organization.

Concerns: The respondent has to go through the same set of twenty pairs of statements for each of the three relationships. This can be seen as too time consuming and repetitious by some respondents.

ORDERING

Where To Order: Teleometrics International
2210 North Frazier
Conroe, Texas 77301
Phone (713) 765-1185

Costs: $3.00 (includes "How to Interpret Your Scores on the Personal Relations Survey" booklet)

MANAGEMENT OF MOTIVES INDEX

Jay Hall

DESCRIPTION

Length: sixty items

Time: *Administering* fifteen to twenty minutes
Scoring ten to fifteen minutes

Scales:

> *Basic Needs*
> *Safety Needs*
> *Belongingness Needs*
> *Ego-Status Needs*
> *Self-Actualization Needs*

The *MMI* uses the same need system (Maslow's) as the *Work Motivation Inventory*. However, the *MMI* is taken from the viewpoint of the manager, while the *WMI* is taken from the viewpoint of the worker. When the manager fills out the *MMI*, he indicates the extent to which he thinks each of Maslow's five needs are important to his workers.

Uses: Comparison of an employee's scores on the *WMI* with his manager's scores on the *MMI* can be instructive in a number of ways. An employer may project his own need system onto his employees. He may treat them all alike, ignoring the fact that there are differences among them in needs. For example, an unmarried employee may use her work situation to fulfill some belongingness needs. For her, the quality of the interpersonal relations where she works will be a consideration in her work satisfaction.

ORDERING

Where to Order: Teleometrics, Int'l.
2210 North Frazier
Conroe, Texas 77301
Phone (713) 756-1185

Cost: $3.00 (Includes "How to Interpret Your Scores on the "Management of Motives Index" booklet)

WORK MOTIVATION INVENTORY

Jay Hall
Martha Williams

DESCRIPTION

Length: sixty items

Time: *Administering* fifteen to twenty minutes
      Scoring   eight to twelve minutes

Scales:

> *Basic Needs*
> *Safety Needs*
> *Belongingness Needs*
> *Ego-Status Needs*
> *Self-Actualization Needs*

Need Systems Serve (Source of Motivation).

> *Basic.* Work conditions, higher wages, creature comforts, leisure.

> *Safety.* Security, order, rules, fringe benefits.

> *Belongingness.* Affiliation, acceptance, harmony, team membership.

> *Ego-Status.* Competence, achievement, recognition, advancement.

> *Self-Actualization.* Creativity, experimentation, meaningfulness, growth.

The *WMI* is a companion to the *Management of Motives Index.*

ORDERING

Where to Order: Teleometrics Int'l.
      2210 North Frazier
      Conroe, Texas 77301
      Phone (713) 756-1185

Cost: $3.00 (Includes "How to Interpret Your Scores on the *Work Motivation Inventory*" booklet.)

SUPERVISORY INDEX

Norman Gekoski
Solomon L. Schwartz

DESCRIPTION

Length: twenty-four sets, four items in each set

Time: *Administering* fifteen to twenty-five minutes
     Scoring ten to fifteen minutes

Scales:

> *Attitude Towards Management*
> *Attitude Towards Supervision*
> *Attitude Towards Employees*
> *Attitutde Towards Human Relations Practices*

The scales measure the supervisor's attitude toward *management* as an entity, *supervision* as a process, *employees* as subordinates, and selected *human relations practices*, plus a total score.

Management. Attitude toward top management, pay, company policy, benefits, plant regulations, company training, and other aspects over which the supervisor has little control.

Supervision. Attitude toward the duties and responsibilities of a supervisor; his annoyances, desires, and needs; the characteristics that make for an "ideal" supervisor; and feelings toward other supervisors.

Employees. Attitude toward the supervisor's subordinates, understanding of their motivations and needs.

Human Relations Practices. Supervisory techniques for handling problems, trouble-making, lateness, apathy, arguments, and low morale.

Total Score. The total is a straightforward sum of the scores on the scales described above. It apparently measures the extent the person holds to a person-centered, "people are basically good" philosophy of management. Total scores related negatively with need for recognition and positively with benevolence.

ORDERING

Where To Order: Science Research Associates, Inc.
          259 East Erie Street
          Chicago, Illinois 60611
          Phone (312) 944-7552

Costs: *Specimen Set* $1.15
         25 Booklets $7.65
         Manual $ .54

PART III
Appendices

Appendix A
LIST OF AUTHORS

Author	Page(s)
Adorno, T.W.	92
Allport, F.H.	175
Allport, G.W.	62, 175
Atkins, S.	260
Bales, R.F.	164
Bass, B.M.	257
Bell, H.M.	110
Bernreuter, R.G.	72
Blake, B.	82
Blansfield, M.G.	74
Briggs, K.C.	101
Burgess, E.W.	192, 195
Byrne, D.	96
Cassel, R.N.	272
Cattell, R.B.	108
Clark, W.W.	124
Cottrell, L.S.	192,195
Crowne, D.	95
Dore, R.	277
Droppleman, L.F.	118
Eber, H.W.	108
Edwards, A.L.	122
Elias, G.	203
Eysenck, H.J.	76
Eysenck, S.B.G.	76
Fisher, V.E.	89
Fleishman, E.A.	271
Frenkel -Brunswik,E.	92
Gekoski, N.	284
Gilner, F.	190
Gordon, L.V.	59, 64, 67, 158
Gough, H.G.	114, 126
Hall, J.	230, 232, 267, 269, 280, 282, 283
Hathaway, S.R.	134
Heilbrun, A.B., Jr.	114
Heist, P.	129
Hemphill, J.K.	233
Heslin, R.	82
Hill, W.F.	207, 217
Jackson, D.N.	131
Jenkins, T.N.	78
Johnson, R.H.	106
Jones, J.	228
Jourard, S.	104
Katcher, A.	260
Kehoe, P.T.	239
LaForge, R.	161
Levinson, D.J.	92
Likert, R.	241
Lindzey, G.	62
Lippitt, G.L.	74
Litwin, G.H.	253
Lorr, M.	118
Lubin, B.	90
Marlowe, D.	95
McKinley, J.C.	134
McNair, D.M.	118
Morrison, L.P.	106
Myers, I.B.	101
Porter, E.H.	228
Reddin, W.J.	80, 239, 263, 265
Rokeach, M.	94
Rundquist, E.A.	202
Sanford, R.N.	92
Schutz, W.C.	85, 139, 152, 179, 197, 243
Schwartz, S.L.	284
Scott, W.A.	69
Shostrom, E.L.	99
Sletto, R.F.	202
Stancik, E.J.	272
Stephenson, R.R.	171
Stern, G.G.	250
Stringer, R.A., Jr.	253
Suczek, R.	161

289

Author	Page(s)	Author	Page(s)
Sullivan, J.B.	80, 265	Tiegs, E.W.	124
Swenson, C.H.	190	Townsend, R.	279
Taylor, R.M.	106	Vernon, P.E.	62
Thelen, H.A.	221	Watson, R.I.	89
Thorndike, R.L.	120	Wile, D.B.	223
Thorpe, L.P.	124	Williams, M.S.	230, 280, 283
Thurstone, L.L.	112	Yonge, G.	129
		Zuckerman, M.	90

Appendix B
LIST OF INSTRUMENTS

Title of Instrument	Page
Adjective Check List, The	114
Adjustment Inventory, The	110
Ascendance-Submission Reaction Study	175
California F-Scale	92
California Psychological Inventory	126
California Test of Personality	124
Coping Operations Preference Enquiry	85
Dimensions of Temperament	120
Dogmatism Scale	94
Educational Values	243
Edwards Personal Preference Schedule	122
Eysenck Personality Inventory	76
Family Adjustment Test	203
Family Scale, The	202
Fundamental Interpersonal Relations Orientation – Behavior	139
Fundamental Interpersonal Relations Orientation – Feeling	152
Gordon Personal Inventory	64
Gordon Personal Profile	67
Group Dimensions Descriptions Questionnaire	233
Group Encounter Survey	230

Title of Instrument	Page
Group Leadership Questionnaire	223
Helping Relationship Inventory	228
Hill Interaction Matrix–B	207
Hill Interaction Matrix–Group	217
How Well Do You Know Yourself	78
Interpersonal Check List	161
Interpersonal Rating Form	164
Inventory of Affective Tolerance	89
Involvement Inventory, The	82
Leadership Ability Evaluation, The	272
Leadership Appraisal Survey	267
Leadership Employee-Orientation and Differentiation	277
Leadership Opinion Questionnaire	271
Life Interpersonal History Enquiry	197
Management Appraisal Survey	269
Management of Motives Index	282
Management Style Diagnosis Test	263
Marital Attitudes Evaluation	179
Marriage Adjustment Scale, The	195
Marriage Prediction Schedule, The	192

Title of Instrument	Page
Minnesota Multiphasic Personality Inventory	134
Multiple Affect Adjective Check List	90
Myers-Briggs Type Indicator	101
Omnibus Personality Inventory	129
Organizational Climate	241
Organizational Climate Index	250
Organizational Climate Questionnaire	253
Organization Health Survey	239
Orientation Inventory, The	257
Personal Growth Inventory	74
Personal Orientation Inventory	99
Personality Inventory, The	72
Personality Research Form	131
Personal Value Scales	69
Personnel Relations Survey	280
Profile of Mood States	118
Psychological Audit for Interpersonal Relations	171

Title of Instrument	Page
Rate Your Boss as a Leader	279
Reactions to Group Situations	221
Repression-Sensitization Scale	96
Scale of Feelings and Behavior of Love	190
Self-Actualization Test	80
Self-Disclosure Questionnaire	104
Sixteen Personality Factor Test, The	108
Social Desirability Scale	95
Study of Values	62
Supervisory Index	284
Survey of Interpersonal Values	158
Survey of Life Orientations, A	260
Survey of Personal Values	59
Taylor-Johnson Temperament Analysis	106
Team Effectiveness Survey	232
Thurstone Temperament Schedule	112
Work Motivation Inventory	283
XYZ Test	265

Scale Name	Page(s)
Abasement	114, 122, 131
Abasement-Assurance	250
Academic achievement	69
Acceptance of aggression	99
Accepting vs. critical	120
Achievement	59, 114, 122, 131, 250
Achievement via conformance	126
Achievement via independence	126
Active	112
Active-social vs. quiet	106
Active vs. lethargic	120
Adaptability-defensiveness	250
Adapting/dealing	260
Aesthetic	62
Affected by feelings vs. emotional stability	108
Affection (administrator-community)	243
Affection (administrator-teacher)	243
Affection behavior/feelings (father)	197
Affection behavior/feelings (mother)	197
Affection (behavior) wanted from wife/husband	179
Affection (behavior) wife/husband wants	179
Affection (expressed)	139
Affection (teacher-child)	243
Affection (teacher-community)	243
Affection (wanted)	139
Affective involvement	82
Affective tolerance	89
Affiliation	114, 122, 131, 250
Aggression	114, 122, 131
Aggression-blame avoidance	250
Aggressive hostility	161, 171
Altruism	129
Ambitiousness	78
Anger-hostility	118
Anti-social tendencies	124
Anxiety	90
Anxiety level	129
Ascendance-submission	175
Ascendancy	67
Ascendancy vs. withdrawing	120
Attack intervention	223
Attitude toward employees	284
Attitude toward family	202
Attitude toward human relations practices	284
Attitude toward management	284
Attitude toward supervision	284
Authoritarianism	92

Scale Name	Page(s)
Authoritarian (System I)	241
Autocratic-aggressive	272
Autocratic-submissive	272
Autonomy	114, 122, 129, 131, 233
Basic needs	282, 283
Behavioral change intervention	223
Behavioral involvement	82
Belongingness needs	282, 283
Benevolence	158
Capacity for intimate contact	99
Capacity for status	126
Cautiousness	64
Change	114, 122, 131
Change and variety	171
Change-sameness	250
Cheerful (objective) vs. gloomy (sensitive)	120
Clarification-confrontation question intervention	223
Cognitive involvement	82
Cognitive structure	131
Communality	126
Communication	239
Community relations	124
Competence (perception of others)	152
Competence (wanted to be perceived by others)	152
Competitive-narcissistic	161
Complexity	129
Compromise management	269
Concern for people	267
Concern for purpose	267
Confidence	72

Scale Name	Page(s)
Conflict	253
Conflict management	239
Conformity	158
Confusion-bewilderment	118
Conjunctivity-disjunctivity	250
Conservative group beliefs	164
Conservative vs. experimenting	108
Conserving/holding	260
Consideration	271
Consultative (System III)	241
Control	233
Control (administrator-community)	243
Control (administrator-teacher)	243
Control (behavior) father	197
Control (behavior) mother	197
Control (behavior) wanted from wife/husband	179
Control (behavior) wife/husband wants	179
Control (expressed)	139
Control (feelings) father	197
Control (feelings) mother	197
Control (feelings) wanted from wife/husband	179
Control (feelings) wife/husband wants	179
Control (school-child)	243
Control (teacher-child)	243
Control (teacher-community)	243
Control (wanted)	139
Controlling/taking	260
Cooperativeness	78, 161
Counseling readiness	114

Scale Name	Page(s)
Counteraction	250
Creativity	239
Creativity (originality)	69
Custodial management	269
Decisiveness	59
Default decision making	230
Defendence	131
Defensiveness	114
Deference	114, 122
Deference-restiveness	250
Dejection	78
Democratic-cooperative	272
Denial	85
Dependency mode	221
Dependent suggestibility	171
Depression	90, 134
Depression-dejection	118
Depressive vs. lighthearted	106
Desirability	131
Devaluation of self	164
Differentiation	277
Docile-dependent	161
Dogmatism	94
Dominance	114, 122, 126, 131
Dominance-submission	72, 161
Dominance-tolerance	250
Dominant	112
Dominant leadership	171
Dominant vs. submissive	106
Dynamism	78
Economic	62
Education, importance of	243
Effectiveness level	263

Scale Name	Page(s)
Ego achievement	250
Ego-status needs	282, 283
Emotional adjustment	110
Emotional control	78, 171
Emotional stability	67
Emotionality-placidity	250
Employee-orientation	277
Endurance	114, 122, 131
Energy-passivity	250
Equalitarianism	164
Estheticism	129
Esthetic pleasures	171
Evaluative	228
Exhibition	114, 122, 131
Exhibitionism-inferiority avoidance	250
Existentiality	99
Expedient vs. conscientious	108
Exposure	232, 280
Expressive-responsive vs. inhibited	106
Extraversion-introversion	76
Family cohesiveness	171
Family relations	124
Fantasied achievement	250
Fatigue-inertia	118
Feedback	232, 280
Feeling of belonging	124
Feeling reactivity	99
Feeling types-thinking types	101
Feelings (not expressed verbally)	190
Femininity	126
Fight mode	221

Scale Name	Page(s)
Flexibility	126, 233
Flight mode	221
Forthright vs. shrewd	108
General adjustment	110
General morale	78
Goal orientation	59
Good impression	126
Good neighbor decision making	230
Group atmosphere interpretation intervention	223
Group dependent vs. self sufficient	108
Group directed intervention	223
Group dynamics interpretation intervention	223
Group dynamics question intervention	223
Group interaction style: Assertive	217
Group interaction style: Confrontive	217
Group interaction style: Conventional	217
Group interaction content: Group	217
Group interaction content: Personal	217
Group interaction content: Relationship	217
Group interaction style: Responsive	217
Group interaction style: Speculative	217
Group interaction content: Topic	217
Harm avoidance	131
Harm avoidance—risk-taking	250

Scale Name	Page(s)
Health adjustment	110
Health concern	171
Hedonic tone	233
Heterosexuality	114, 122
Home Adjustment	110
Homogeneity	233
Honesty	69
Hostile vs. tolerant	106
Hostility	90
Human resource management	239
Humanities—social science	250
Humble vs. assertive	108
Hypercriticalness	78
Hypochondriasis	134
Hypomania	134
Hysteria	134
Identity	253
Impulse expression	129
Impulsive	112
Impulsive—deliberation	250
Impulsiveness	78
Impulsive vs. planful	120
Impulsivity	131
Inclusion (administrator-community)	243
Inclusion (administrator-teacher)	243
Inclusion (behavior) father	197
Inclusion (behavior) mother	197
Inclusion (behavior) wanted from wife/husband	179
Inclusion (behavior) wife/husband wants	179
Inclusion (expressed)	139

Scale Name	Page(s)
Inclusion (feelings) father	197
Inclusion (feelings) mother	197
Inclusion (feelings) wanted from wife/husband	179
Inclusion (feelings) wife/husband wants	179
Inclusion (teacher-community)	243
Inclusion (wanted)	139
Independence	69, 158
Independence needs	80
Individualistic isolationism	164
Infrequency	131
Inner directed/other directed	99
Inquiry mode	221
Integrated decision making	230
Intellectual efficiency	126
Intellectual rigidity	171
Intellectualism	69
Intensity	161
Interaction-orientation	257
Interpretive	228
Intimacy	233
Intraception	114, 122
Intra-family homeyness—homelessness	203
Introversion-extraversion	72
Introverts-extraverts	101
Intuitives-sensing types	101
Irritability	78
Isolation	85
Kindness	69
Lability	114

Scale Name	Page(s)
Laissez-faire	272
Leader experience intervention	223
Leader feeling intervention	223
Leadership	158, 239, 279
Less intelligent vs. more intelligent	108
Lie scale	76
Lovability (perception of others)	152
Lovability (wanted to be perceived by others)	152
Love-hate	161
Loyalty	69
Managerial-autocratic	161
Marriage-adjustment	195
Marriage-prediction	192
Masculinity-femininity	129, 134
Material success and power	164
Member feeling intervention	223
Mind (development of)	243
Models of management	263
Monetary concern	171
Narcissism	250
Nature of man	99
Need for approval	95
Nervousness	78
Nervous symptoms	124
Nervous vs. composed	106
Neuroticism	76
Neurotic tendency	72
Nonverbal intervention	223
Novelty-loving	78
Number of favorable adjectives checked	114

Scale Name	Page(s)
Number of unfavorable adjectives checked	114
Nurturance	114, 122, 131, 250
Nurturant helpfulness	171
Objectivity-projectivity	250
Occupational adjustment	110
Occupation relations	124
Order	114, 122, 131
Order and routine	171
Order-disorder	250
Orderliness	59
Organization structure	239
Original thinking	64
Outdoor interests	171
Pairing mode	221
Paranoia	134
Parental approval (perceived) father	197
Parental approval (perceived) mother	197
Participation	233, 239
Participative (System IV)	241
Participative management	269
Past and parents intervention	223
Paternalistic (System II)	241
People-centered management	269
Perceptives-judging types	101
Permeability	233
Persistence	78
Personal adjustment	114, 124
Personal growth (estimation of another person)	74
Personal growth (self-estimate)	74
Personal integration	129

Scale Name	Page(s)
Personal interaction style: Assertive	207
Personal interaction style: Confrontive	207
Personal interaction style: Conventional	207
Personal interaction content: Group	207
Personal interaction content: Personal	207
Personal interaction content: Relationship	207
Personal interaction style: Responsive	207
Personal interaction style: Speculative	207
Personal interaction content: Topic	207
Personal life intervention	223
Personal relations	64
Physical affection	171
Physical development	69
Physical needs	80
Placid vs. apprehensive	108
Placid vs. irritable	120
Play	131
Play-work	250
Polarization	233
Political	62
Political conservatism	171
Potency	233
Practicality	78
Practical mindedness	59
Practicalness-impracticalness	250
Practical outlook	129

Scale Name	Page(s)
Practical vs. imaginative	108
Probing	228
Productivity	239
Projection	85
Psychasthenia	134
Psychodynamic interpretation intervention	223
Psychological-mindedness	126
Psychological support	171
Psychopathic deviate	134
Punctuality	78
Reassurance-approval intervention	223
Rebellious-distrustful	161
Recognition	158
Reflective	112
Reflective vs. practical	120
Reflectiveness	250
Regression	85
Rejection of conservative group beliefs	164
Relationships needs	80
Relationships orientation	263
Relaxed vs. tense	108
Religious	62
Religiousness	69
Religious orientation	129
Repression-sensitization	96
Reserved vs. outgoing	108
Respect needs	80
Response bias	129
Responsibility	67, 126, 253
Responsible-hypernormal	161
Responsible vs. causal	120
Reward	253
Risk	253

Scale Name	Page(s)
Risk ratio	207
Role-playing intervention	223
Safety needs	282, 283
Schizophrenia	134
Science	250
Security needs	80
Self-acceptance	99, 126, 171
Self-actualization	80
Self-actualization needs	282, 283
Self-actualizing value	99
Self-confidence	114
Self-control	69, 114, 126
Self-disciplined vs. impulsive	106
Self-disclosure	104, 190
Self-effacing-masochistic	161
Self-orientation	257
Self-regard	99
Self-rejection	171
Self-reliance	124
Self-sufficiency	72
Self-sufficient decision making	230
Sense of personal freedom	124
Sense of personal worth	124
Sense of well-being	126
Sensuality-puritanism	250
Sentience	131
Seriousness	78
Sexuality-prudishness	250
Shy vs. venturesome	108
Significance (perception of others)	152
Significance (wanted to be perceived by others)	152
Silence intervention	223
Sober vs. happy-go-lucky	108
Sociable	72, 112

Scale Name	Page(s)
Sociable vs. solitary	120
Sociability	67, 126
Social	62
Social adjustment	110, 124
Social extraversion	129, 171
Socialization	126
Social presence	126
Social recognition	131
Social skills	69, 124
Social standards	124
Spontaneity	99
Social status	171
Stability	233
Stable	112
Standards	253
Status	69
Stratification	233
Structure	253, 271
Structure intervention	223
Subjective vs. objective	106
Submissiveness	78
Submissive passivity	171
Subtle guidance intervention	223
Succorance	114, 122, 131
Supplication-autonomy	250
Support	158, 253
Supporting/giving	260
Supportive	228
Support (material evidence)	190
Support (non-material evidence)	190
Sympathetic vs. indifferent	106
Synergy	99
Task-centered management	269

Scale Name	Page(s)
Task-orientation	257, 263
Tension-anxiety	118
Theoretical	62
Theoritical orientation	129
Theory X	265
Theory Y	265
Theory Z	265
Therapist activity	217
Thinking introversion	129
Time competent/time incompetent	99
Tolerance	126, 190
Total acceptance score	207
Total involvement	82
Total number of adjectives checked	114
Tough-minded (masculine) vs. tender-minded (feminine)	120
Tough-minded vs. tender-minded	108
Traditional decision making	230
Trusting vs. suspicious	108
Turning against the self	85
Understanding	131, 228, 250
Undisciplined self-conflict vs. control	108
Variety	59
Verbal expression	190
Vigor	64
Vigor-activity	118
Vigorous	112
Viscidity	233
Vocational assurance	78
Warmth	253
Withdrawing tendencies	124

Atkins-Katcher Associates, Inc.
8383 Wilshire Boulevard, Beverly Hills, California 90211
(213) 653-0672

Basic Books, Inc.
10 East 53rd Street, New York, New York 10022
(212) 593-7057

Bureau of Business Research
1775 South College Road, Columbus, Ohio 43210
(614) 422-6446

Consulting Psychologists Press, Inc.
577 College Avenue, Palo Alto, California 94306
(415) 326-4448

CTB/McGraw-Hill
Del Monte Research Park, Monterey, California 93940
(408) 373-2932

Educational and Industrial Testing Service
Box 7234, San Diego, California 92107
(714) 222-1666

Educational Testing Service
Princeton, New Jersey 08540
(609) 921-9000

Executive Analysis Corp.
76 Beaver Street, New York, New York 10017
(212) 867-0471

Fawcett World Library
Fawcett Place, Greenwich, Connecticut 06380
(203) 661-6700

Harcourt, Brace and World, Inc.
757 Third Avenue, New York, New York
(212) 572-5000

Harcourt, Brace, Jovanovich
757 Third Avenue, New York, New York
(212) 572-5000

Harvard Business School
Division of Research, Boston, Massachusetts, 02103
(617) 495-6000

Holt, Rinehart and Winston
383 Madison Avenue, New York, New York 10017
(212) 688-9100

Houghton Mifflin Company
53 West 43rd Street, New York, New York 10036
(212) 867-8050

Institute for Personality and Ability Testing
1602 Coronado Drive, Champaign, Illinois 61820
(217) 352-4739

Alfred A. Knopf
201 East 50th Street, New York, New York 10022
(212) 751-2600

Leadership Resources, Inc.
1750 Pennsylvania Avenue, N.W., Washington, D.C. 20006
(202) 298-7092

McGraw-Hill Book Company
1121 Avenue of the Americas, New York, New York 10020
(212) 997-1221

W. W. Norton Co., Inc.
55 5th Avenue, New York, New York 10003
(212) 255-9210

Oregon Research Institute
Eugene, Oregon 97401
(503) 343-1674

Organizational Tests, Ltd.
Box 324, Fredericton, New Brunswick, Canada
(506) 475-8366

Psychological Corporation, The
304 East 45th Street, New York, New York 10017
(212) 679-7070

Psychological Publications, Inc.
5300 Hollywood Boulevard, Los Angeles, California 90027
(213) 465-4163

Psychological Research Center
Syracuse University, Syracuse, New York 13210
(315) 476-5541

Psychometric Affiliates
Box 3167, Munster, Indiana 46321
(219) 836-1661

Rand McNally
Box 7600, Chicago, Illinois 60600
(312) 267-6868

Research Psychologists Press, Inc.
36 St. Johns Street, Goshen, New York 10924
(914) 294-6383

Science Research Associates, Inc.
259 East Erie Street, Chicago, Illinois 60611
(312) 944-7552

Sheridan Supply Co.
Box 837, Beverly Hills, California, 90213
(213) 474-1744

Richard R. Stephenson
3912 3rd Avenue, San Diego, California 92103
(714) 298-1477

Teleometrics, Int'l
2210 North Frazier, Conroe, Texas 77301
(713) 756-1185

University Associates Publishers and Consultants
Box 615, Iowa City, Iowa 52240
(319) 351-7322

Van Nostrand Reinhold Co.
450 W. 33rd Street, New York, New York 10001
(212) 594-8660

Western Psychological Services
12031 Wilshire Boulevard, Los Angeles, California 90025
(213) 478-6730

John Wiley and Sons, Inc.
605 Third Avenue, New York, New York 10016
(212) 867-9800

Youth Studies Center
University of Southern California, Los Angeles, California 90007
(213) 746-6292

Appendix E
RESOURCES

REVIEWS OF INSTRUMENTS

Buros, Oscar K. *Personality Tests and Reviews*. Highland Park, N.J.: Gryphon Press, 1970

This is an excellent resource which includes scale titles, research references, initial reviews, prices, and publishers of a number of projective and non-projective personality instruments.

SOURCES OF INSTRUMENTS

Shaw, Marvin E., and Wright, Jack M. *Scales for the Measurement of Social Attitudes*. New York: McGraw-Hill, 1967.

The book has a section on measurement theory, and it includes a variety of scales to measure various attitudes. There are a number of scales to measure individual attitudes, for example, there are seven scales to measure attitudes toward Negroes and seven scales to measure attitudes toward religion.

Miller, Delbert C. *Handbook of Research Design and Social Measurement*. New York: McKay, 1964.

Miller has a section on research design and one on statistics. The remainder of the book is devoted to "Selected Sociometric Scales and Indexes." The major focus is on measuring social rather than personal variables, *i.e.*, social class, group cohesiveness, social distance, community solidarity, although there is a description of the MMPI and a reprint of one of the versions of the F-Scale.

Robinson, John P., and Shaver, Phillip R. *Measures of Social Psychological Attitudes*. Ann Arbor, Michigan: Institute of Social Research, University of Michigan, 1969.

An excellent resource for measures of self-esteem, alienation, values, cognitive rigidity, and attitudes. In most cases, the scales are presented in their entirety.

Pfeiffer, J. William, and Jones, John E. *The 1972 Annual Handbook for Group Facilitators*. Iowa City, Iowa: University Associates, 1972.

These handbooks contain sections on "Structured Experiences," "Lecturettes," theoretical papers, and instruments. The instruments are reproduced in their entirety, with answer forms and scoring keys.

Jones, John E., and Pfeiffer, J. William. *The 1973 Annual Handbook for Group Facilitators.* Iowa City, Iowa: University Associates, 1973.

The *1973 Annual* follows the same organization as the *1972 Annual.* There is no overlapping content.

Pfeiffer, J. William, and Jones, John E. *A Handbook of Structured Experiences for Human Relations Training.* Volumes I, II, III, and IV. Iowa City, Iowa: University Associates, 1969, 1970, 1971, and 1973.

The handbooks contain exercises and other procedures for getting acquainted, increasing people's awareness of their personal and interpersonal styles, their leadership styles, the social climate in their organizations, the ways in which they (as individuals or as a group) make decisions, and how to observe group process. Several brief instruments are included.

MEASUREMENT THEORY AND TECHNIQUE

Cronbach, Lee J. *Essentials of Psychological Testing.* (3rd edition.) New York: Harper & Row, 1970.

This is a well-respected book on testing, although it could be clearer and more direct in its organization. It is aimed primarily at the graduate-level student.

Anastasi, Anne *Psychological Testing.* (3rd edition.) New York: McMillan, 1968.

Anastasi's book is at about the same level as Cronbach, but it is more readable, clearer, and better organized. Students find her review of statistical concepts very useful.

Karmel, Louis J. *Measurement and Evaluation in the Schools.* New York: Mac-Millan, 1970.

Karmel's book is easier reading than either of the above two books; it is appropriate for both advanced undergraduates and graduate students. It is somewhat more appropriate for the classroom teacher than for the counselor or psychologist.

RESEARCH AND STATISTICAL METHODS

Downie, Norville M., and Heath, R.W. *Basic Statistical Methods* (3rd edition.) New York: Harper & Row, 1970.

This book is a readable, well-organized presentation of basic statistics. It contains discussions of the various measures of average (*e.g.*, mean) and score spread (*e.g.*, standard deviation) plus measures of association between sets of scores (*e.g.*, correlation), and differences between sets of scores (*e.g.*, t-ratios and basic analyses of variance).

Hays, William. *Statistics for Psychologists* New York: Holt, Rinehart & Winston, 1963.

This book is more advanced than Downie and Heath's book, and it is also well written.

Campbell, Donald, and Stanley, Julian. *Experimental and Quasi-Experimental Designs for Research.* Chicago, Illinois: Rand McNally, 1966.

This is an excellent discussion of methods of research design for use in the real world (as opposed to the laboratory) when the researcher cannot completely control the human variables affecting the outcomes of the study.

Scott, William A., and Wetheimer, Michael. *Introduction to Psychological Research.* New York: Wiley, 1962.

This is a source book to help solve many of the basic problems and avoid many of the pitfalls of research in the behavioral sciences.

Cooper, C.L., and Mangham, I.L. *T-Groups: A Survey of Research.* New York: Wiley-Interscience, 1971.

This is the most comprehensive, up-to-date survey of available evidence about the outcomes of human relations training. The book includes treatments on research design, change, facilitators, group composition, group dynamics, and group development.

SEMINARS AND INSTRUMENT PACKAGES

Listed below are several organizations that market instrument seminars. They sell an instrument (or a package of instruments), and hold public and contracted seminars on the use of those instruments.

Teleometrics, Int'l. (Jay Hall, President)
2210 North Frazier
Conroe, Texas 77301
Phone (713) 756-1185

Organizational Tests Limited (William J. Reddin, President)
P. O. Box 324
Fredericton, N.B., Canada
Phone (506) 455-8366

Atkins-Katcher Associates, Inc. (Stuart Atkins and Allan Katcher)
8383 Wilshire Boulevard
Beverly Hills, California 90211
Phone (213) 653-0672

Scientific Methods, Inc. (Robert Blake, President)
Box 195
Austin, Texas 78767
Phone (512) 477-5781

The University Associates public and contracted workshops include an eclectic seminar entitled "Uses of Instrumentation in Human Relations Training," in which fifteen to twenty-five instruments are surveyed. The workshop takes two and a half days. The contents of the workshop varies, depending on the needs and background of the participants. Typically it includes the FIRO series, one or two instruments from both the Organizational Tests Ltd. and Teleometric series, Personal Orientation Inventory, Orientation Inventory, Survey of Interpersonal Values, Survey of Personal Values, A Survey of Life Orientations, Hill Interaction Matrix, and the Group Leadership Questionnaire.